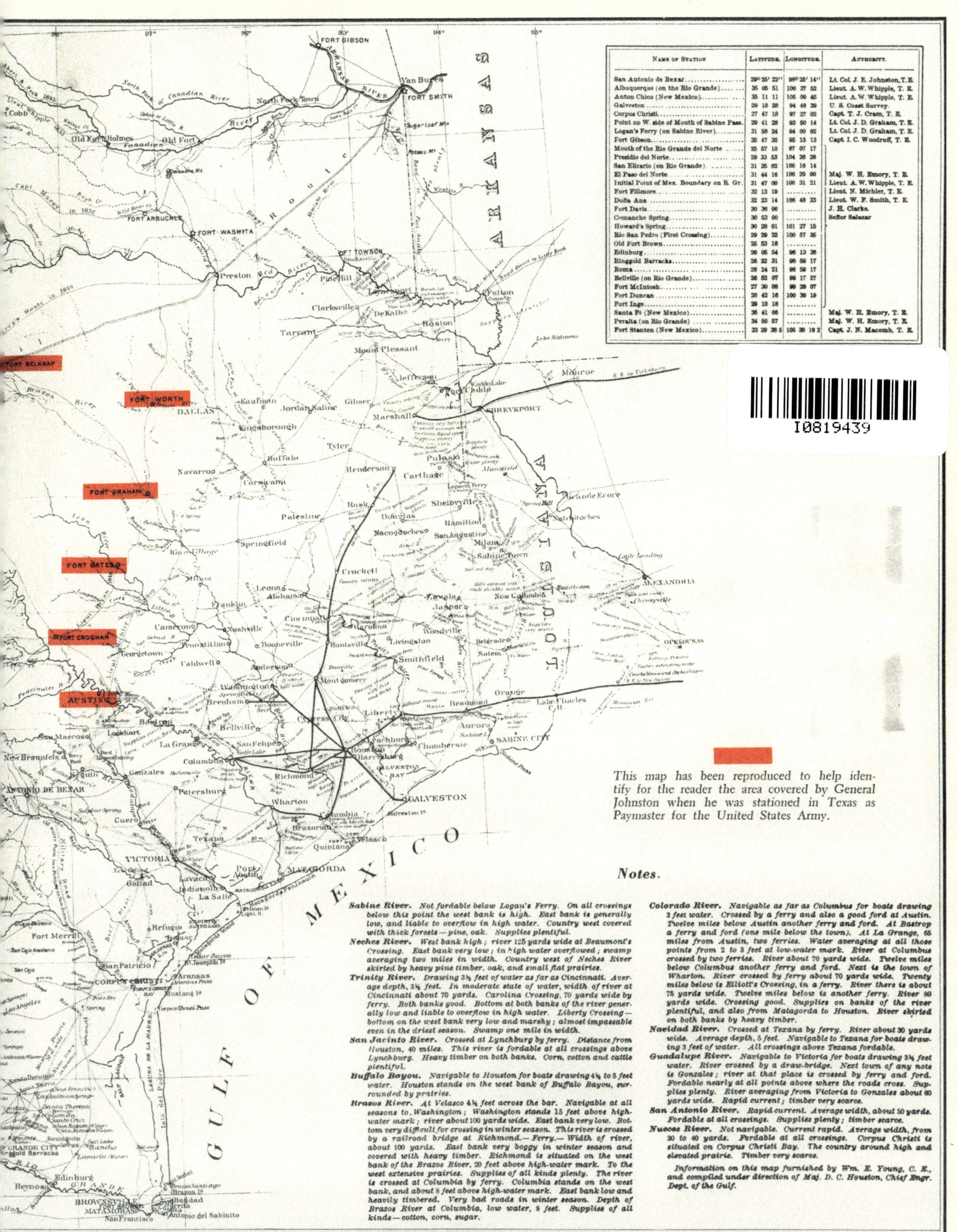

NAME OF STATION	LATITUDE.	LONGITUDE.	AUTHORITY.
San Antonio de Bexar	29° 25′ 22″	98° 25′ 14″	Lt. Col. J. E. Johnston, T. E.
Albuquerque (on the Rio Grande)	35 06 51	106 37 52	Lieut. A. W. Whipple, T. E.
Anton Chico (New Mexico)	35 11 11	105 09 45	Lieut. A. W. Whipple, T. E.
Galveston	29 18 28	94 46 39	U. S. Coast Survey.
Corpus Christi	27 47 18	97 27 02	Capt. T. J. Cram, T. E.
Point on W. side of Mouth of Sabine Pass.	29 41 28	93 50 14	Lt. Col. J. D. Graham, T. E.
Logan's Ferry (on Sabine River)	31 58 24	94 00 02	Lt. Col. J. D. Graham, T. E.
Fort Gibson	35 47 35	95 15 13	Capt. I. C. Woodruff, T. E.
Mouth of the Rio Grande del Norte	25 57 10	97 07 17	
Presidio del Norte	29 33 53	104 26 28	
San Elizario (on Rio Grande)	31 35 02	106 16 14	
El Paso del Norte	31 44 16	106 29 00	Maj. W. H. Emory, T. E.
Initial Point of Mex. Boundary on R. Gr.	31 47 00	106 31 21	Lieut. A. W. Whipple, T. E.
Fort Fillmore	32 13 19	....	Lieut. N. Michler, T. E.
Doña Ana	32 23 14	106 48 33	Lieut. W. F. Smith, T. E.
Fort Davis	30 36 06	....	J. H. Clarke.
Comanche Spring	30 53 00	....	Señor Salazar
Howard's Spring	30 28 01	101 27 15	
Rio San Pedro (First Crossing)	29 29 22	100 57 36	
Old Fort Brown	25 53 16	....	
Edinburg	26 06 54	98 13 38	
Ringgold Barracks	26 22 31	98 50 17	
Roma	26 24 21	98 59 17	
Bellville (on Rio Grande)	26 52 07	99 17 27	
Fort McIntosh	27 30 08	99 29 07	
Fort Duncan	28 42 16	100 30 19	
Fort Inge	29 10 18	....	
Santa Fé (New Mexico)	35 41 06	....	Maj. W. H. Emory, T. E.
Peralta (on Rio Grande)	34 50 57	....	Maj. W. H. Emory, T. E.
Fort Stanton (New Mexico)	33 29 38 5	106 38 19 2	Capt. J. N. Macomb, T. E.

This map has been reproduced to help identify for the reader the area covered by General Johnston when he was stationed in Texas as Paymaster for the United States Army.

Notes.

Sabine River. *Not fordable below Logan's Ferry. On all crossings below this point the west bank is high. East bank is generally low, and liable to overflow in high water. Country west covered with thick forests—pine, oak. Supplies plentiful.*

Neches River. *West bank high; river 125 yards wide at Beaumont's Crossing. East bank very low; in high water overflowed; swamp averaging two miles in width. Country west of Neches River skirted by heavy pine timber, oak, and small flat prairies.*

Trinity River. *Drawing 3½ feet of water as far as Cincinnati. Average depth, 3½ feet. In moderate state of water, width of river at Cincinnati about 70 yards. Carolina Crossing, 70 yards wide by ferry. Both banks good. Bottom at both banks of the river generally low and liable to overflow in high water. Liberty Crossing—bottom on the west bank very low and marshy; almost impassable even in the driest season. Swamp one mile in width.*

San Jacinto River. *Crossed at Lynchburg by ferry. Distance from Houston, 40 miles. This river is fordable at all crossings above Lynchburg. Heavy timber on both banks. Corn, cotton and cattle plentiful.*

Buffalo Bayou. *Navigable to Houston for boats drawing 4½ to 5 feet water. Houston stands on the west bank of Buffalo Bayou, surrounded by prairies.*

Brazos River. *At Velasco 4½ feet across the bar. Navigable at all seasons to Washington; Washington stands 15 feet above high-water mark; river about 100 yards wide. East bank very low. Bottom very difficult for crossing in winter season. This river is crossed by a railroad bridge at Richmond.—Ferry.—Width of river, about 100 yards. East bank very boggy in winter season and covered with heavy timber. Richmond is situated on the west bank of the Brazos River, 20 feet above high-water mark. To the west extensive prairies. Supplies of all kinds plenty. The river is crossed at Columbia by ferry. Columbia stands on the west bank, and about 8 feet above high-water mark. East bank low and heavily timbered. Very bad roads in winter season. Depth of Brazos River at Columbia, low water, 8 feet. Supplies of all kinds—cotton, corn, sugar.*

Colorado River. *Navigable as far as Columbus for boats drawing 3 feet water. Crossed by a ferry and also a good ford at Austin. Twelve miles below Austin another ferry and ford. At Bastrop a ferry and ford (one mile below the town). At La Grange, 65 miles from Austin, two ferries. Water averaging at all those points from 2 to 3 feet at low-water mark. River at Columbus crossed by two ferries. River about 70 yards wide. Twelve miles below Columbus another ferry and ford. Next is the town of Wharton. River crossed by ferry about 70 yards wide. Twenty miles below is Elliott's Crossing, in a ferry. River there is about 75 yards wide. Twelve miles below is another ferry. River 80 yards wide. Crossing good. Supplies on banks of the river plentiful, and also from Matagorda to Houston. River skirted on both banks by heavy timber.*

Navidad River. *Crossed at Texana by ferry. River about 30 yards wide. Average depth, 5 feet. Navigable to Texana for boats drawing 3 feet of water. All crossings above Texana fordable.*

Guadalupe River. *Navigable to Victoria for boats drawing 3½ feet water. River crossed by a draw-bridge. Next town of any note is Gonzales; river at that place is crossed by ferry and ford. Fordable nearly at all points above where the roads cross. Supplies plenty. River averaging from Victoria to Gonzales about 60 yards wide. Rapid current; timber very scarce.*

San Antonio River. *Rapid current. Average width, about 50 yards. Fordable at all crossings. Supplies plenty; timber scarce.*

Nueces River. *Not navigable. Current rapid. Average width, from 30 to 40 yards. Fordable at all crossings. Corpus Christi is situated on Corpus Christi Bay. The country around high and elevated prairie. Timber very scarce.*

Information on this map furnished by Wm. E. Young, C. E., and compiled under direction of Maj. D. C. Houston, Chief Engr. Dept. of the Gulf.

TEXAS WILD FLOWERS

By

ELIZA GRIFFIN JOHNSTON

TEXAS WILD FLOWERS

BY

ELIZA GRIFFIN JOHNSTON

The original copy was a gift to her husband

GENERAL ALBERT SIDNEY JOHNSTON, C.S.A.

Preserved for future generations by
The Daughters of the Republic of Texas
and the
William Barret Travis Chapter of
The Daughters of the Republic of Texas

FOREWORD BY LUCI BAINES JOHNSON

with a biography of Mrs. Johnston by
DR. MILDRED PICKLE MAYHALL

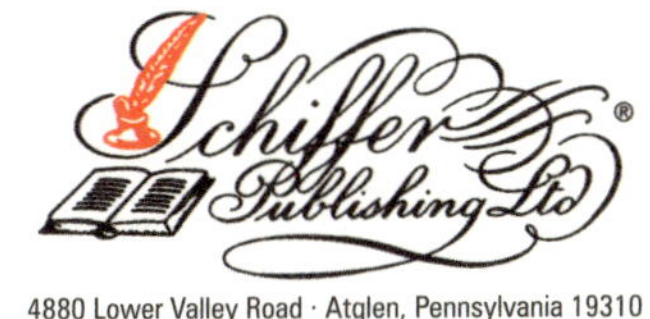

4880 Lower Valley Road · Atglen, Pennsylvania 19310

Schiffer Books are available at special discounts for bulk purchases for sales promotions or premiums. Special editions, including personalized covers, corporate imprints, and excerpts can be created in large quantities for special needs. For more information contact the publisher:

Published by Schiffer Publishing Ltd.
4880 Lower Valley Road
Atglen, PA 19310
Phone: (610) 593-1777; Fax: (610) 593-2002
E-mail: Info@schifferbooks.com

For the largest selection of fine reference books on this and related subjects, please visit our website at **www.schifferbooks.com**
We are always looking for people to write books on new and related subjects. If you have an idea for a book, please contact us at the above address.

This book may be purchased from the publisher.
Include $5.00 for shipping.
Please try your bookstore first.
You may write for a free catalog.

In Europe, Schiffer books are distributed by
Bushwood Books
6 Marksbury Ave.
Kew Gardens
Surrey TW9 4JF England
Phone: 44 (0) 20 8392 8585; Fax: 44 (0) 20 8392 9876
E-mail: info@bushwoodbooks.co.uk
Website: www.bushwoodbooks.co.uk

Library of Congress Control Number: 2011932371

Type set in Shelley Andante/Times New Roman

ISBN: 978-0-7643-3863-2

Printed in China

FOREWORD

Texas Wild Flowers by Eliza Griffin Johnston is an exquisite collection of wildflower paintings but it is so much more. It is a tribute to the natural beauty of Texas that makes our landscape thrilling beyond compare. And it is a lasting memorial to a love story steeped in the history of Texas between a young bride and her heroic husband and their love of this great state.

It is so right that this beautiful work belongs to the Daughters of the Republic of Texas who have seen to its preservation. And it is to the Daughters eternal credit that they have had it so elegantly published for future generations of Texans to enjoy.

The Daughters of The Republic of Texas and my family like Eliza and her family, have had a lasting and treasured relationship. The DRT honored my family on March 2, 1932 when they interred my great, great, great uncle, John Wheeler Bunton, in the Texas State Cemetery "in recognition of his patriotic services on behalf of Texas." John Wheeler Bunton's service to Texas was substantial. He signed the Texas Declaration of Independence, "was a member of the committee to draft the Texas Constitution, and was on General Sam Houston's staff at the Battle of San Jacinto." His younger brother, Robert Howell Bunton, was my great, great Grandfather.

I have had the privilege by accident of birth to be the descendant of not only a Republic of Texas hero, but the first Texan to serve as President of the United States. Thus, I have a keen respect for those who cherish their Texas legacy.

I feel especially honored that the Daughters of The Republic of Texas would ask me to write the foreword to *Texas Wild Flowers* by Eliza Griffin Johnston because of my father's Texas roots and my mother's love of Texas wildflowers. A love of Texas unites the Johnstons and the Johnsons across the generations.

The common links between our families seem to be infinite. Eliza Griffin Johnston was a Christmas baby born on December 26, 1821. My mother, Claudia Alta Taylor Johnson, "Lady Bird," was also a Christmas baby born on December 22, 1912.

When Eliza Johnston was four years old, her parents died and my mother was only five when her mother died. But the ties that bind these two great ladies are far greater than genealogy. They cover the waterfront of their substantial interests.

Both sought solace in the love of Texas's native plants. Eliza was a highly skilled artist and created a collection of 101 exquisite hand-painted wildflowers from the 1840's and 1850's as a present to her husband. Mother, an eloquent wordsmith, wrote about them in her book, *Wildflowers Across America*, as part of her effort to awaken our nation's conscience to the importance of our native plants.

Both women were educated and sophisticated well ahead of their time and eager to share their knowledge. Both knew the challenging roles of being a spouse of a man who was also married to serving his state and country.

Eliza's husband was in government service as an Army Officer including an appointment by Sam Houston to command the Texas Army and as Secretary of War under Texas President Mirabeau Lamar. And of course Mama's husband spent decades of service to his state and country as Congressman and Senator, finishing his career as U.S. President.

I felt like Eliza was a natural mentor of Mother. But I have no idea if Mother ~a history and journalism major from the University of Texas~ ever knew of her predecessor's enormous contribution to the preservation of the natural history of Texas that Mother loved so dearly.

What I do know is they were each other's kindred spirits though more than a hundred years separated them. They found comfort in an orphaned childhood in nature and meaning as adults in sharing their love and considerable knowledge of the native plants of Texas with future generations. Both offered invaluable support to their husbands' careers in public service and each left the world a more beautiful place than they found it.

How grateful I am that the Daughters of The Republic of Texas through my lifelong friend, Judy Day, asked me to write this foreword. Had they not, I might have missed getting to know the beauty of these common bonds that tie one family to another across generations. I might even have missed this important chapter in our states history. I might have missed the gift that the Daughters of The Republic of Texas gives all of us ~ a personal love for our state and all who've gone before us to make her great.

—Luci Baines Johnson

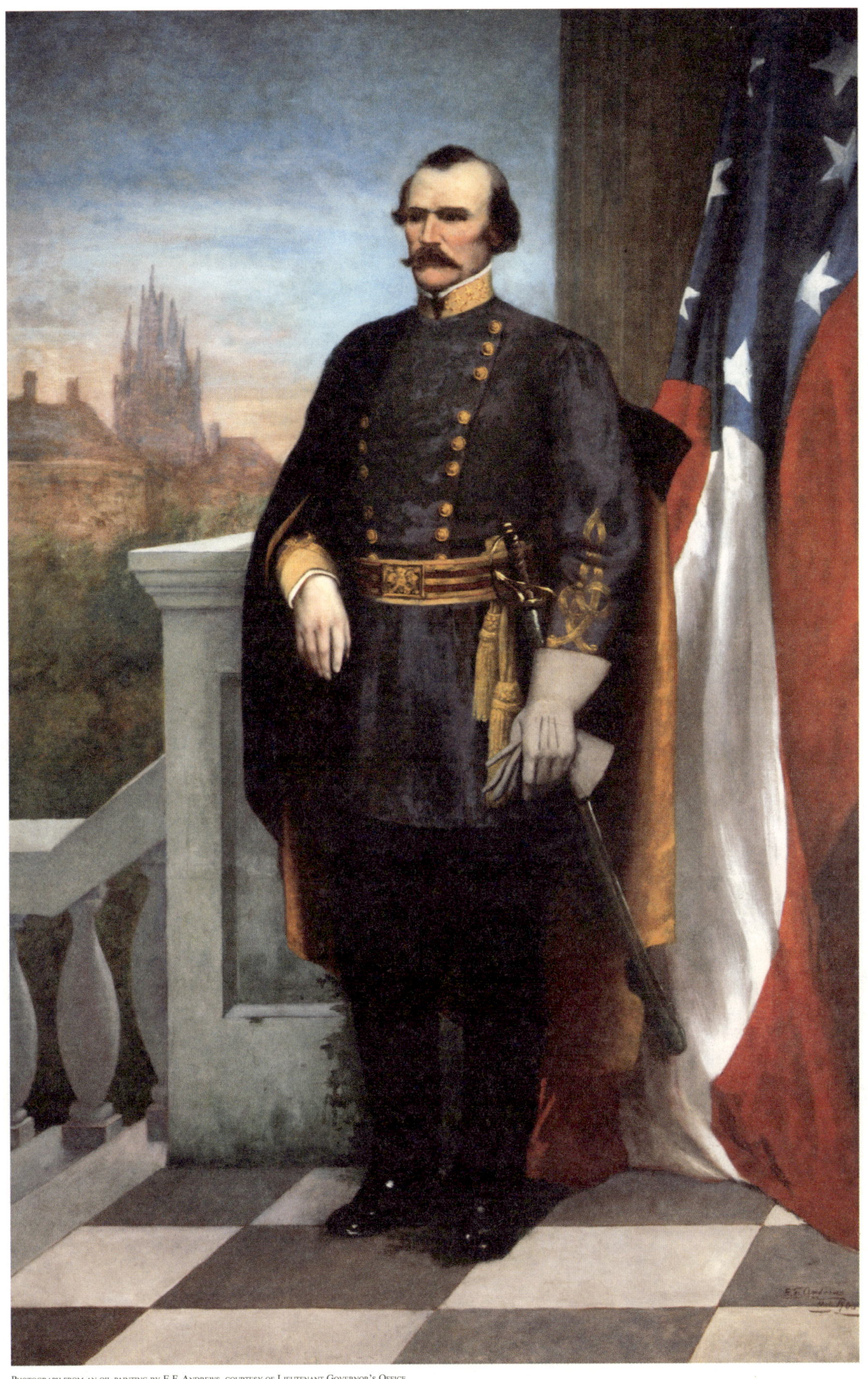

Photograph from an oil painting by E.F. Andrews, courtesy of Lieutenant Governor's Office

General Albert Sidney Johnston, C.S.A

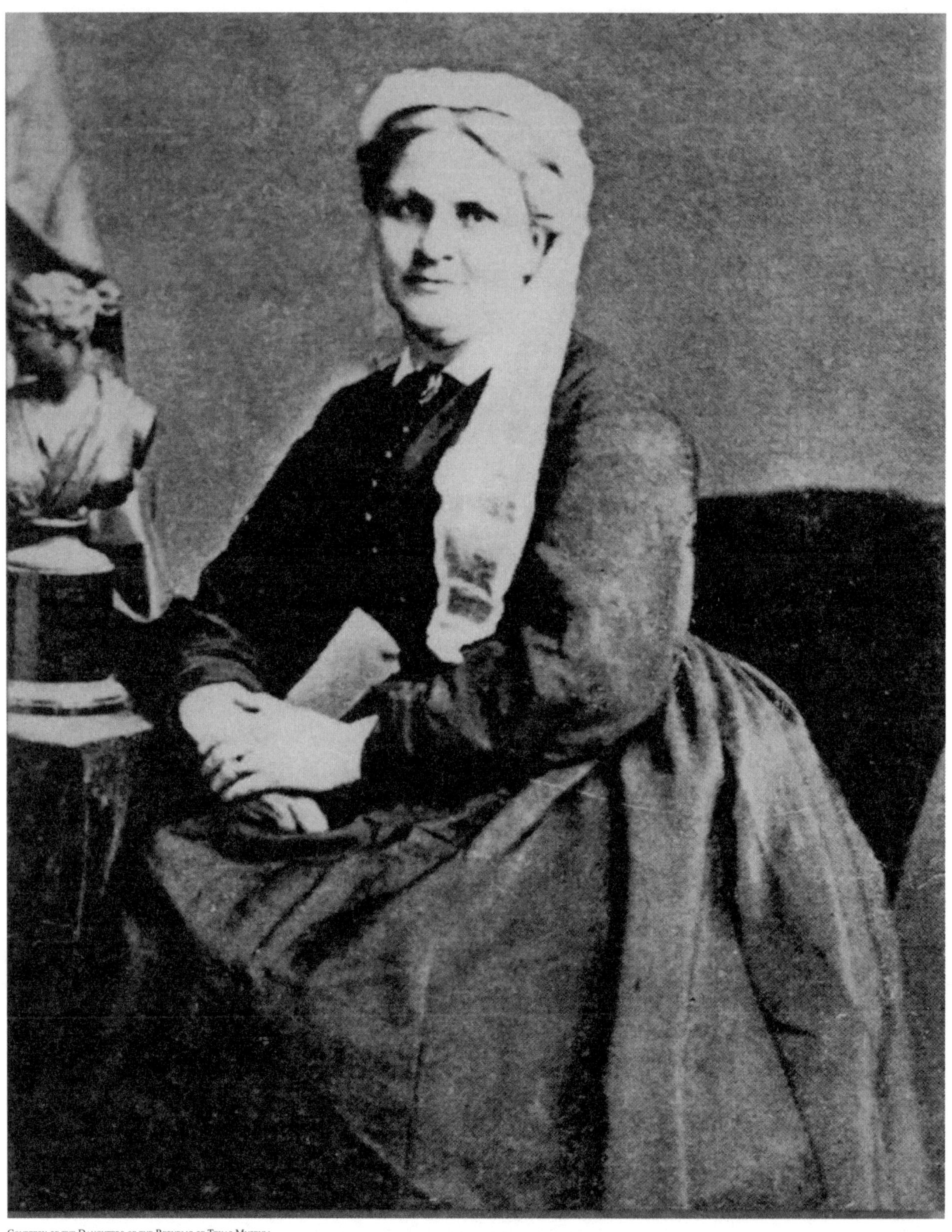

Courtesy of the Daughters of the Republic of Texas Museum

ELIZA GRIFFIN JOHNSTON

FROM A PHOTOGRAPH, TAKEN ABOUT THIRTY-FIVE YEARS AFTER HER MARRIAGE, GIVEN TO THE DAUGHTERS OF THE REPUBLIC OF TEXAS MUSEUM BY REYNOLDS LOWREY, GREAT-NEPHEW OF THOMAS F. MCKINNEY.

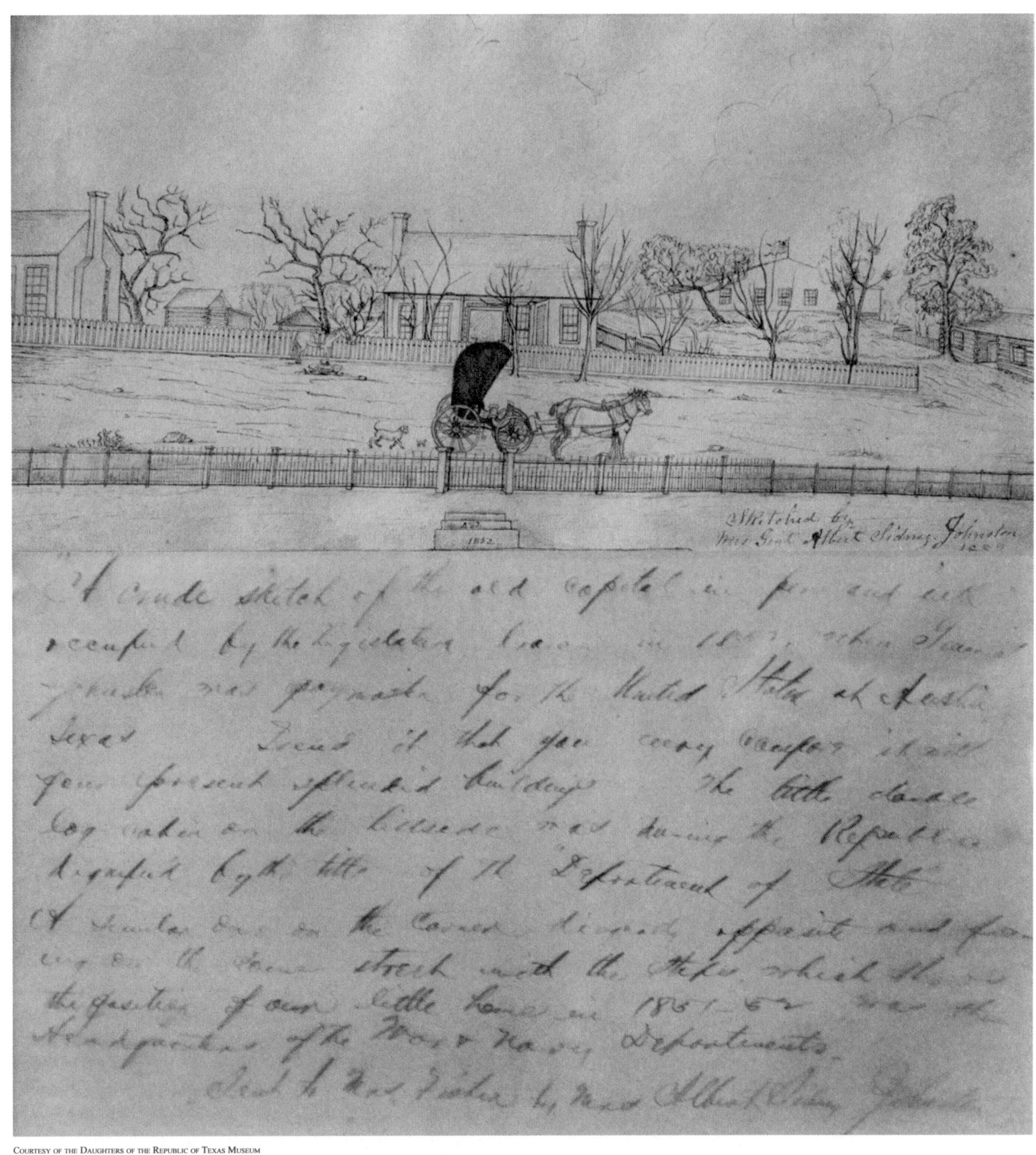

Eliza Johnston's Sketch of Their Home in Austin, 1852

In the background is the old Capitol Building on the corner of Eighth and Colorado streets.

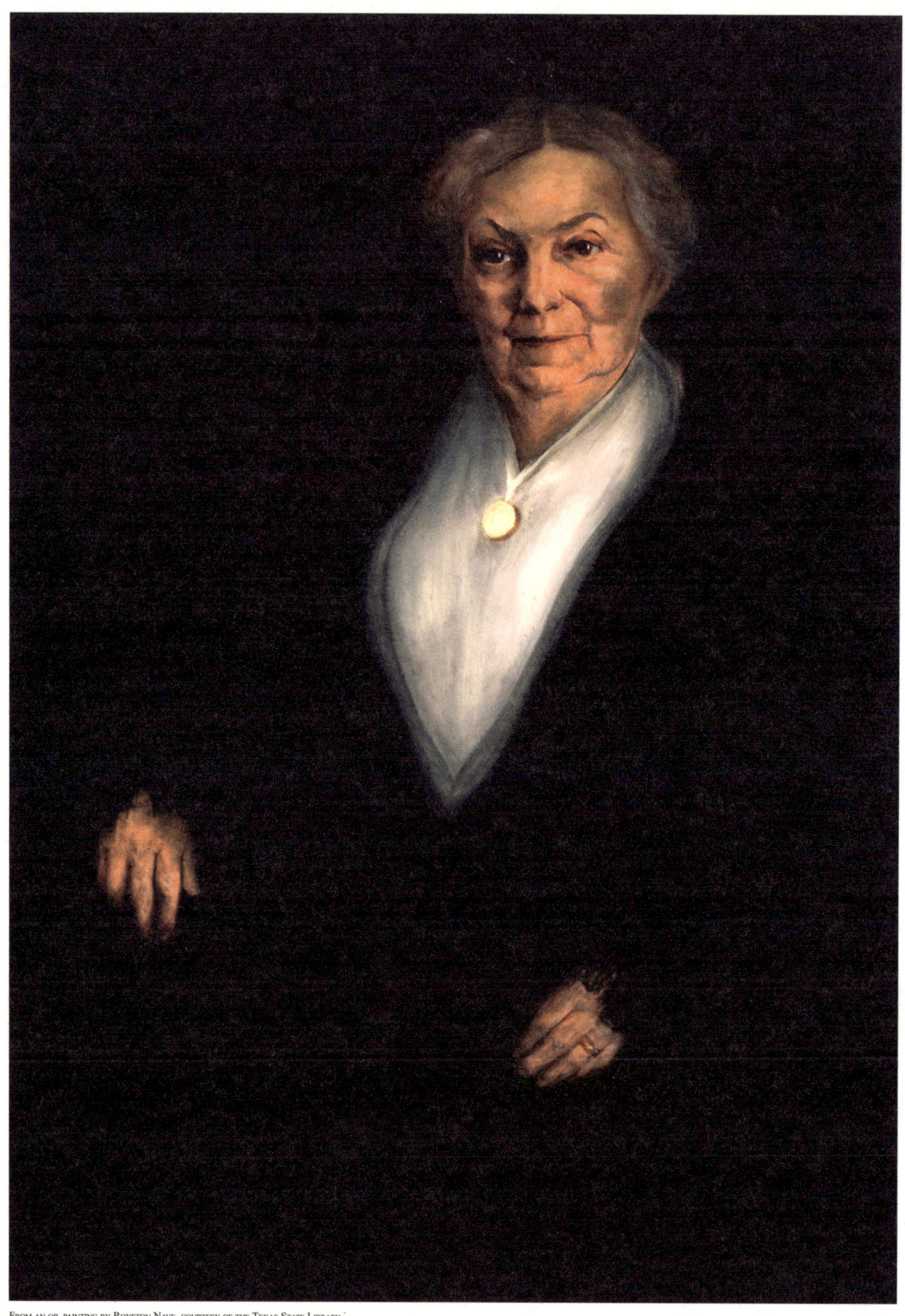

From an oil painting by Royston Nave, courtesy of the Texas State Library

Rebecca Jane Fisher

Charter Member and first President of William B. Travis Chapter, Daughters of the Republic of Texas; President General, 1908 to 1927

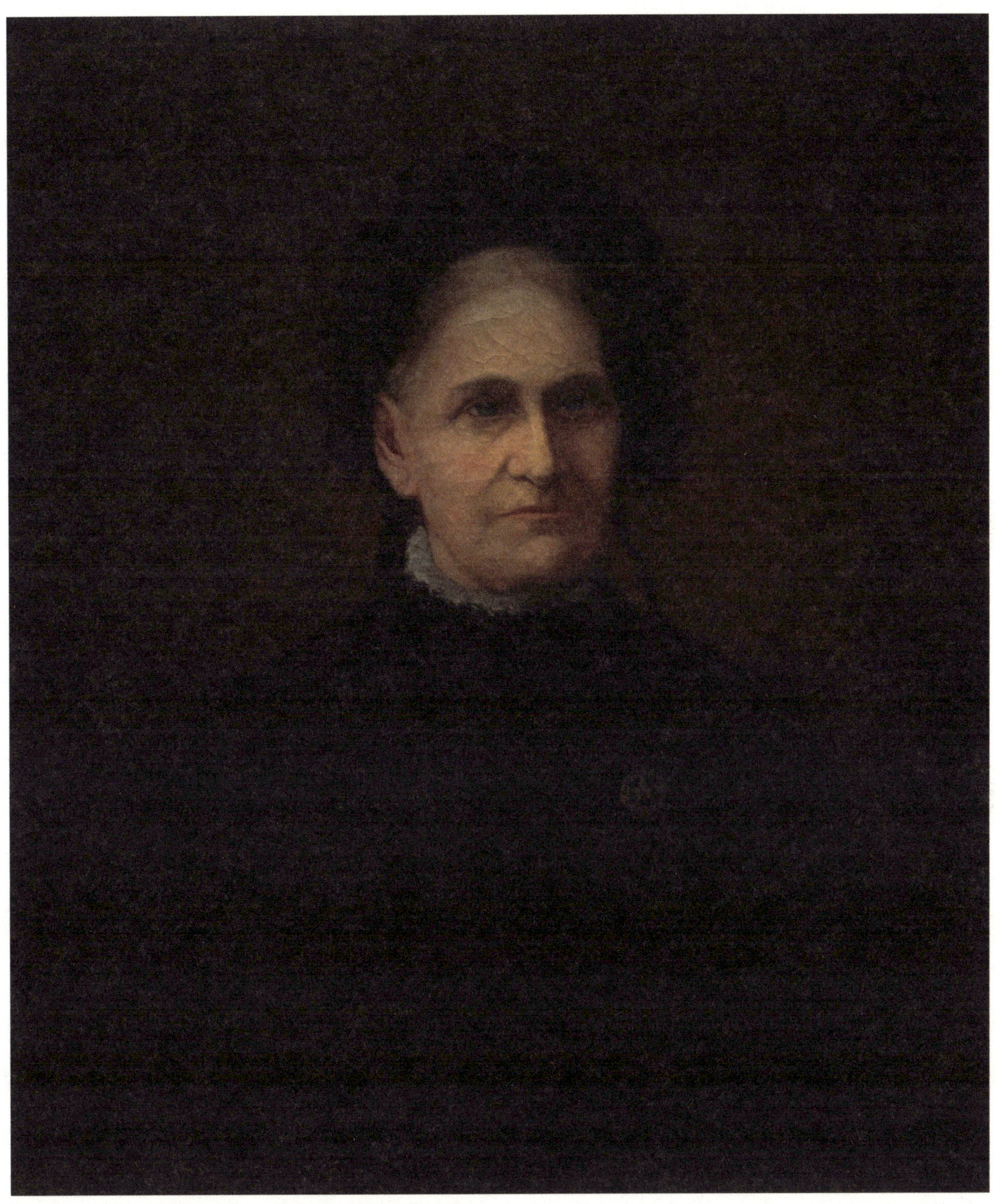

From an oil painting by Florence C. Eager, courtesy of the Daughters of the Republic of Texas Museum

Mrs. Anson Jones

Wife of the last President of the Republic of Texas, and first President General of the Daughters of the Republic of Texas

ELIZA GRIFFIN JOHNSTON

BY MILDRED P. MAYHALL

Eliza Griffin was born on December 26, 1821, at Fincastle, Virginia. She was the youngest child of John Caswell Griffin and his wife, Mary Hancock Griffin. Eliza had three older brothers. When she was four years old, both of her parents died, and her maternal grandmother, Margaret Strother Hancock, took her into her home. In 1830 they moved to Louisville, Kentucky. After Mrs. Hancock's death, Eliza lived in the home of her uncle, Colonel George Hancock, son of the elder Colonel George Hancock of Virginia.

Eliza was well educated, considering the educational opportunities for young women of that day and time, receiving an education which stood her in good stead when she became an army officer's wife. A bright and intelligent student, she studied several languages, wrote and spoke French, and was accomplished in music. She completed her studies in Philadelphia at Mrs. Segoigne's School.[1]

A beautiful young lady, popular with young people, and much sought after by beaux—in the parlance of the time Eliza Griffin was a "belle." She was slightly above medium stature and slender but with a well proportioned figure, with large brown eyes and brown hair, which would turn silvery in later life. She had a charming personality and made friends easily. Eliza was an artist, painting in both watercolors and oil. She had a soprano voice and sang and played the piano with skill, often writing her own compositions.

Eliza was about eighteen years old when Albert Sidney Johnston took bright notice of her and shortly thereafter began to court her. He was almost twice her age, a lonely widower whose two young children were being cared for by their grandmother. An aura of adventure about Johnston stemming from his career in the army and the almost fatal duel he had fought in Texas made the difference in age seem of no importance. Johnston was a fine looking man, in stature one inch over six feet, with dark brown hair and blue eyes. Straight and slender, he had a handsome, soldierly bearing.

[1]Alberta Johnston Denis, "Mrs. Albert Sidney Johnston," Texas Magazine, I (May, 1897), 429-430; and "Albert Sidney Johnston," *ibid.*, 426-428. Alberta was the youngest daughter of Eliza, and was the author of *Spanish Alta California* (New York, Macmillan, 1927).

Eliza was the cousin of Johnston's first wife, Henrietta Preston Johnston. The girls were daughters of sisters. Certainly Eliza must have admired him as all her family did long before he became a suitor. Johnston had resigned his commission in the United States Army in 1833 when Henrietta became gravely ill. After Henrietta died of tuberculosis in August of 1835, Johnston's two young children were left to live with their grandmother in Louisville. Johnston left Kentucky to visit his brother near Alexandria, Louisiana, and went to Nacogdoches, Texas, on July 13, 1836.

Johnston had long been interested in Texas. Two of his older brothers were in the 1812 1813 Gutierrez-Magee Expedition to Texas, which was a part of the Mexican Revolution against Spain. Johnston was already sympathetic to the Texas Revolution against Mexico when he heard Stephen F. Austin speak in Louisville early in 1836, while Austin and the Texan Commissioners to the United States were recruiting men and money in the interest of Texas.

In Nacogdoches Johnston met Sam Houston, who had just returned from New Orleans where he had received medical care for his shattered ankle and other wounds sustained in the successful Battle of San Jacinto on April 21, 1836. Johnston left Nacogdoches to seek out and join the Texas Army.

Early in 1837 he was appointed to command the Texan Army by Sam Houston, president of the new republic. Felix Huston, then second in command and temporarily in charge of a somewhat unruly group of volunteers after San Jacinto, refused to recognize Johnston's superiority and challenged him to a duel. Johnston accepted and was badly injured by a bullet that went through the pelvis, fracturing bones and disturbing the sciatic nerve. The wounds took months to heal and would give him years of pain. When he could finally assume command, Huston conceded the job. Late in 1838 Johnston was appointed Secretary of War by President Mirabeau B. Lamar.

Several times he returned to Kentucky to see his son, William Preston, and his daughter, Henrietta, whom he called "Will" and "Henny". He also had some property to look after and sell. On one trip he met Eliza again, now grown to womanhood, and fell in love with her. It took several years for the romance to culminate in marriage. Back in Texas, Johnston heard about Eliza from friends and relatives. Perhaps he felt a little twinge of jealousy when in 1839 one wrote that Eliza was visiting relatives, the Bentons, in St. Louis and was said to be engaged to George Clark. He remembered the parties that the Bentons and Clarks gave for Henrietta Preston when he was a lieutenant at Jefferson Barracks.

Johnston and Eliza had an interest in each other that quickened with each meeting and was kept alive despite Johnston's long absences while in service in Texas. Theirs was to be a love story that would last to Shiloh and forever after.

Eliza perhaps favored military men although she did not lack for suitors. Military service was important in her family and among her forebears. The Griffins, Prestons, and others of her family line had served in the Revolutionary War and in the War of 1812. Her three brothers were commissioned in military service. Captain George H. Griffin, United States Army, was an aide to General Zachary Taylor, a kinsman. George H. Griffin died in the war against the Seminoles in Florida while serving with General Taylor. Lieutenant William P. Griffin died in the service of the United States Navy. Dr. John S. Griffin was a surgeon in the United States Army. After his retirement he lived in Los Angeles, California, where his sister Eliza would later live.

Despite good friends, card games, good conversations, and brandy and tobacco after dining, Johnston got lonely and thought of Eliza. In 1839 he was in Texas's new capital, Austin, serving as Secretary of War and sharing a two room log cabin with Dr. James Harper Starr, Secretary of the Treasury. Johnston loved Austin with its fine climate and beautiful hills. He was also in love with Eliza and became irritated when he did not get letters on time. In 1840, he returned to Kentucky with an indefinite leave of absence.

From 1840 to 1843 Johnston came back to Texas for visits, as he was anxious to be on hand if war with Mexico developed. Mexico threatened war twice with invasions in 1841 and 1842 but each time President Houston, who took office for a second term on December 13, 1841, would authorize nothing but defensive action. In the time before his second marriage, Johnston's friends wanted him to enter politics. James Love, Thomas F. McKinney, James Hamilton and others wanted him to run against Houston for the presidency. Johnston and Houston had become estranged over Johnston's prosecution of the removal of the Cherokees, initiated by President Mirabeau B. Lamar. Johnston was, however, more interested in returning to the army than in entering politics.[2]

Eliza and Albert Sidney were married in the home of Eliza's uncle, George Hancock, at Lynch's Station near Louisville, Kentucky, on October 3, 1843. Johnston's son and daughter thought Eliza would be a wonderful stepmother. The observant young stepson, William, then about thirteen years old, said that Eliza was "a young lady of great beauty, talent, and accomplishments."[3]

Texas friends sent congratulations and urged Johnston and his wife to come to Texas. Among the well wishers were two former Kentuckians—James Love, a lawyer, and Thomas F. McKinney, famed financier of the Texas Revolution. In November, shortly after their marriage, the Johnstons set out for Texas, by way of New Orleans. At Galveston they visited Johnston's close friend James Love and his wife. They wanted to check on Johnston's plantation at China Grove and possibly sell the place.

Before his marriage, Johnston and some of his friends had invested in land in Texas. As the population of the Republic of Texas grew, land was appreciating rapidly and some fortunes were in the making. Johnston had suffered losses in East Texas land because of title difficulties, but he was still hopeful. He and Albert T. Burnley bought a plantation called China Grove

[2]William Preston Johnston, *The Life of General Albert Sidney Johnston* (New York, D. Appleton and Company, Inc., 1878), 120-128. William Preston Johnston wrote a detailed biography of his famous father, after serving in the Civil War as an aide to Jefferson Davis. Later he was president of Tulane University in New Orleans. He also wrote *The Johnstons of Salisbury* (New Orleans, L. Graham and Son, Ltd., 1897).

[3]William Preston Johnston, *The Life of General Albert Sidney Johnston*, 129. The quotation is from "The Diary of Eliza (Mrs. Albert Sidney) Johnston, The Second Cavalry Comes To Texas," edited by Charles P. Roland and Richard C. Robbins. The Southwestern Historical Quarterly, LX, No. 4 (April, 1957), 463-500; reference 463-464. Hereinafter called Eliza Johnston, "Diary." The diary is in the Mrs. Mason Barret Collection of Albert Sidney and William Preston Johnston Papers, Tulane University Archives, New Orleans.

on Oyster Creek in Brazoria County about forty miles from Galveston. A thousand of the more than five thousand acres was in cotton, but most of it was unbroken prairie, glorious in vegetation and wild flowers—beautiful to look at but overpriced. Johnston, having trouble paying off the indebtedness, hoped to get a release on the place, even at a discount, or sell it.[4] It was Eliza's first look at Texas and she loved it.

Warren D. C. Hall, who had been with Dr. James Long's expedition into Texas in 1819 - 1821, was the original owner. Unable to pay off the judgment against the place, he had remained as tenant after Johnston and Burnley bought it. Johnston decided to leave the place rented. He resigned from the army and with Eliza returned in the spring to Kentucky, where their first child was born on April 8, 1845. Named Albert Sidney, Junior, he was called "Sid."

Johnston tried to dispose of China Grove for over two years. At last, he decided to live on the place and cultivate as much of the acreage as possible. Perhaps he could make it productive enough to pay the debt. Johnston and his family returned to Texas, and while they were visiting the Loves at Galveston, news came that the Unites States was at war with Mexico. Johnston welcomed the news. He enlisted for six months and was chosen by the men to be Colonel of the First Texas Infantry Regiment. Later, when the six month recruits did not re-enlist, General Zachary Taylor made Johnston an Inspector General with Major William O. Butler, Commander of the Volunteers. Johnston was an outstanding leader in the Battle of Monterrey, but when another command was not available afterwards, he returned to his family in Galveston. Then they decided to live on the plantation.

The Johnstons spent three years at China Grove, and Eliza came to love Texas as her husband did. She enjoyed the sweep of prairies along the Gulf Coast with their many grasses, shrubs, and wild flowers, and the beauty of sky and sea. The wild animals caught her attention, especially the birds of diverse types, many of which she painted.

[4]Charles P. Roland, *Albert Sidney Johnston, Soldier of Three Republics* (Austin, University of Texas Press, 1964), 117-119 and note 59, page 118, citing William Preston Johnston, "History of China Grove Plantation," Johnston Papers, Barret Collection, Tulane University, New Orleans, Louisiana.

A letter from the Johnstons, written from China Grove in March of 1848, describes springtime in Texas:

> We are now in the midst of spring. Everything around us is very beautiful. The grounds about our cabin are filled with china trees in full bloom; large monthly roses, also, are blooming and the Cherokee rose hedge, is dark green spangled with large white roses; the Quasatic [Huisache], a species of acacia, 'waves its yellow hair'; and the air is redolent of sweets.[5]

It was a busy life with hard, physical work to do, but the place was lovely with cultivated plants such as roses besides wild plants everywhere. There were also wild animals such as deer, turkey, and panther. They often shot wild game and had a wealth of venison, prairie hens, and turkeys for food. They also had milk cows and poultry. A vegetable garden furnished produce and there were melons and figs.

Eliza's second child was born at China Grove in 1848. He was named Hancock McClung Johnston, and called "Clungy." A daughter, Mary Hancock Johnston, named for Eliza's mother, was born in 1850.

Four Negro slaves and a hired white man (who often got drunk) helped cultivate the soil but, although all on the plantation worked hard, debts continued to pile up. Johnston became tired and frustrated; he was ill with sciatica at times, and the early wounds plagued him. Sometimes the seclusion made them lonely. Colonel Hall and his family lived on a sugar plantation a few miles away and the Halls and Johnstons became good friends. James Love and his wife often visited China Grove, which made enjoyable interludes in the farm work. In the spring of 1847, Johnston's oldest son, William Preston, came from Kentucky to visit at China Grove for three months. William planned to attend Yale and later to study law in Kentucky.

After the Mexican War, Johnston was pleased by General Zachary Taylor's election as President of the United States. Eliza was a relative of President Taylor and hoped for an appointment for her husband, but Johnston would not apply for a post, believing that his military merits should speak for him. Eliza was worried about his health. His high spirits were being worn down

[5]Alberta Johnston Denis, op. cit., 428.

by increasing debts. He was doing no good at farming and wanted to get back into the army with a military command, but few commands were available. Finally friends and relatives urged President Taylor to give Johnston an appointment which he would not solicit for himself. Taylor had not even known that Johnston was interested in an appointment, but he tried to locate something.

In the fall of 1849, the creditors sold China Grove at auction for $2,000. Johnston had paid $16,000 for it, and his own notes as well as those he had taken over from his partner left a debt of $8,000 after the sale.

In 1849 the President appointed Johnston Paymaster of the Army with a major's rank. He accepted the commission in November because Eliza pled with he to do so. He took his family back to Kentucky, then returned alone in the spring of 1850 to Texas. He reported to San Antonio in July for duty as paymaster but made his home in Austin, a town that he loved.

His first duty as paymaster took him to New Orleans to get the money, $40,000. After returning by boat to Galveston, he made the trip north to Forts Croghan, Gates, Graham and Worth to pay the soldiers. His first trip was completed in November. Plans were made for Eliza and the children to join him when he went back to New Orleans.

Eliza and family left Kentucky and met her husband in New Orleans for the boat trip to Texas. Johnston was shocked to learn then of the death of the baby daughter. Letters telling of that sad event had not reached him. From New Orleans they took passage to Galveston, then went by stagecoach to Austin to make their home. For a while they lived, as Mrs. Elisha Pease, wife of Governor Pease, said "for the longest time in the Palm House." This was the August B. Palm rock home with a rock fence around it, bought from De Chaumes (an architect and builder of the rock Texas Capitol in 1853) and rented to the Johnstons. It was east of Congress Avenue, on the corner of Brazos and Ash Street later known as Ninth Street. Later they lived west of Congress, near the old Capitol Building on Hickory Street, later known as Eighth, and Colorado.

In Austin the family spent many happy times, especially when Johnston came home and had some leisure time between trips. When her husband left, Eliza kept busy with her paintings. It was in 1852 and 1853 that she painted constantly. Some earlier sketches she transcribed to canvas and some to a portfolio developing a series of wild flower paintings that she later gave her husband for his birthday. Laughingly, she said: "Who knows that I may not make as much by [painting] (if I conclude to honour the world by its publication) as Mrs. [Harriet] Beecher Stowe did by Uncle Tom's Cabin"?[6] Viewing her paintings today, we can agree with Eliza; she was an artist who captured beauty and mood in her painting with perception and sensitivity to nature. The Johnstons enjoyed their Austin years, perhaps the happiest period of their lives. A year after they settled in Austin, Margaret, later called "Mag," was born.

The paymaster's job was not easy and was often dangerous because of hostilities of the Plains Indians who came in increasing numbers to Texas. Pioneer settlements moved rapidly west and north in the 1850s into the old hunting grounds of the early Texas tribes which now included the hunting area of the hostile Comanches, Kiowas, Kiowa-Apaches, Southern Cheyennes and Southern Arapahos. The tribes often raided in concert after they joined in a treaty in 1840.

At times, however, Johnston's trips were monotonous. The job necessitated three journeys a year to New Orleans to pick up the money. Johnston went by stagecoach from Austin to Houston, by steamboat to Galveston, then by steamboat to New Orleans. He was accompanied by one clerk to New Orleans. When he went north to pay the troops in the forts, he traveled from Austin, with an escort of the Second Dragoons from the Austin Post, in a covered wagon, called an ambulance, with his Negro slave John driving four mules, and with his slave, Randolph, who did the cooking. The locked money chest was placed back of the seat in the ambulance. Another wagon with food and provisions supplied Johnston and the slaves and the escort with food and necessities. Often the wagons carried material for the soldiers, for Johnston served as friend and buyer for the soldiers who ordered horses, books, guns,

[6]Roland, A*lbert Sidney Johnston*, 159.

watches and other personal items. These he took along and delivered to the respective purchasers.

The country traveled over was beautiful in its varied seasons, especially spring and fall. Johnston's party covered about thirty miles a day. After new forts were built farther north, the party had to take extra precautions against raids by Indians or bandits. The escort usually comprised twelve cavalry men under a non-commissioned officer to provide protection against marauders or robbers. The early trips covered 620 miles from Austin to the posts and back. Later more forts were added and six trips a year were made. From the Austin Post, headquarters of the Second Dragoons commanded first by General William S. Harney, Johnston went north to Fort Croghan near present Burnet, on to Fort Gates near present Gatesville; Fort Graham near present Hillsboro; and on to Fort Worth, site of the present city of that name; then back to Austin. In 1854 the route was extended northwest, adding about 250 miles, to include Fort Belknap near present Graham; Fort Phantom Hill near present Abilene; Fort Chadbourne on Oak Creek tributary of the Colorado; and Fort McKavett on the San Saba River; then back to Austin. Later some of the forts were abandoned. In 1853, Fort Croghan was abandoned save for a military guard to protect materials stored there but the guards still had to be paid. The commander of Fort Croghan, Major Henry Hopkins Sibley, moved his companies of Second Dragoons to Phantom Hill, leaving Lieutenant Newton Curd Givens to pack up and close the fort, then march the remainder to Fort Phantom Hill, called Post on the Clear Fork of the Brazos, the most northwestern fort at that time. Fort Graham was also abandoned.

As the work increased, the salary did not. Johnston's annual salary of $2,500 was considered good at that time, but he was still in debt and could not manage to save anything. He hoped to build a home in Austin for Eliza and the children but never was able to do so. He also hoped to bring his two older children from Kentucky to Texas to live with him but could never afford it. They did visit occasionally, however. He was a loving and indulgent father, and, while they lived comfortably but not expensively, they were still in debt.

Eliza and the children were permitted to take some of the trips with Major Johnston. In her letters to family and friends, Eliza mentioned visiting the charming little town of New Braunfels, recently settled by emigrants from Germany, sponsored by the *Adelsverein* under Prince Carl of Solms-Braunfels. Johnston took the whole family in the summer of 1852 over the first two hundred miles of the route but would not take them into the area menaced by the Comanches and Kiowas, fearing an all too real danger. In 1854, when Sid was thirteen years old, his father took him on the whole journey.

Johnston's oldest son, William Preston, accompanied him on the trip in the spring of 1854, and by Johnston's special invitation again in the spring of 1855. William had graduated from Yale in 1852 and finished his law studies at the University of Louisville. It was in 1852 that he signed notes to purchase China Grove and his father's notes. The investment returned a long delayed profit when the plantation was sold for $20,000 in 1860. William discovered that the trusted slave, John, was stealing money from the strongbox with a duplicate key. A total of $3,900 was missing over a period of about two years, which Johnston increased his debts to repay. The slave was sold for $1,000 to help pay the debt but was allowed to pick his new owner from several who wanted him. John had spent the money for gifts for his pretty quadroon wife, and some $700 was found in his wife's trunk, part of it the especially marked coins of the 1855 trip. A gambler had made the key for John.[7]

William wrote of his visits to northwest Texas in 1854 and 1855 in his "Journal."[8] He described the country with much the same interest that his stepmother, Eliza, had. He said:

> Our route for the most part, lay across high rolling prairies, the rich soil of which was clothed with its earliest verdure and spangled with hyacinth, coryopsis, verbena, pink phlox, yellow primrose and other flowers just beginning to bloom.[9]

---

[7]Roland, *Albert Sidney Johnston*, 166-167.

[8]Marilyn McAdams Sibley (ed.), "With Albert Sidney Johnston in West Texas: Austin To Fort Chadbourne, March, 1855," in West Texas Historical Association, Year Book, XXXV (October, 1964), 121-145. William Preston Johnston's "Journal" is in the Mrs. Mason Barret Collection, Tulane University Library, New Orleans.

[9]Johnston, *The Life of Albert Sidney Johnston*, 173. The author also noted with interest the Penateka Comanches who were visiting and talking with the officers at Fort Belknap, preparatory to settling on the reservation. *Ibid.*, 139, 145.

After five years of paying the army, and constantly being on the road in all sorts of weather, Johnston tired of the job. The work had doubled since the beginning. Eliza worried about her husband, who was getting tired and thin. Johnston again had hopes of getting an army command, and Eliza played an important part in getting that command for him—entirely unknown to him.

Johnston did not know that Eliza and her cousin, William Preston, Representative in congress from Kentucky, brother of Johnston's first wife Henrietta, were able diplomats who would help secure for him an appointment as Commander of the newly created Second Cavalry Regiment. Although Johnston was in line for promotion to such a position, he might have been passed over had not Eliza, William Preston, and William's wife Margaret, called his qualifications to the attention of President Franklin Pierce and Secretary of War Jefferson Davis. Davis was a life-long friend of Johnston, a fellow student at West Point two classes below Johnston, and they had been soldiers together in the Mexican War. After the Battle of Monterrey, Johnston's quick action in forcing a Mexican officer to take him and Davis to the Mexican general to receive a written surrender may have saved both of their lives when they faced Mexican soldiers' guns upon them. Davis favored Johnston over numerous applicants for the position and chose him for the commission. The Texas Legislature also supported Johnston and urged United States Senator Thomas J. Rusk to endorse him. In the campaign waged to get a command for Johnston, Margaret Preston was especially active. Her husband credited her letter to Secretary of War Davis, asking him to consider Johnston for a regimental command as the most effective of their efforts. The families were old friends and Davis's first wife was the daughter of Zachary Taylor, a relative of the Prestons and Griffins.

Johnston was appointed by President Pierce, on Davis's recommendation, on March 9, 1855, to command the Second Cavalry. In May 0f 1855, he left Austin for Louisville, Kentucky, to take over the command from Robert E. Lee who was temporarily in charge. Eliza and the children visited relatives, then joined Johnston in Louisville where he made his headquarters for several months.

While stationed at Louisville, Johnston and Major William J. Hardee of the Second Cavalry went to Washington, D.C., to adopt uniforms and equipment for the two new regiments, as members of the Cavalry Equipment Board. The uniforms were to be blue coats with yellow trim, gray trousers, and black hats with the right side pinned up with ostrich plumes slanted to the back from the crown. Gutta-percha cloaks (rain coats) and woolen overcoats were also provided. The rakish plumed hats were later replaced with visor caps. Arms included carbines, Navy revolvers, and sabers.[10] The Second Cavalry was later called "a crack regiment." It also had horses of thoroughbred stock bought in Kentucky for not less than a hundred dollars apiece which were of matched color for each company. In September Johnston moved regimental headquarters to Jefferson Barracks, Missouri, to prepare for and await field service.

On October 27, 1855, the regiment started for Texas with 850 men. There were twenty six supply wagons in the caravan plus some privately owned wagons and teams. There were also sutlers to buy fresh supplies along the way. Families of four of the officers, with their hired servants and slaves, followed the cavalry in covered wagons. The wagons were formed in order of rank with Eliza and her children in the first. It was going to be a new experience, at times dramatic and at times difficult for Eliza and her family.

Lieutenant Colonel Robert E. Lee, second in command, was left at Leavenworth to complete business details, before going to Texas by way of the Mississippi River to New Orleans and the Texas Coast. From there he would go to San Antonio, then north to Camp Cooper on the Clear Fork of the Brazos to rejoin the regiment.

Officers of the Second Cavalry under Colonel Johnston's command were: Lieutenant Colonel Robert E. Lee, second in command; Majors William J. Hardee and George Bell Thomas; Captains Earl Van Dorn, Edmund Kirby Smith, Innis N. Palmer, and George Stoneman; and a number of lieutenants,

---

[10]George F. Price, Across the Continent with the Fifth Cavalry (New York, D. Van Nostrand Company, Inc., 1883), 26-29. See also John K. Herr and Edward S. Wallace, *The Story of the U.S. Cavalry, 1775-1942* (Boston, Little, Brown and Company, 1953) for details about the Second Cavalry.

among whom were John Bell Hood, Nathan G. Evans, Charles W. Field, Richard W. Johnson,[11] and Kenner Garrard.

Eliza wrote a remarkable journal of the trip. Eliza's letters were always interesting but it is in her "Diary"[12] that she really comes alive. With perceptive observation and candid appraisal of persons, gossip, and experiences along the way, she recounts the journey through southern Missouri, a part of Arkansas, Indian Territory, then into Texas. They reached Fort Belknap in a blizzard and camped under difficulties.

One duty of the Second Cavalry was to establish a new fort, Camp Cooper, on the Comanche Reserve, forty miles to the west of Fort Belknap. Major Hardee with a detachment of four companies set out to establish it. The fort was designed to protect the peaceful Indians from the hostiles. Texas supplied the land and the Bureau of Indian Affairs of the Interior Department of the United States supplied the Indian Agents and maintenance. In the summer of 1855, the Indians began to settle on the two new reserves, the Brazos Reserve in present Young County and the Comanche Reserve on the Clear Fork of the Brazos in present Throckmorton County.

There were fewer than 500 Penateka Comanches who remained there—the only ones who would agree to settle down. They comprised about one fifth of the Penatekas under Chief Ke-tum-see; the other four-fifths of the Penateka band of the Comanches had split up under separate war chiefs and had turned against Ke-tum-see's group as well as the whites. John R. Baylor was the Indian Agent.

Fifteen miles below Fort Belknap was Brazos Reserve where the displaced and almost destitute tribes of East and Central Texas were being located. These were village and agricultural settlements of peaceful Indians, now under the protection of Fort Belknap. Shapley P. Ross became the long-time Indian Agent there after several others had served this group.

---

[11]Richard W. Johnson, *A Soldier's Reminiscences in Peach and War* (Philadelphia, J. B. Lippincott Company, 1886.) Johnson wrote about the Second Cavalry in Texas and some friends of Van Dorn wrote about his experiences in *A Soldier's Honor: With Reminiscences of Major-General Earl Van Dorn*. By his comrades. (New York, Abbey Press, 1902.)

[12]Eliza Johnston, "Diary," 463-500.

The regiment left Fort Belknap and continued on its way. On January 3, 1856, it crossed the Clear Fork on ice and headed for Fort Mason where the journey would end at the headquarters for the Second Cavalry on January 14. Eliza had begun her diary on October 29, 1855. She continued the account while they were at Fort Mason and ended it on May 7, 1856.

Looking over Eliza's account of the trip from Missouri to Texas, we note particularly what she wrote about the countryside, vegetation, and wild flowers. On November 6, 1855, her entry in the diary stated that she had seen no wild flowers except a kind of "lilac coloured astor [sic]." After crossing the Gasconade River, not far from Lebanon, Missouri, she wrote that she "saw Purple Verbena growing wild, and in bloom, leaf like the cultivated verbena & not like that which grows wild in Texas."[13]

On November 19, when the caravan camped about fifty miles from Springfield, she wrote that around her tent "were Grapes, Raspberry, Gooseberries, Blackberrys, Walnuts & Hazlenuts."[14] On November 20 she said: "This country is rich in wild Roses of two or three kinds, it must look beautiful in Spring when all are blooming."[15]

There were no flowers in bloom when they reached Fort Belknap, Texas, in a blizzard with sleet and snow and a temperature around four degrees below zero. Eliza noted that "our land" was near there, referring to land that Johnston had preempted when he was on the Clear Fork as paymaster. On January 8, 1856, they traveled through "beautiful country" with the temperature nine degrees above zero. After crossing the Colorado and reaching Brady Creek, Eliza wrote that they were in a "beautiful Country of fine grass, live-oak and mesquite, very fine & extensive views."[16]

---

[13]Ibid., 471-472

[14]Ibid., 475.

[15]Ibid., 475.

[16]Ibid., 489.

Eliza's "word pictures" of the country show her interest in nature. While camped on the San Saba River, she wrote that they

> today passed through one of the most beautiful portions of Texas. we could see over a vast extent of Country covered with live-oaks & other growth dotted over the Prairie seemingly as ornaments to the landscape. the green trees & brown grass & bright sunshine gave the scene all the effect of a midsummer harvest it was like a dream of August. but only a dream, for while we gazed admiringly we were shivering from cold.[17]

They went on to Fort Mason, their destination. Here they shared a four-room house with three other families—a family to a room. Cooking was carried on in tents placed outside. After settling down, Eliza managed to get some painting done, even in the crowded house. On March 30 she wrote:

> I have painted for Uncle the female of the species of Quail I gave him last summer. Maj. Van Dorn offered to paint my Mag's miniature for me. When I get a daguerreotype from Ky, he will copy it for me.[18]

On March 30, Colonel Robert E. Lee stopped at Fort Mason on his way to take command of Camp Cooper on the Clear Fork. Eliza was not impressed with him. She wrote that he would not stop long enough to help an old friend by serving as a character witness in a court-martial. She said that she supposed that he feared "to become unpopular," and it was "a mean act" in her opinion.

Lee, however, wrote a nice comment on Eliza:

> Mrs. Johnston is a pretty and sweet woman, intelligent and well adapted to her position in life. She teaches her own children—two boys and a girl—and occupies herself in painting birds and flowers of the country.[19]

[17]Ibid., 489.

[18]Ibid., 493. Major Van Dorn was interested in art and poetry. He was also an active Indian fighter. See note 9 above.

[19]Carl Coke Rister, *Robert E. Lee in Texas* (Norman, University of Oklahoma Press, 1946), 17.

On March 31 Eliza wrote that "Capt Eastman gave me his sketch book yesterday with 6 sketches he has illustrated Schoolcrafts book upon Indians."[20]

That same day an express arrived to notify Johnston that he was to be in command of the Department of Texas, at San Antonio, in addition to his regimental command. He was to replace Brevet Brigadier General Persifor F. Smith. Eliza could afford to gloat a bit, perhaps remembering her part in her husband's last promotion. She wrote:

> So rolls the wheel of fate, last year at this time my husband was traveling here as Paymaster, now today an Express arrived from San Antonio to tell him he is in command of this department we leave on Friday for S. Antonio.[21]

Life in San Antonio was pleasant. They lived in the home previously occupied by General Smith—a stone house on the bank of the San Antonio River. The site was an acre well planted with pecan and peach trees and flowering shrubs. Birds, busy with springtime, nesting and singing, inhabited the grounds. Here Eliza enjoyed time for painting, music, and receiving guests. The two boys were placed in a private school and did well. Colonel Johnston enjoyed the leisure time he had with his family and taught the children to swim in the river. They lived economically but comfortably. San Antonio had much to offer after the cramped quarters of one room and a kitchen tent at Fort Mason. There was a lot to do and a social gathering now and then was fun but Eliza still found time to paint. On April 9 she

[20]Eliza Johnston, "Diary," 495. Captain Seth Eastman was in Texas in 1848-1849. He was given leave to go to Washington, D. C., to illustrate Henry Rowe Schoolcraft's compilation of materials on Indians gathered by the Bureau of Indian Affairs and published in *Historical and Statistical Information Respecting the History, Conditions and Prospects of the Indian Tribes of the United States*, 6 Parts (Philadelphia, Grambo and Company, 1851-1857).
Eastman knew the Indians around Fort Snelling well. His first wife was a Sioux Indian by whom he had one daughter. In Texas his sketches were of buildings and landscapes and only one sketch of an Indian encampment near Fredericksburg. Unfortunately this marvelous painter of Indians did no Indian portraits in Texas. Eastman returned to Texas after being on leave in Washington. See also Seth Eastman, *A Seth Eastman Sketchbook, 1848-1849* with introduction by Lois Burkhalter (San Antonio, Marion Koogler McNay Institute, and Austin, University of Texas Press, 1961. Eastman's biography is given in John Francis McDermott, *Seth Eastman, Pictorial Historian of the Indian* (Norman, University of Oklahoma Press, 1961).

[21]Eliza Johnston, "Diary," 494.

wrote: "Yesterday I drew the old Alamo from Mrs. Baylors. I will go down soon and sketch the old mission."[22]

The last entry in her diary was on May 7. At that time she was worried about her children catching scarlet fever. She said:

> Heard yesterday that Mr I McKinney had lost his eldest daughter Ella as well as his only son Lockiel. Mrs T McK[inney] is coming to see us soon. I trust she will not, as I greatly dread her bringing scarlet fever in her clothing among my little flock. I feel perfectly nervous about that disease. . . . We ride out every evening when the weather permits.[23]

These were the last sentences in her diary, Mary 7, 1856. Eliza's third son was born in San Antonio in the spring of 1857, and was named Griffin Hancock Johnston. The "Griffin" was for her father, and "Hancock" was for Eliza's uncle, George Hancock, in whose home Eliza lived before her marriage.

In the spring of 1857, Brigadier General David E. Twiggs took over the command of the Department of Texas, and the Johnstons returned to Fort Mason. Two months later Johnston was instructed to report to Washington, D.C., for a new assignment. He turned over the command to Colonel Robert E. Lee who left Camp Cooper for Fort Mason, still the headquarters of the Second Cavalry. Johnston took his family to Kentucky and went on to Washington.

There he learned he was to take command of the expedition that was on its belated way to Utah, relieving General William S. Harney. The expedition was a punitive one against the Mormons. It was a difficult expedition that would encounter losses from both freezing weather and Mormons and finally become a tiresome adventure. Eliza and the children were to stay in Kentucky while her husband would be gone for three lonely years.

---

[22]Ibid., 499. Mrs. Baylor was the widow of Dr. John Walker Baylor. One of her sons, John R. Baylor, was the Indian Agent at the Comanche Reserve. One of her daughters was Frances, wife of Major James A. Belger in San Antonio. Her husband's brother was Reverend Robert E. B. Baylor for whom Baylor University was named. Baylor Letters, University of Texas Archives, Eugene C. Barker Texas History Center, Austin.

[23]Ibid., 500. They rode in a horse drawn carriage. The reference to "Mrs. T. McK" was to Mrs. Thomas F. McKinney.

On April 16, 1857 Johnston became a brigadier general. In the fall of 1858 he had 2,900 men at Camp Floyd and 400 at Fort Bridger. In March of 1859, he was at last free of the Mormon War and left Utah for California to take ship for home. After almost three years of separation, he arrived in Louisville for a leave of absence before his next assignment—a pleasant leave of seven months. Then, in charge of the Department of the Pacific which comprised both California and Oregon, he and his family took passage in December of 1860 for California, going by way of New York to Panama, thence up the coast. He was stationed at San Francisco on January 15, 1861. Secession began while the Johnstons were on the way west. After three months in San Francisco, Johnston resigned on April 8, 1861. Later, he determined to return to the South and join the Confederacy.

Johnston left California with a group of Southerners organized by Captain Alonzo Ridley, on June 16, 1861, leaving his family in Los Angeles. Eliza was expecting a baby that summer and could not make the trip. But she was not alone; her brother, Dr. John Griffin, had settled there. Johnston took with him Randolph (the slave he had emancipated) who wished to return, as well as a wagon and horses and a saddle horse. At times he rode horseback and at times he rode in the wagon with Ran. The party rode in midsummer heat across 800 miles of desert and plain from southern California to New Mexico and then to Texas.

Johnston's letters to Eliza on the way expressed his love and tried to explain his need to leave. Eliza would remember these, such as: "Love & hope cheer me on to discharge a great duty. . . . I will always love my dear wife—Kiss my dear children."[24] She would not see him again.

Johnston stopped in Mesilla, New Mexico, for three weeks to aid the Confederate interests there, then went to El Paso, San Antonio, and Houston. When he reached New Orleans, he was unable to take a ship because of the Federal blockade, so he left by rail for Richmond. Jefferson Davis was delighted to have him. He was appointed full general and given command of the Department of the West. He left at once for Nashville, Tennessee. Here he met his son, William Preston, on his way to join his Kentucky regiment in northern Virginia. They would not meet again.

---

[24]Roland, A*lbert Sidney Johnston*, 256, citing Johnston to Eliza Johnston, June 26, 1861, Johnston Papers, Barret Collection.

In California, Eliza had a daughter born on August 31, 1861. She named the baby Eliza Alberta Johnston. This was her sixth child.

Albert Sidney Johnston died at the Battle of Shiloh, also called the Battle of Pittsburg Landing, on April 6, 1862. It was early spring and the peach trees and dogwood were in bloom near the little Church of Shiloh, Tennessee, and in the orchards that became a battlefield. Fifteen minutes after a Minié ball struck below and behind Johnston's right knee, cutting the popliteal artery, he died. It was a great loss for the Confederacy—and for Eliza.

After her husband's death, Eliza remembered that he had said: "When I die, I want a handful of Texas earth on my breast." And she wanted him buried in Texas. Temporarily he was buried in New Orleans but later was reinterred in the State Cemetery in Austin. Still later, the sculptress, Elisabet Ney, carved in white marble a monument of his reclining figure to grace his last resting place in a mausoleum.

Eliza made her home in Los Angeles for the rest of her life, but she did not forget her Texas friends. One was Rebecca Jane Fisher who had known General Albert Sidney Johnston from her childhood. She was grateful to him for saving her from Comanche bondage. Johnson Gilleland, father of Rebecca, brought his family to Texas in 1837 and settled near Refugio. In 1840, while Gilleland was at home on leave from the Texas Army, Comanche Indians attacked and killed the elder Gillelands, carrying off Rebecca and her brother William as captives. General Johnston, stationed at Texana, with a detachment of soldiers followed the Comanches and rescued Rebecca and William, taking them to Victoria, then to Galveston to live with an aunt.

In 1844 Rebecca entered Rutersville Academy where, after graduation, she married Reverend Orceneth Fisher. Mrs. Fisher later lived in Austin. She was a charter member of the Daughters of the Republic of Texas, founded in 1892. She was state president of the organization for the last thirty-two years of her life and also served as president of the William Barret Travis Chapter and aided Clara Driscoll in saving the Alamo. Rebecca Jane Fisher's friendship for the Johnston was lifelong and cordial.[25]

[25]Webb, Walter Prescott and H. Bailey Carroll (eds.), *The Handbook of Texas*, I, 602-603.

In 1894, after some previous correspondence with Mrs. Rebecca Fisher of Austin, Eliza wrote:

Los Angeles, Cal
Oct-18-1894

My dear Mrs. Fisher:

Your kind letter has been received with the enclosures for which, and your cordial invitation to visit Austin this Winter I thank you sincerely. I desire much to accept. I am pleased to think that my coming might be a desired pleasure for some as you assert, but the journey is beyond my strength.

I have been unavoidably deterred from attention to your previous letter, or any of its requests, all of which I still hold in rem[em]brance.

Today I sent by express the souvenirs I have with much Diplomacy induced my children to relinquish. I regret the incompleteness of the Book of Texas Flowers, which, had I returned to that state would not have occurred.

Four Plates have been stolen, A vine with bunch of native grapes, a vine of Texas Sarsaparilla, each crowding a full page. A small landscape with yellow prairie-flower and horned Toad, and one other all of which the Thief selected with judgement from the best.

The Grey uniform sleeve of the Coat worn at Shiloh or a part of such as could be saved from the moths, when I received it, some years after the War packed away in a trunk, it had become a heap of insects & their cocoons.

I am sorry to say that the sketches of the Texas Flag were so crude that no use could be made of them as a guide. Now, if your friend desires to paint one for his book, please say that it must necessarily be accurate, I will paint one with pleasure, if he will send me the exact measure of the paper to fit his book, together with a small accurately drawn & colored flag, or some small lithographed or chromo as a model, the present one in use the best I think. I thought of painting one on a Plaque for your Bazar.

Mrs. Prichard is prevented just now from sending her papers, will do so shortly.

With sincere regard I am
Your friend
Eliza Griffin Johnston[26]
to Mrs. Rebecca J. Fisher
No 300 East 13th St
Austin
Texas.

[26]Eliza Griffin Johnston to Mrs. Rebeca J. Fisher, October 18, 1894, Daughters of the Republic of Texas Museum (in Johnston Museum Case), 510 East Anderson Lane, Austin, Texas.

In 1894 Eliza was living in the home of her daughter Alberta. Her last days were happy ones, for she loved the land and the people of Los Angeles and the company of her brother and many friends. She died there on September 25, 1896, survived by three of her children. They were Hancock McClung Johnston, Mrs. Margaret Johnston Prichard, and Eliza Alberta Johnston, wife of George J. Denis of New Orleans and later of Los Angeles. Pictures of Eliza and of Albert Sidney Johnston and others of the Johnston family were given to the Daughters of the Republic of Texas by Alberta Johnston Denis. Eliza Griffin Johnston was a member of William Barret Travis Chapter of the Daughters of the Republic of Texas and many of its members were her lifelong friends. Many of these attended a memorial service for General Albert Sidney Johnston when the Elisabet Ney Monument was dedicated in the State Cemetery, in honor of this famous family.

Eliza's *Book of Texas Flowers* has rested in the Daughters of the Republic of Texas Museum since 1894. These delicate watercolors are well over a century old, some having been painted in Texas in the 1840s and 1850s. Eliza's paintings are beautiful and accurately portrayed because Eliza was both artist and botanist.

At long last Eliza's wild flowers will be enjoyed by many people.

Lithographs

of the

Water Color Paintings

of

Texas Wild Flowers

painted by

Eliza Griffin Johnston

~All plates are reproduced 81% of original size~

Botanical and common names of the flowers, where missing in Mrs. Johnston's handwritten text, were supplied by Dr. Mildred P. Mayhall

Is a shrub, varying from five to seven feet in height, with many grey coloured stems, springing from the same root with Spinose leaves, the flower bearing stems dark red, long and slender and rich with clusters of fragrant blossoms from about the 20th of Feb 'till the middle of March, bears a red berry which ripens in April, and is called by the people of the country "wild currant" having a pleasant acid taste resembling that fruit, it is frequently used for tarts. Its locality is upon hills, and overhanging cliffs, soil, clay and gravel. It is an evergreen.

No. 1

Agarita — *Agaritia trifoliolata* Moric.

Is a shrub, varying from five to seven feet in height, with many grey coloured stems, springing from the same root with spinose leaves, the flower bearing stems dark red, long and slender and rich with clusters of fragrant blossoms from about the 20th of Feb 'till the middle of March, bears a red berry which ripens in April, and is called by the people of the country "wild currant" having a pleasant acid taste resembling that fruit, it is frequently used for tarts. Its locality is upon hills, and overhanging cliffs, soil, clay and gravel. It is an evergreen.

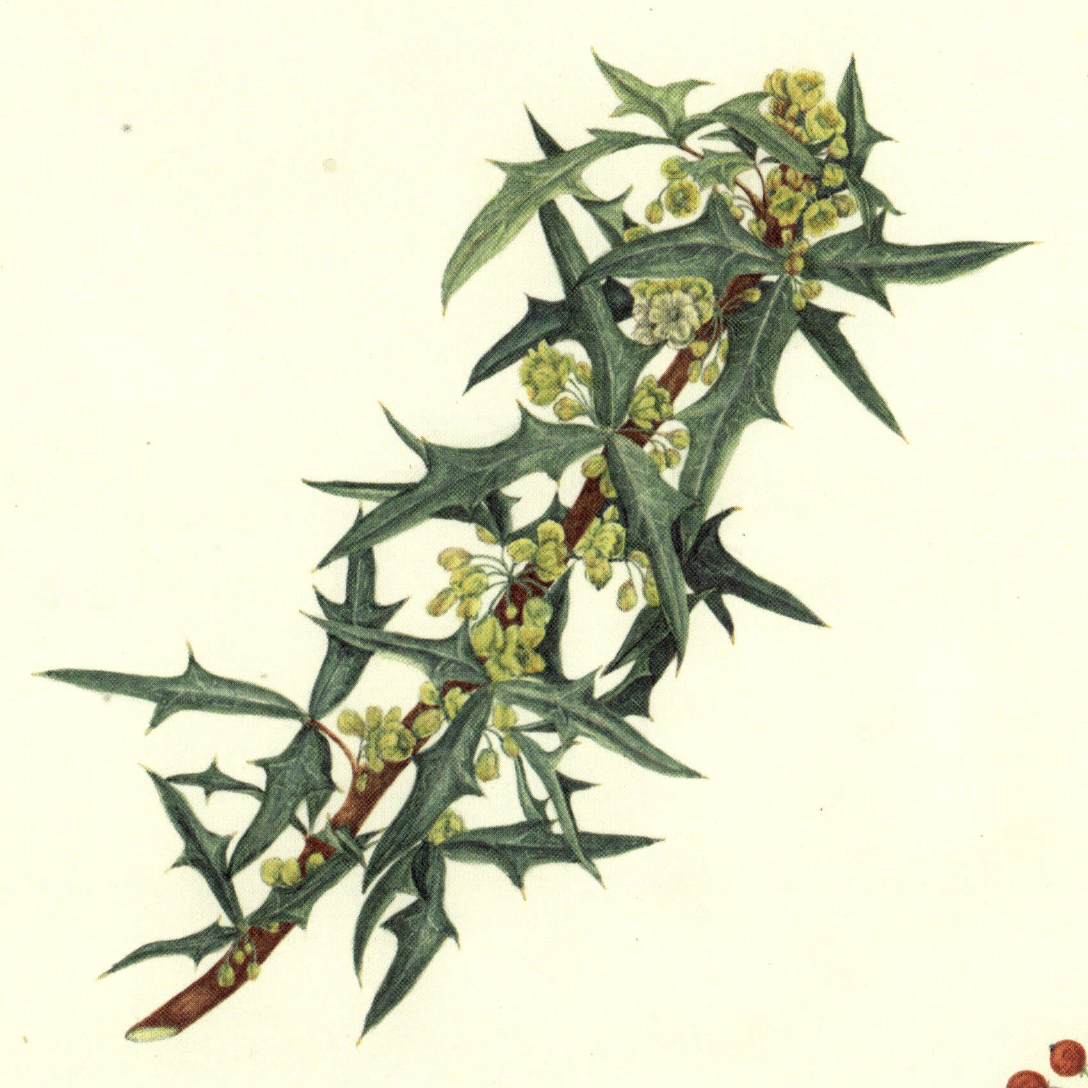

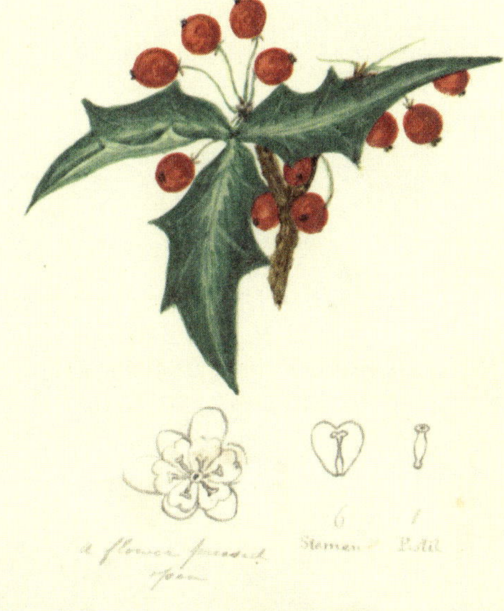
a flower pressed open
6
Stamens
1
Pistil

Is a modest little flower with no peculiar merit, but as the first flower of a Texan spring, it has a bulbous root, and blooms as early as the 4th of Feb, it flourishes in a thin soil with red clay substratum.

No. 2

Anemone — *Anemone decapetala* Ard.

Is a modest little flower with no peculiar merit, but as the first flower of a Texan spring, it has bulbous root, and blooms as early as the 4th of Feb, it flourishes in a thin soil with red clay substratum.

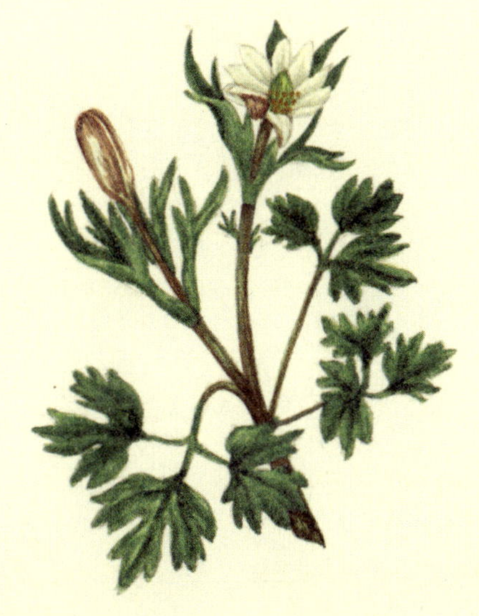

10 Petals

1 Pistil 24 Stamens

This is a pretty little bulbous plant, blooming about the last of Feb in good rich soil.

No. 3

Star-flower — *Androstephium coeruleum* Scheele

This is a pretty little bulbous plant, blooming about the last of Feb in good rich soil.

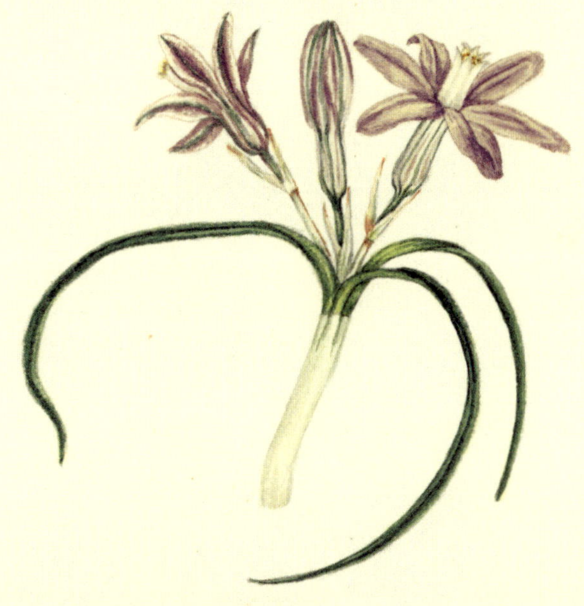

Wild Hyacinth

Feb. 27

Blooms early, peeping its sunny face just above
the short spring grass, early in March its corolla is
crimped, resembling Crape Myrtle, it is a prolific
bloomer, and lasts about six weeks, root tuberous,
growing in rich gravelly soil.

No. 4

Puccoon — *Lithospermum incisum* Lehmann.

Blooms early, peeping its sunny face just above the short spring grass, early in March its corolla is crimped, resembling Crape Myrtle, it is a prolific bloomer, and lasts about six weeks, root tuberous, growing in rich gravelly soil.

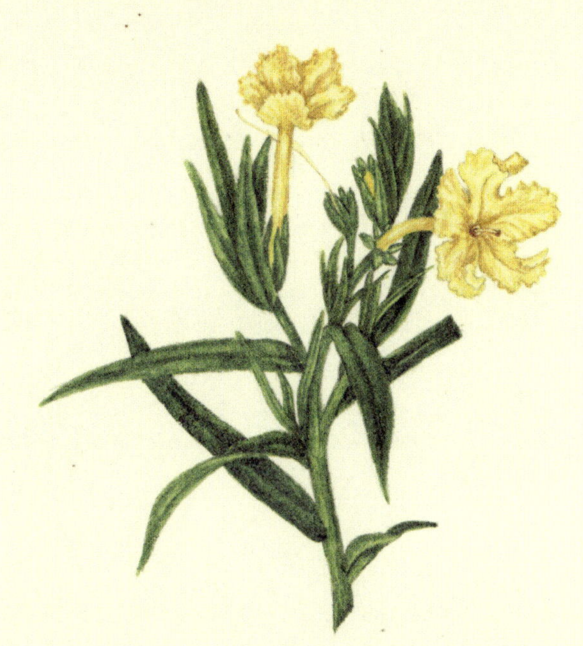

March 1st

Grows in great profusion, in rich Prairie land, the bulb is edible, when boiled, it resembles in flavour, boiled chesnuts,

No. 5

Celestial — Nemastylis geminiflora Nutt.

Grows in great profusion, in rich Prairie land, the bulb is edible, when boiled, it resembles in flavour, boiled chestnuts.

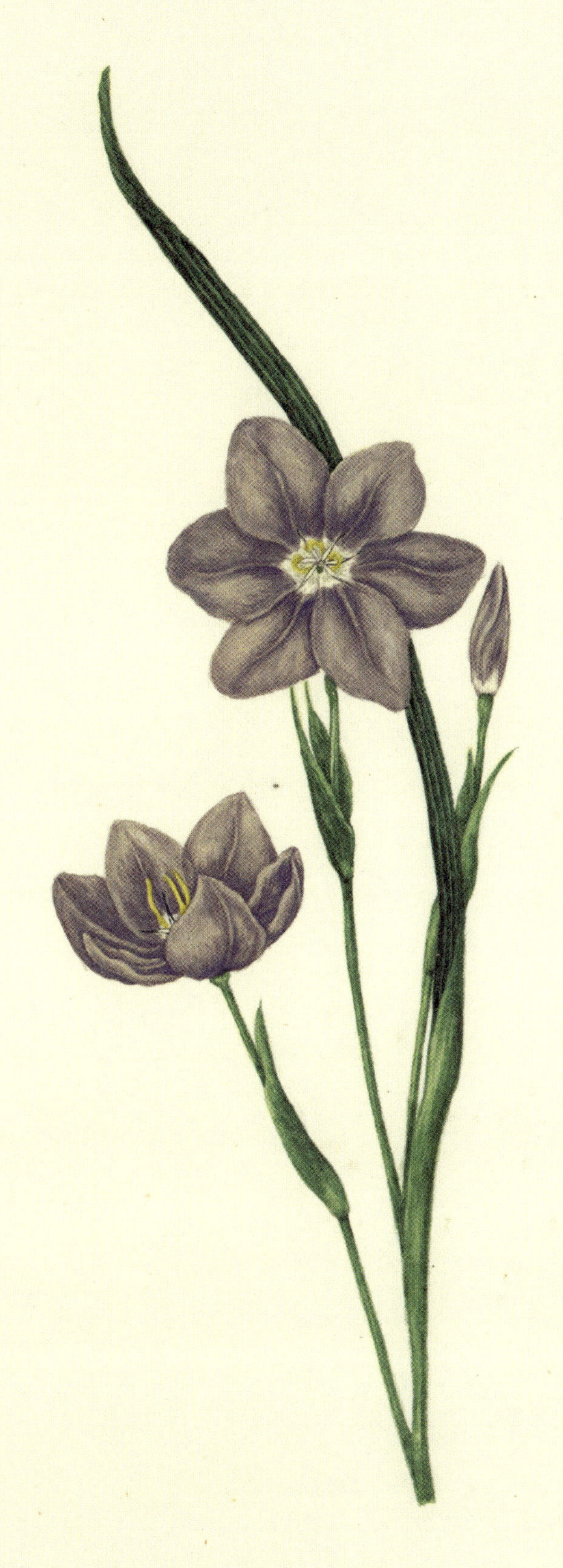

March 13th

One of the most brilliant evergreens of Texas, it blooms in March. and is a small tree or shrub from ten to fifteen feet in height; the blossoms form racemes of rich purple bunches, which shed an over-powering fragrance, it bears a pod enclosing a beautiful glossy red bean, the Mexicans call it "Frijolia," or bean tree, it is a highland shrub, but flourishes much better in sheltered nooks of the hills, than when exposed to the full glare of the sun, upon the Mountain side.

No. 6

Mountain Laurel or Mescal Bean — *Sophora secundiflora*

Ortega., D.C.

One of the most brilliant evergreens in Texas, it blooms in March, and is a small tree or shrub from ten to fifteen feet in height; the blossoms form racemes of rich purple bunches, which shed an overpowering fragrance, it bears a pod enclosing a beautiful glossy red bean, the Mexicans call it "Frijolia," or bean tree, it is a highland shrub, but flourishes much better in sheltered nooks of the hills, than when exposed to the full glare of the sun, upon the Mountain side.

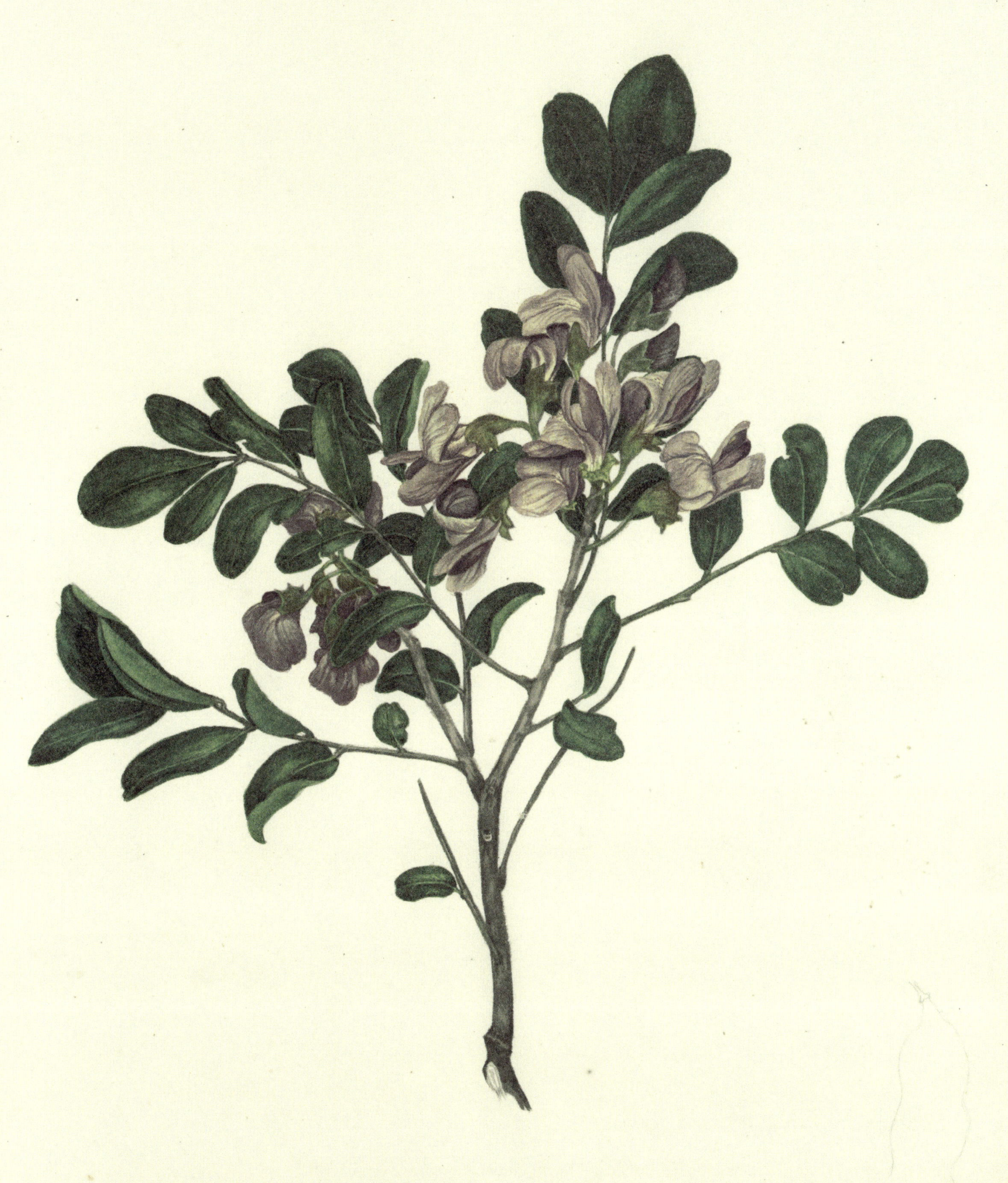

A well known Phlox, it blooms from the middle of March 'till the last of April, in rich soil.

No. 7

Dwarf Phlox — *Phlox nana* Nutt.

A well known Phlox, it blooms from the middle of March 'till the last of April, in rich soil.

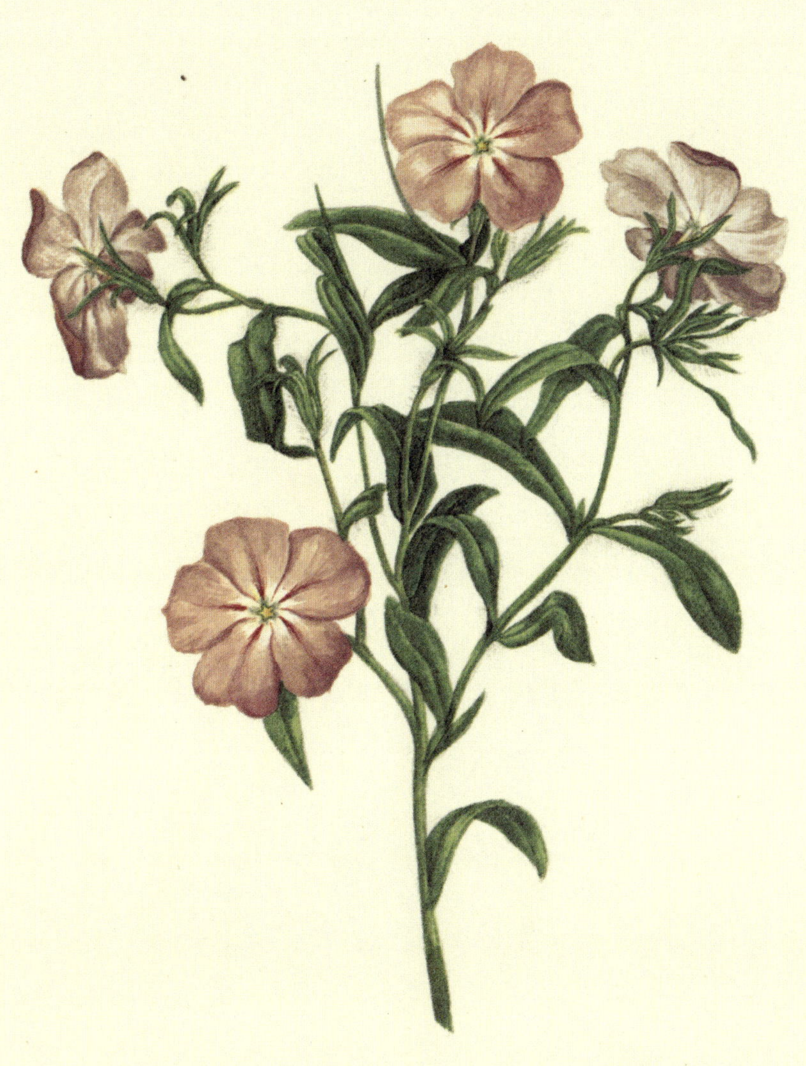

Mexican Buckeye, a shrub ten feet high, it grows near the margin of small streams, in very wet soil. blooms in the middle of March, the flowers have a very pleasant odour it bears a small buckeye the size of a hazel nut, three in a pod, has an agreeable flavour but when eaten produces giddiness, there is also a shrub Buckeye with long spikes of crimson flowers, growing in the same locality.

No. 8

Mexican Buckeye — *Aesculus flava* Art.

(The crimson buckeye mentioned by Mrs. Johnston is *Aesculus pavia* L.)

Mexican Buckeye, a shrub ten feet high, it grows near the margin of small streams, in very wet soil, blooms in the middle of March, the flowers have a very pleasant odour it bears a small buckeye the size of a hazel nut, three in a pod, has an agreeable flavour but when eaten produces giddiness, there is also a shrub Buckeye with long spikes of crimson flowers, growing in the same locality.

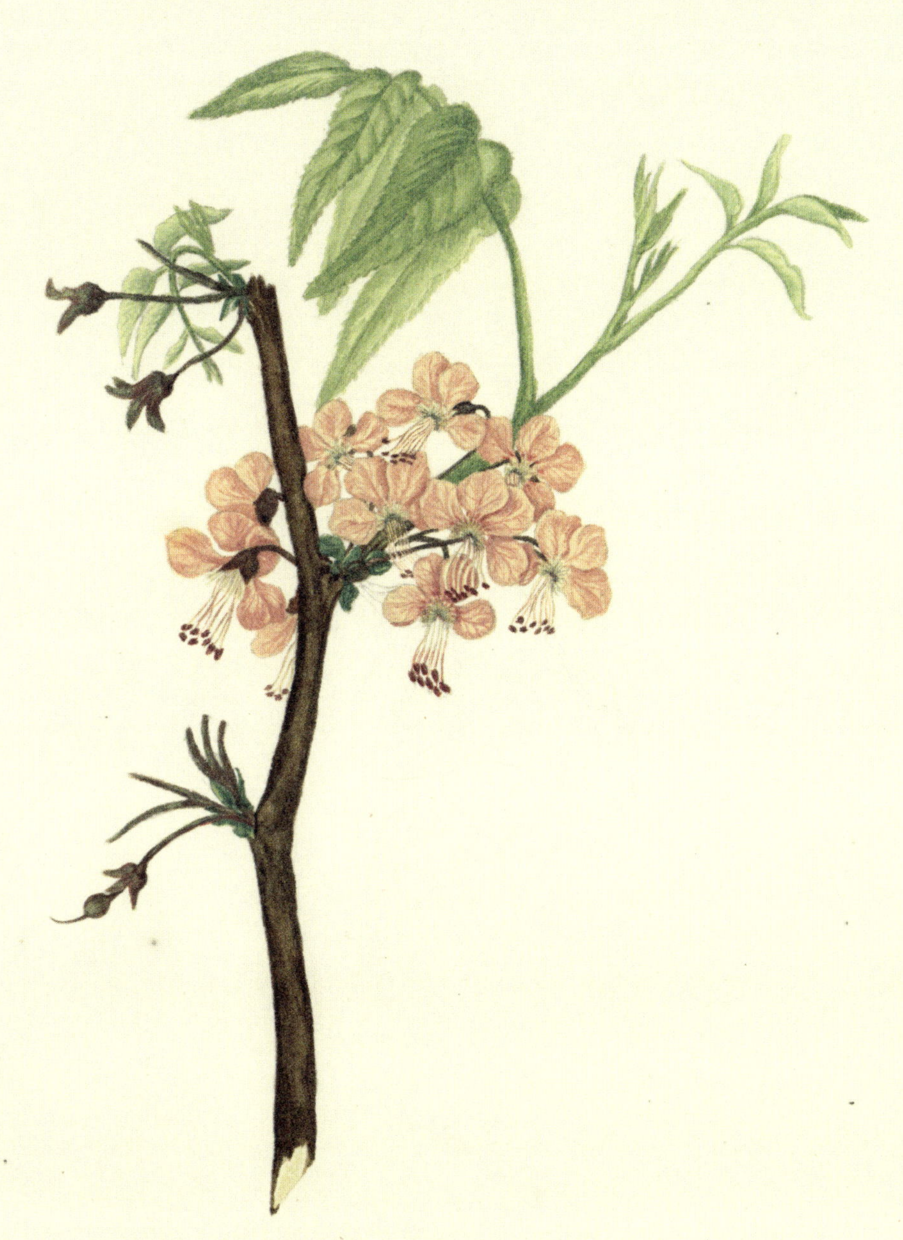

The well known Red Bud, a shrub or small tree, blooms in Texas during the month of March

No. 9

Redbud — *Cercis canadensis* L.

The well known Red Bud, a shrub or small tree, blooms in Texas during the month of March.

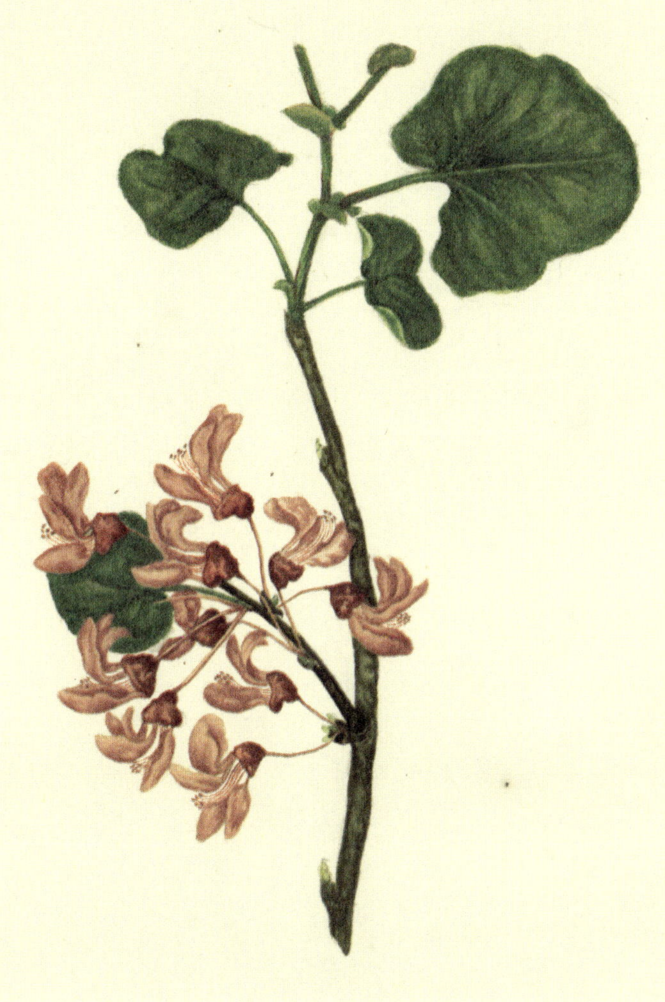

A Marigold, blooms in profusion, from 18 March during a period of 8 or 10 weeks, flourishes in a good soil.

No. 10

Yellow Daisy — *Tetraneuris scaposa* D. C.

A Marigold, blooms in profusion, from 18 March during a period of 8 or 10 weeks, flourishes in a good soil.

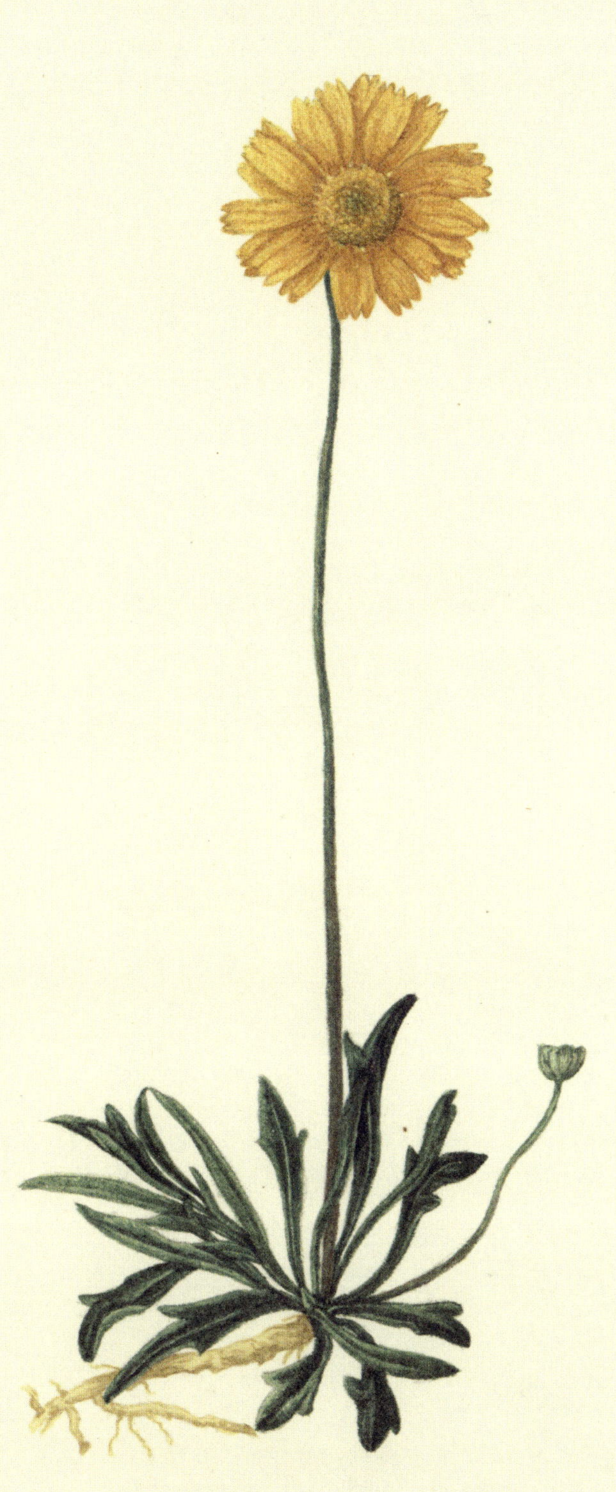

A very beautiful little plant, blooms profusely for about four weeks from the 20 March. The stem is covered with very fine bristles it grows upon sandy hill sides. the leaves also are setaceous.

No 11

Phacelia — *Phacelia patuliflora* Englem. and Gray

A very beautiful little plant, blooms profusely for about four weeks from the 20 March. The stem is covered with very fine bristles it grows upon sandy hill sides, the leaves also are setaceous.

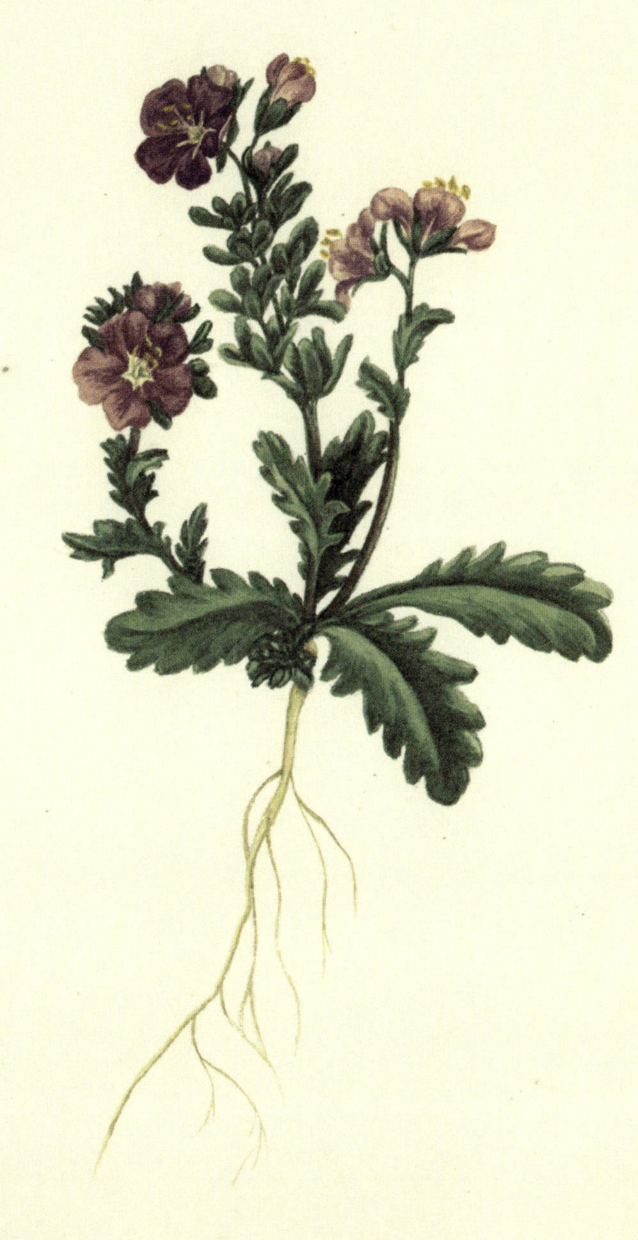

Blooms about the 21st of March, lasting three of four weeks, it springs from the dry sandy hill sides.

No. 12

Bladder-pod or Cloth-of-Gold — *Lesquerrella lasiocarpa* (Gray) Wats var. *lasiocarpa*

Blooms about the 21st of March, lasting three of four weeks, its springs from the dry sandy hill sides.

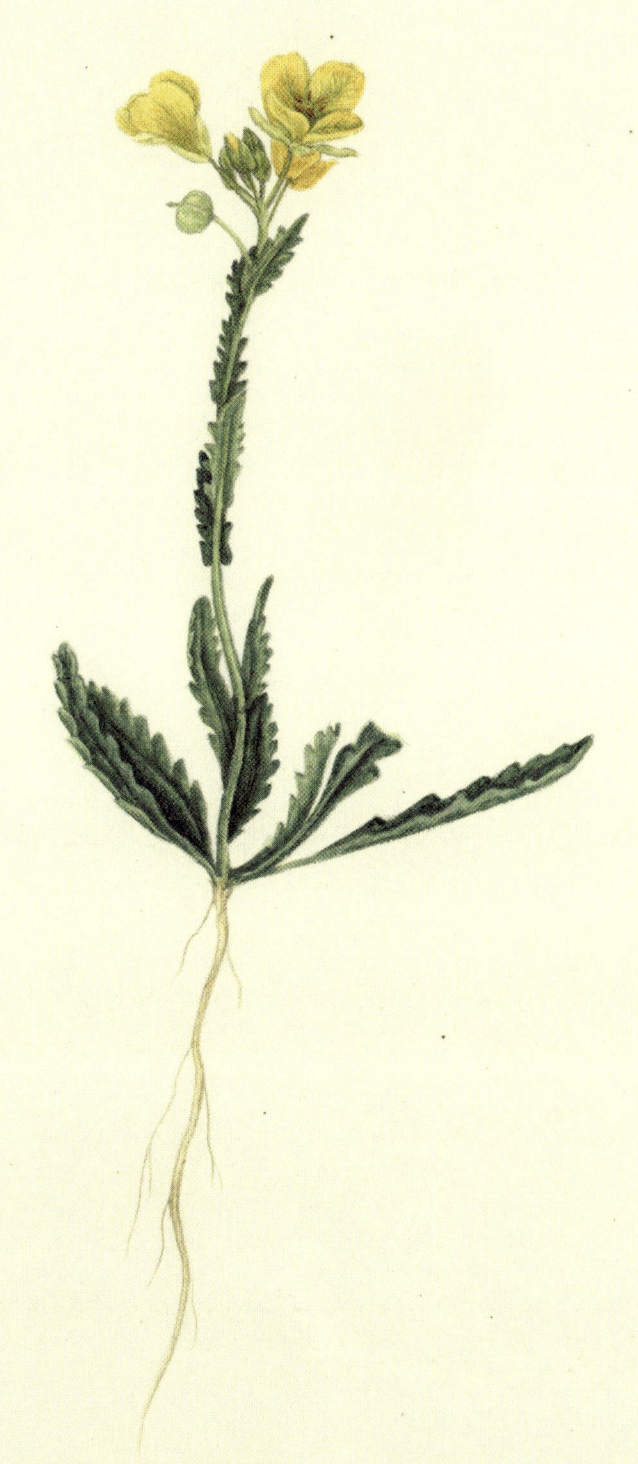

A delicate, and beautiful plant, worthy a place in the garden, Stalk and leaves setaceous, blooms from the middle of March three or four weeks, it is found only on sandy hills or river banks.

No. 13

Baby Blue-eyes — *Nemophila phacelioides* Nutt.

A delicate, and beautiful plant, worthy a place in the garden. Stalk and leaves setaceous, blooms from the middle of March three or four weeks, it is found only on sandy hills or river banks.

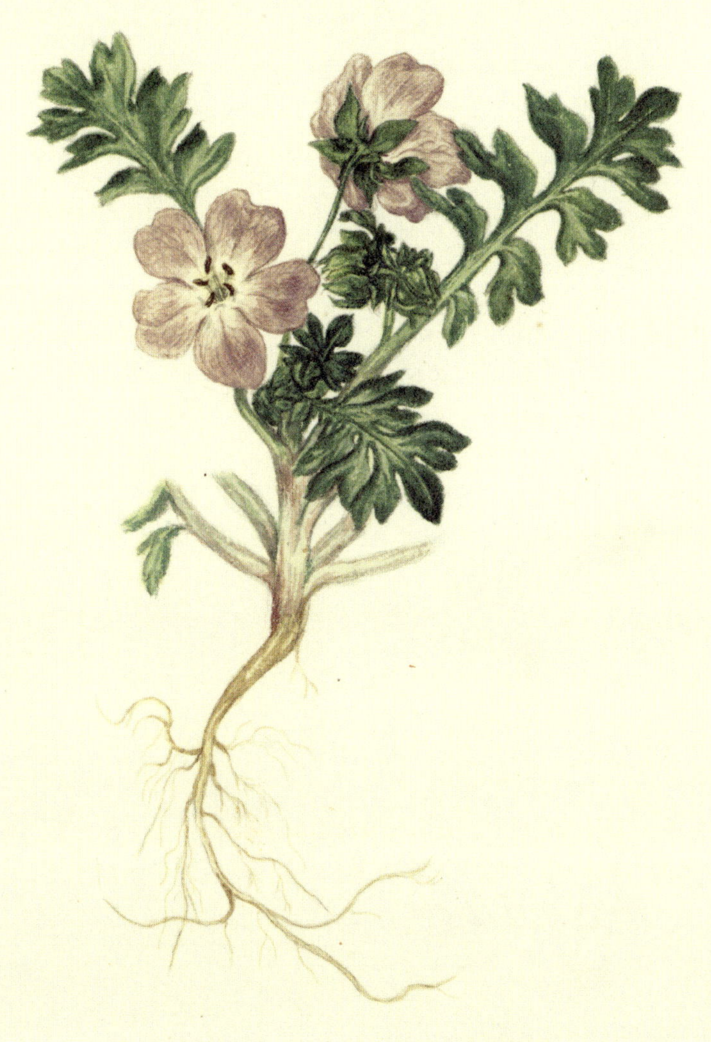

Black Haw, well known, blooms in Texas about the 21st of March, in rich soil.

No. 14

Black Haw — *Bumelia lanuginosa* Michx., Pers.

Black Haw, well known, blooms in Texas about the 21st of March, in rich soil.

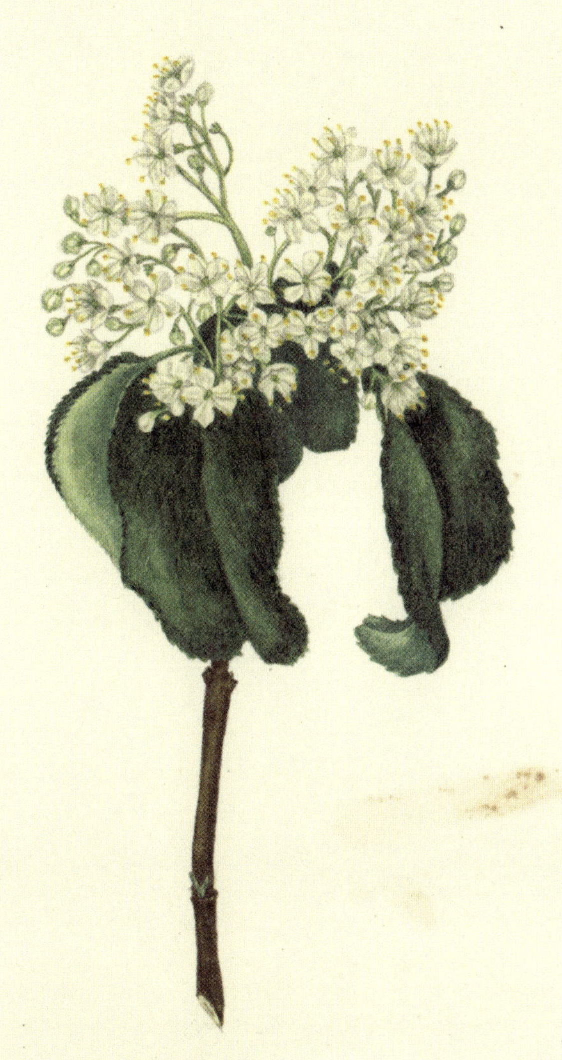

Black Haw

A plant of the sunflower species. found in rich soil. there are many fine varieties of this class of plants, which are indigenous in Texas.

No. 15

Texas Star Daisy or Linheimer's Daisy — *Lindheimera texana* Gray and Englem.

A plant of the sunflower species, found in rich soil, there are many fine varieties of this class of plants, which are indigenous in Texas.

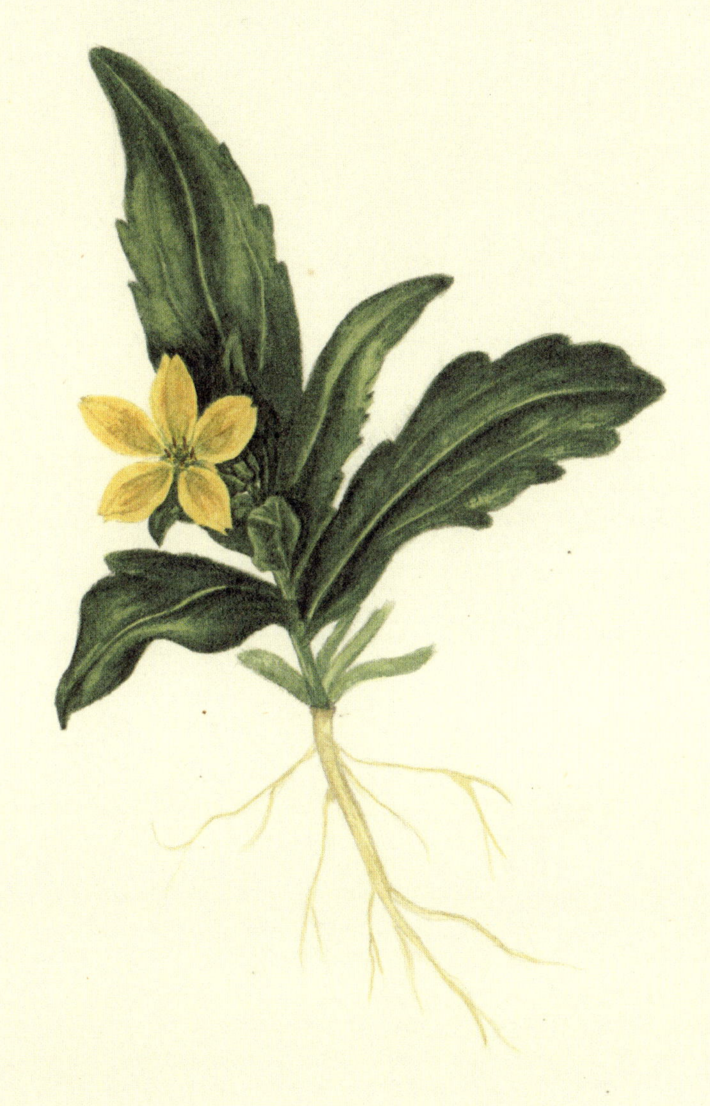

Is a flower of peculiar appearance, in some localities grows in such profusion that the prairie seems coloured with it, it is from two to three feet high and seldom has more than two flowers on a stalk, blooms about the 25th March and lasts only a few weeks.

No. 16

Wild Honeysuckle — *Gaura suffulta* Engelm.

Is a flower of peculiar appearance, in some localities grows in such profusion that the prairie seems coloured with it, it is from two or three feet high and seldom has more than two flowers on a stalk, blooms about the 25th March and lasts only a few weeks.

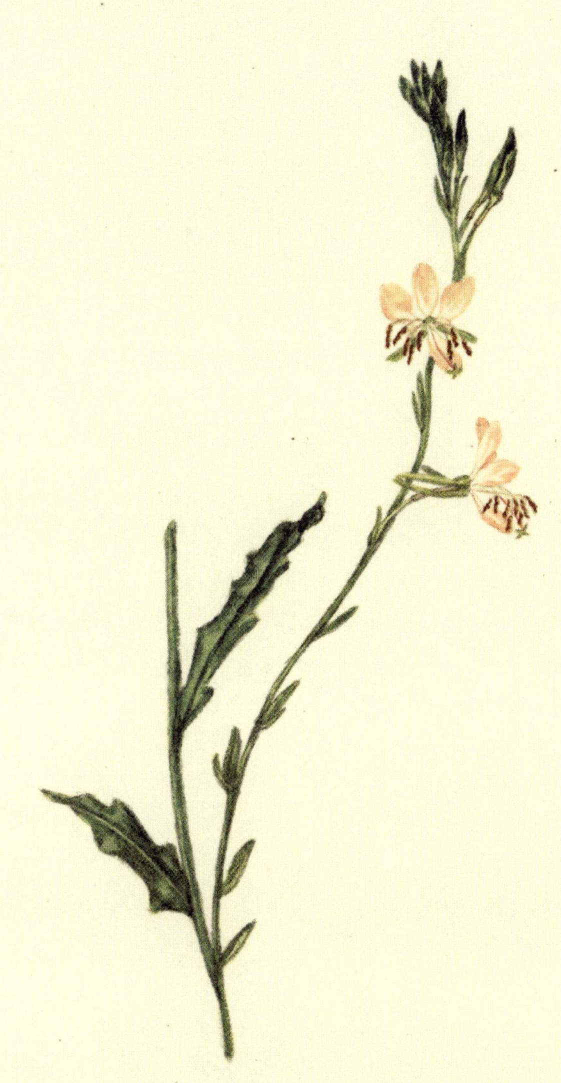

Is a small pea, which grows in the Prairie grass, prostrate and creeping, Cattle are exceedingly fond of it, and eat it, with great eagerness. it flourishes in every variety of soil

No. 17

Texas Climbing Vetch — *Vicia texana* Torr, and Gray, Small

Is a small pea, which grows in the Prairie grass, prostrate and creeping. Cattle are exceedingly fond of it, and eat it, with great eagerness, it flourishes in every variety of soil.

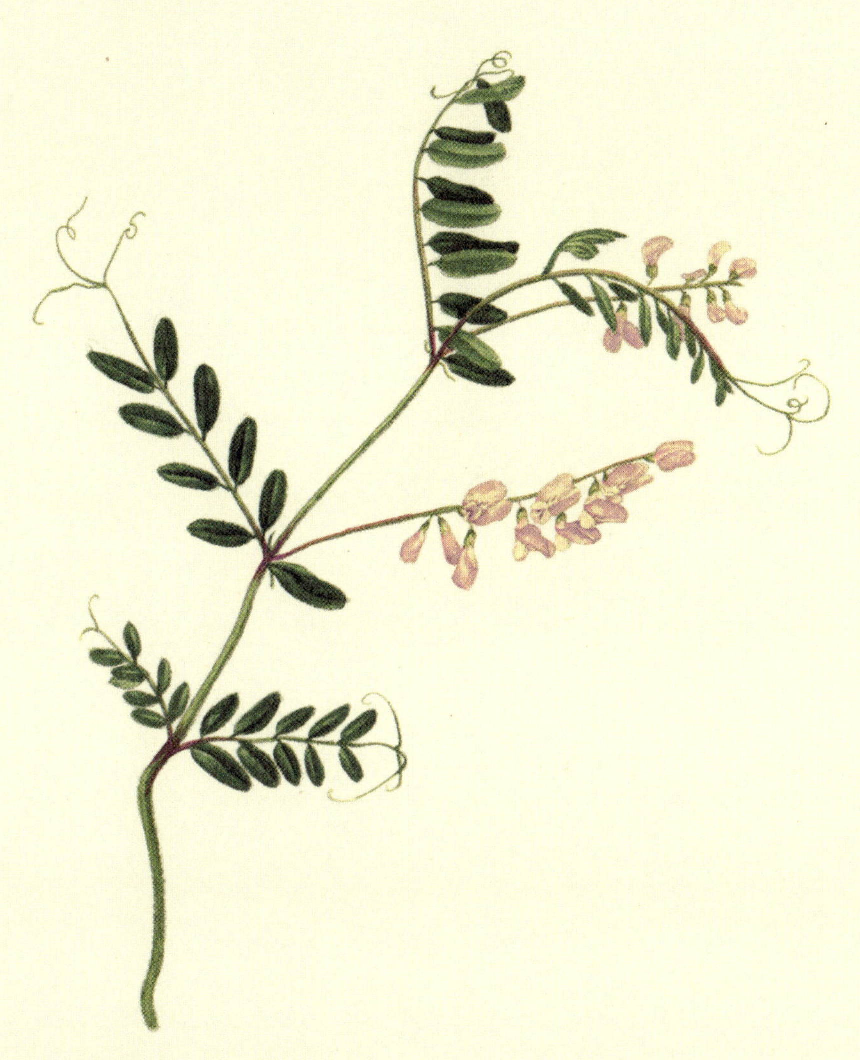

Grows in moist sand, near running water blooms about the last of March, continuing about three weeks.

No. 18

Texas Corydalis or Scrambled Eggs — *Capnoides curvisiliquum* Englem., Kuntze.

Grows in moist sand, near running water blooms about the last of March, continuing about three weeks.

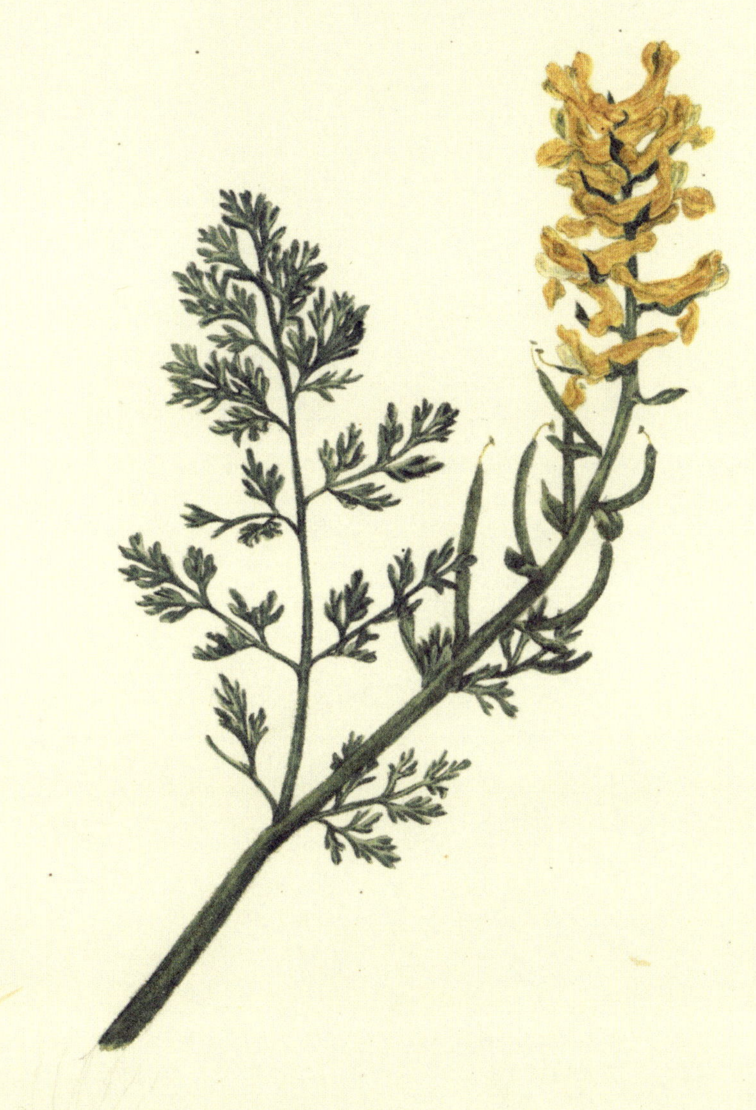

The Lupin, called by the people of the country "Bonnet flower", it grows in such profusion that the Prairie in the distance, often closely resembles the blue waters of a lake, and again on the horizon, one can scarcely tell where earth and sky meet, it blooms for seven or eight weeks from the last of March.

No. 19

Bluebonnet — *Lupinus texenis* Hook.

The Lupin, called by the people of the country "Bonnet flower", it grows in such profusion that the Prairie in the distance, often closely resembles the blue waters of a lake, and again on the horizon, one can scarcely tell where earth and sky meet, it blooms for seven or eight weeks from the last of March.

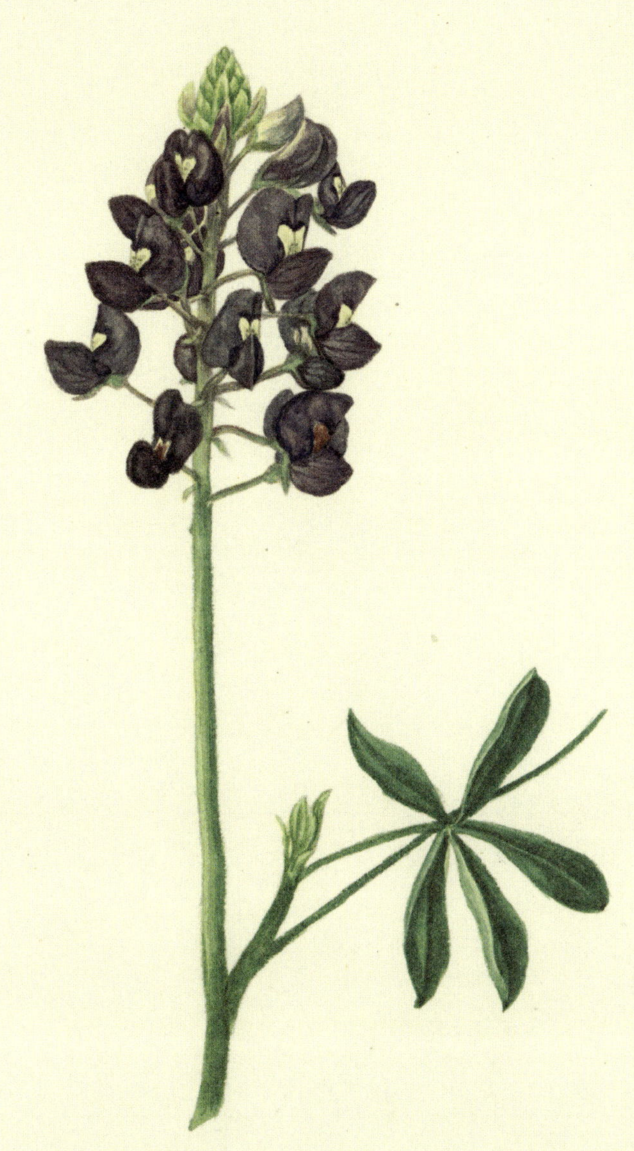

Blooms about the last of March, never more than two on a plant, is fond of sandy loam.

No. 20

Large-flowered Buttercup or Crow-foot — *Ranunculus macranthus* Scheele.

Blooms about the last of March, never more than two on a plant, is fond of sandy loam.

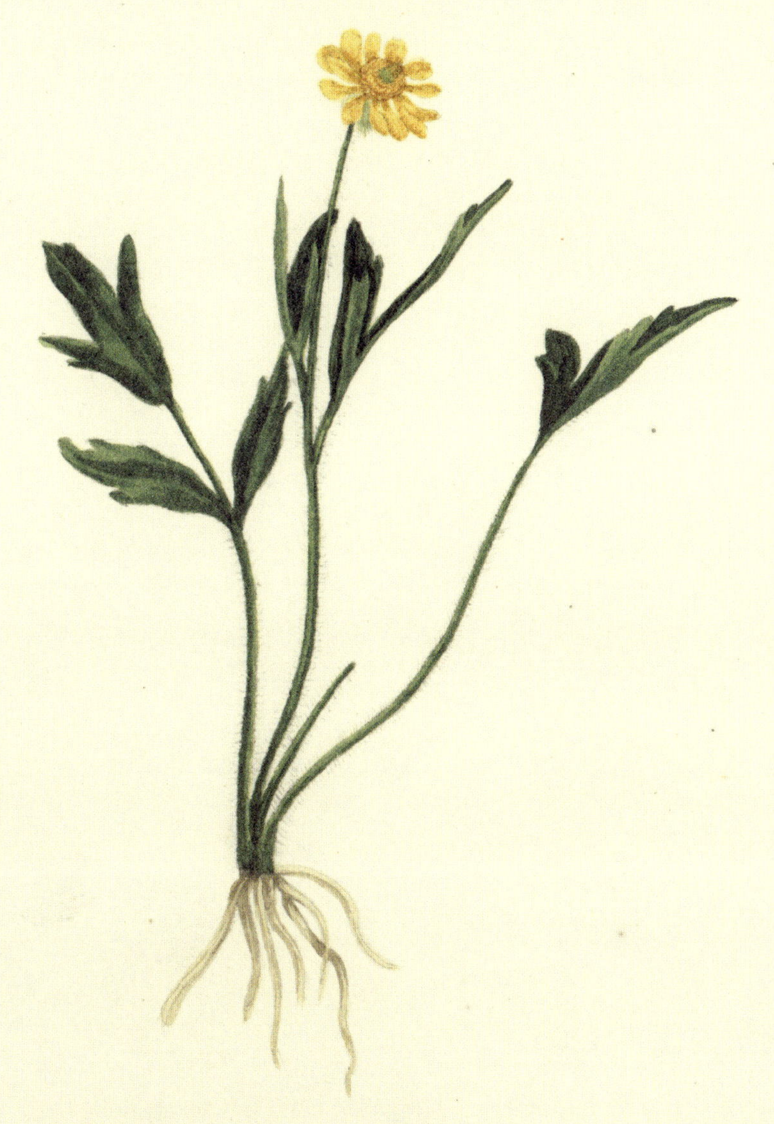

March 29

Is a very rich gay flower, prostrate and slightly creeping, it is called familiarly by children "wild Holly hock" it blooms the last of March on sandy hill sides.

No. 21

Wine Cup — *Callirhoe digitata* Nutt.

Is a very rich gay flower, prostrate and slightly creeping, it is called familiarly by children "wild Holly hock" it blooms the last of March on sandy hill sides.

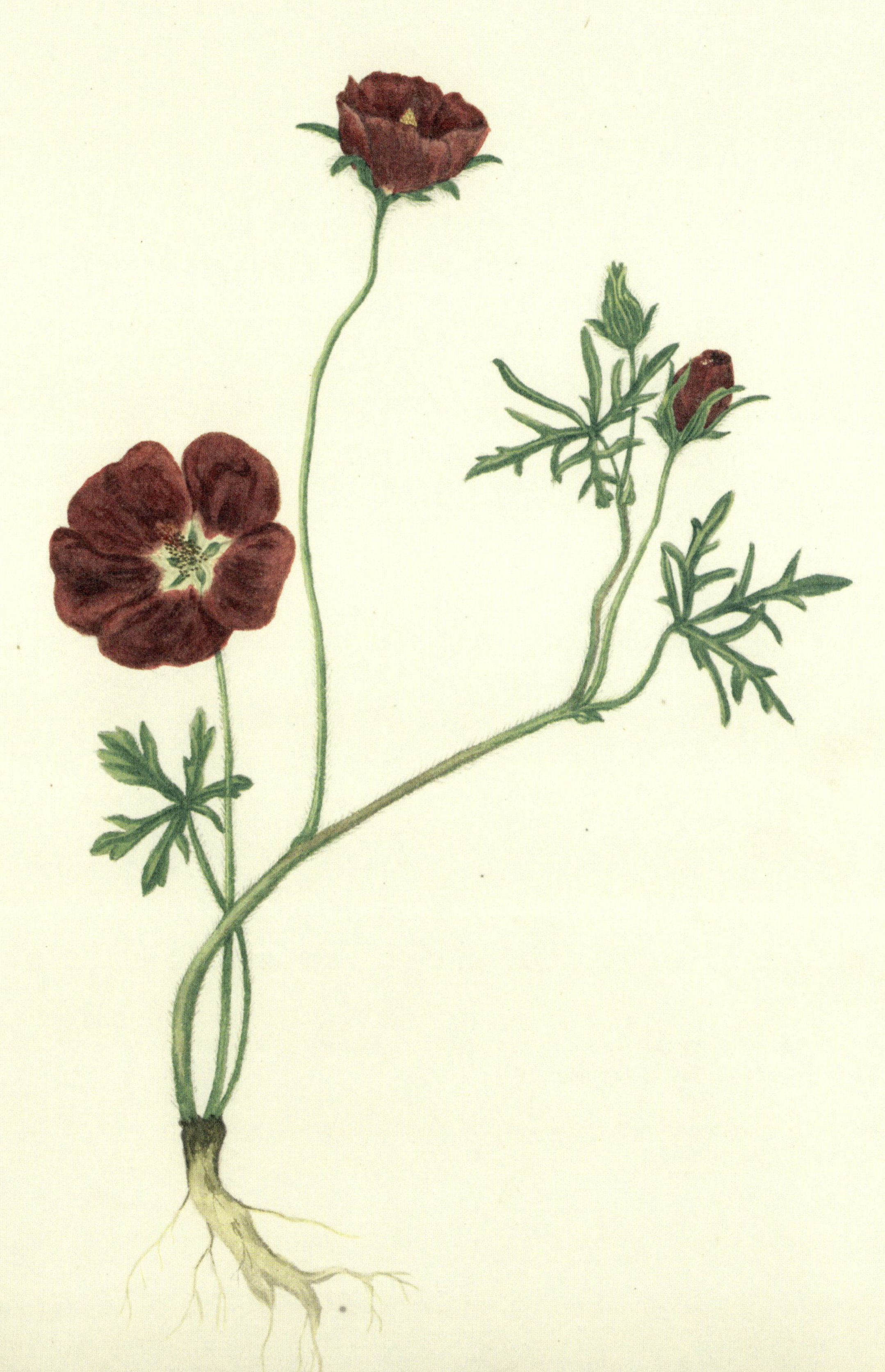

A plant which grows in sandy soil, and blooms freely from the last of March throughout the Spring, Summer and Autumn.

No. 22

Cut-leaved Evening Primrose — *Oenothera laciniata* Hill (= *O. laciniata grandiflora* Wats., Robins.)

A plant which grows in sandy soil, and blooms freely from the last of March throughout the Spring, Summer and Autumn.

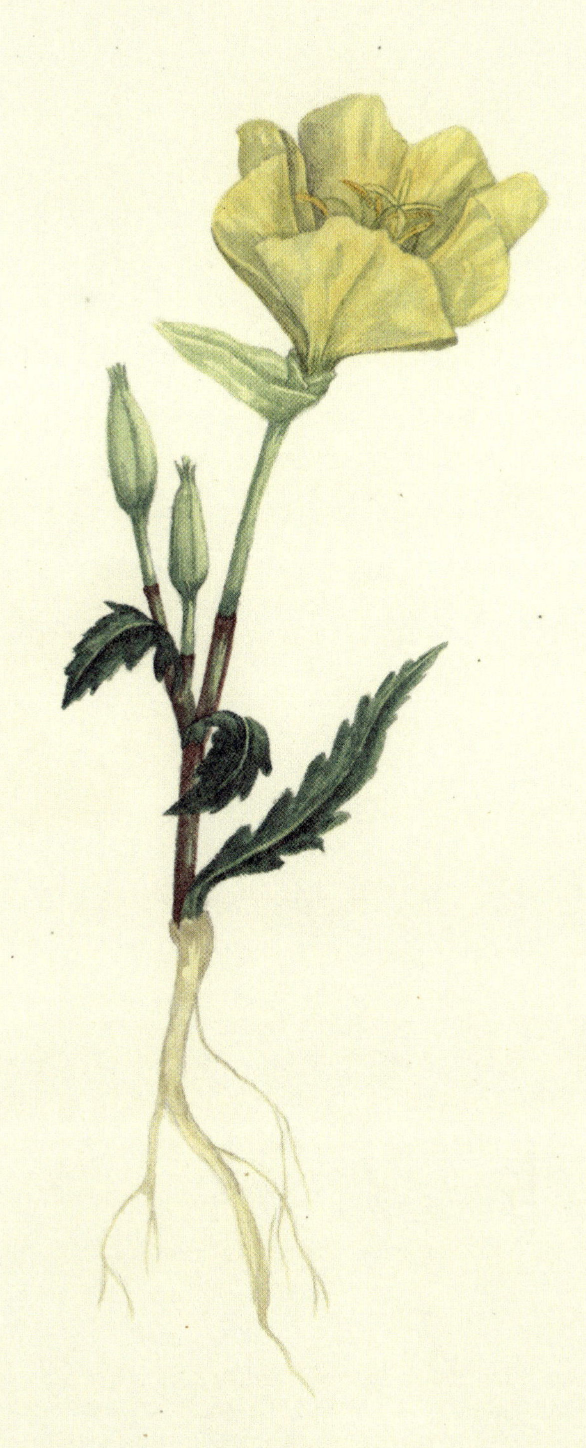

The "Yo Pohn" shrub, or small tree, from 15 to 20
feet high, blooms about the last of March, deciduous,
in Carolina, the leaves are sometimes dried; and
used as a substitute for green tea, during the fall
and winter it is covered with scarlet berries, which,
together with the brilliant evergreens of Texas, give
the forests a gay appearance. it affects alluvials.

No. 23

Yaupon or Cassine — *Ilex vomitoria* Ait.

The "Yo Pohn" shrub, or small tree, from 15 to 20 feet high, blooms about the last of March, deciduous, in Carolina, the leaves are sometimes dried; and used as a substitute for green tea, during the fall and winter it is covered with scarlet berries, which, together with the brilliant evergreens of Texas, give the forest a gay appearance, it affects alluvials.

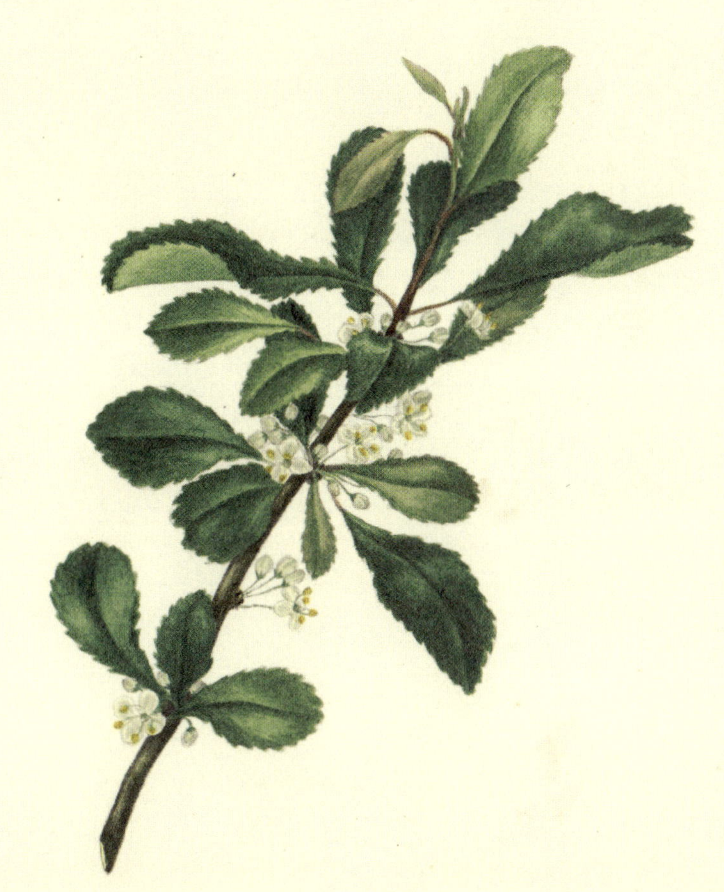

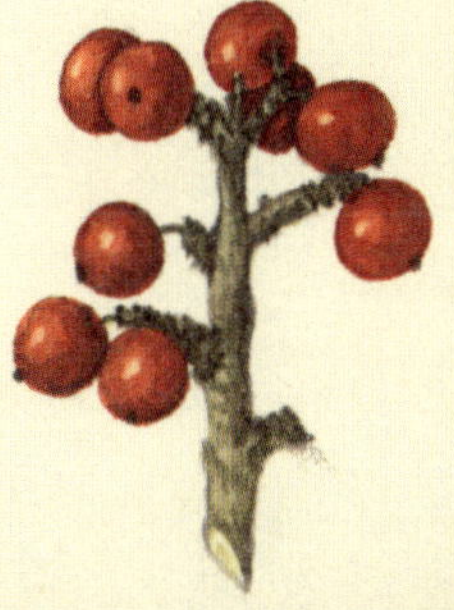

Digitalis. blooms in great perfection, in rich soils, about the last of March.

No. 24

False Foxglove — *Penstemon cobaea* Nutt.

Digitalis, blooms in great perfection, in rich soils, about the last of March.

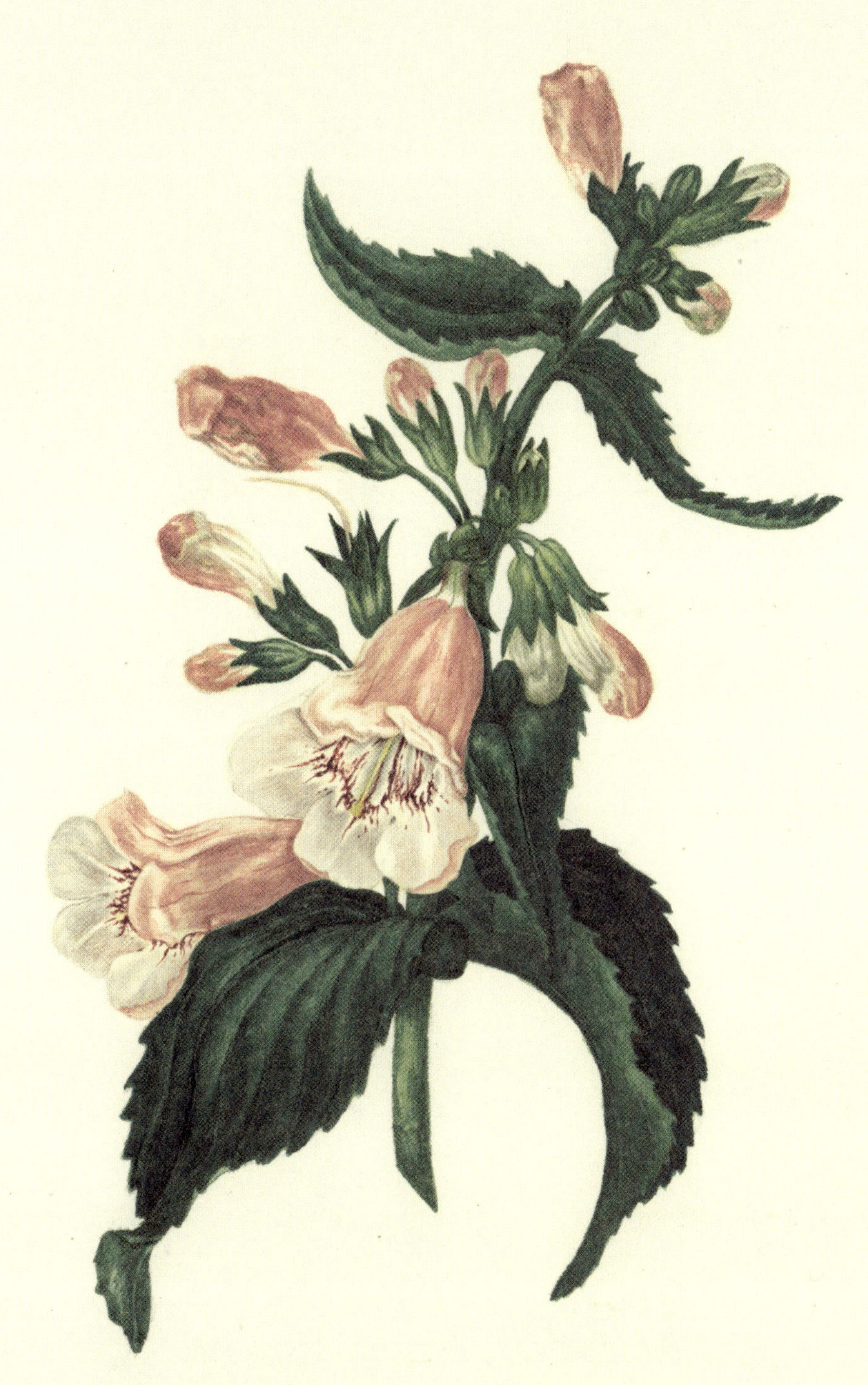

Verbena, blooms from April 'till December, in great abundance, in rich soil.

No. 25

Wild Verbena — *Verbena bipinnatifida* Nutt.

Verbena, blooms from April 'till December, in great abundance, in rich soil.

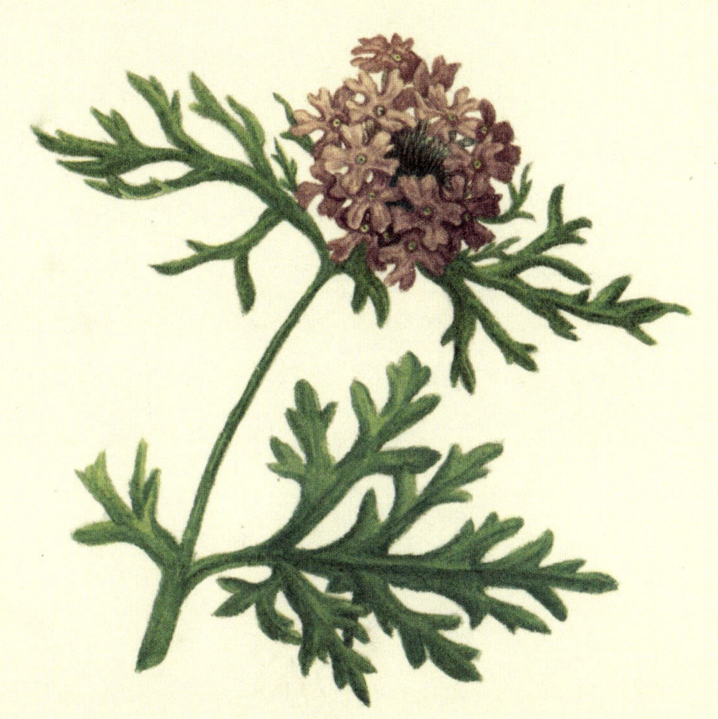

Verbena

April – 3

Crocus, Blooms from early in April, throughout the spring, after every shower, there is also saffron coloured crocus, with dots of red upon the petals, which blooms during summer.

No. 26

Giant Rain-lily — *Cooperia pedunculata* Herb.
(=*Zephyranthes drummondii* D. Don.)

Crocus. Blooms from early in April, throughout the spring, after every shower, there is also saffron coloured crocus, with dots of red upon the petals, which blooms during summer.

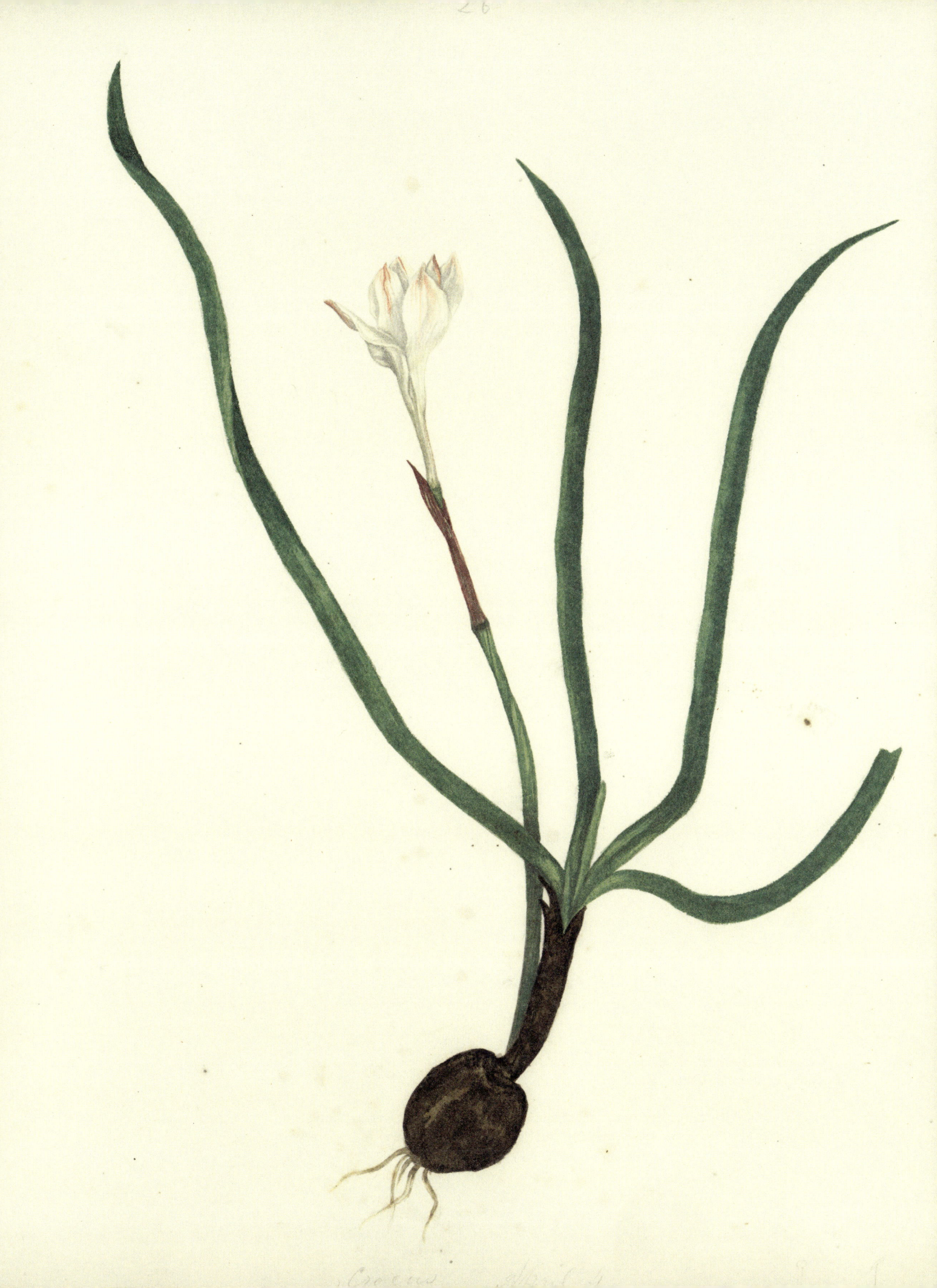

A very beautiful plant from one, to two feet high, blooms during 6 or 8 weeks from the begining of April, ligneous in its structure, and grows in fine gravel and loamy soils, there is also another variety of this precisely similar, except that the inside of the Calyx is a deep blue black.

No. 27

Buttercup or Day Primrose — *Oenothera serrulata* Nutt.
(=*Meriolix serrulata* Nutt., Raf.)

A very beautiful plant from one to two feet high, blooms during 6 or 8 weeks from the beginning of April, ligneous in its structure, and grows in fine gravel and loamy soils, there is also another variety of this precisely similar, except that the inside of the calyx is a deep blue black.

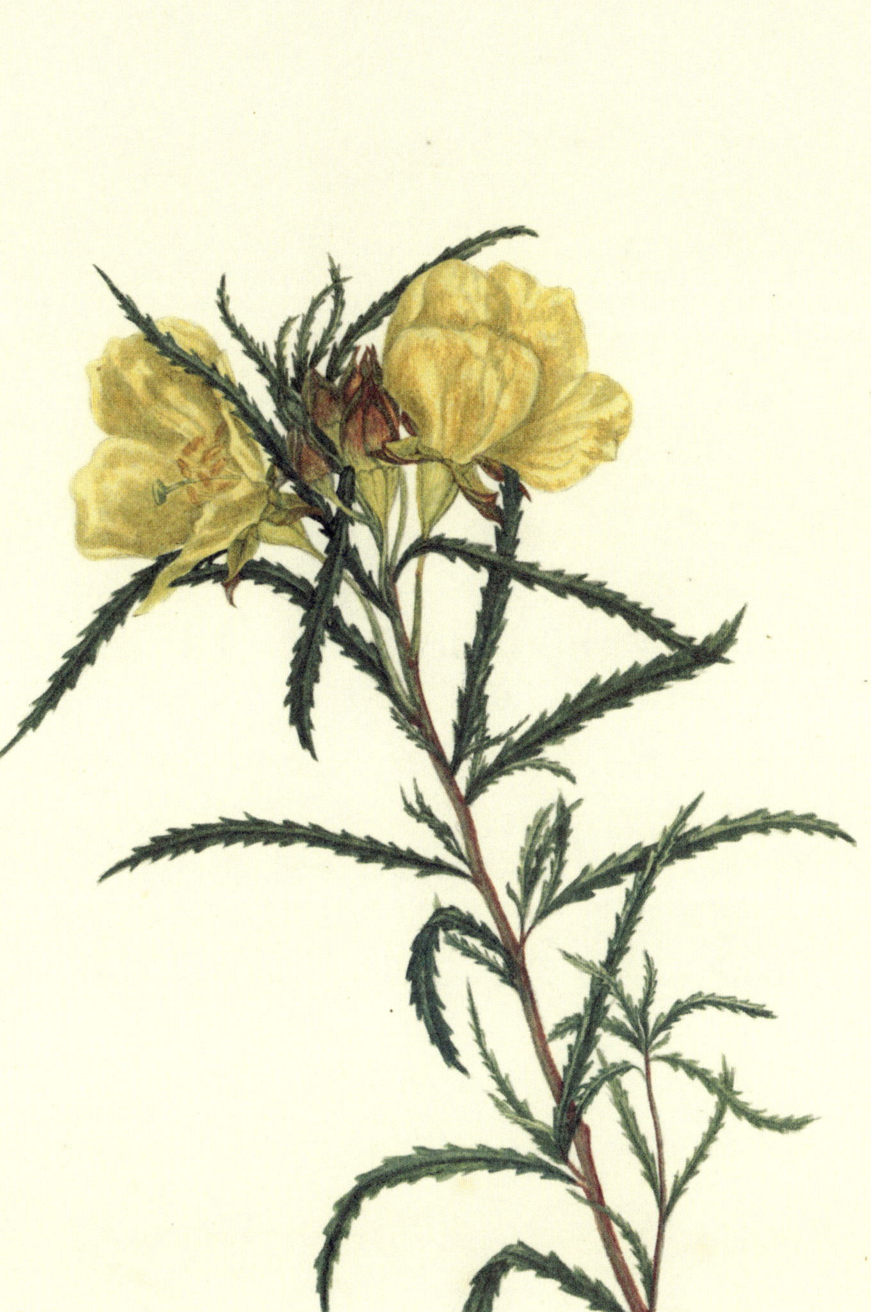

A Shrub from 8 to 12 feet high, thinly clad with very small leaves, which, when broken yield a pleasant spicy odour, the delicate little flower has a sweetness peculiar to itself it grows upon alluvial lands and bears flowers from the begining of April till late in the fall.

No. 28

Bee Brush — called Colorado Myrtle by Mrs. Johnston)
Aloysia Ligustrina Lag., Small)=*Lippia lycioides* Steud.)

A shrub from 8 to 12 feet high, thinly clad with very small leaves, which, when broken yield a pleasant spicy odour, the delicate little flower has a sweetness peculiar to itself it grows upon alluvial lands and bears flowers from the beginning of April till late in the fall.

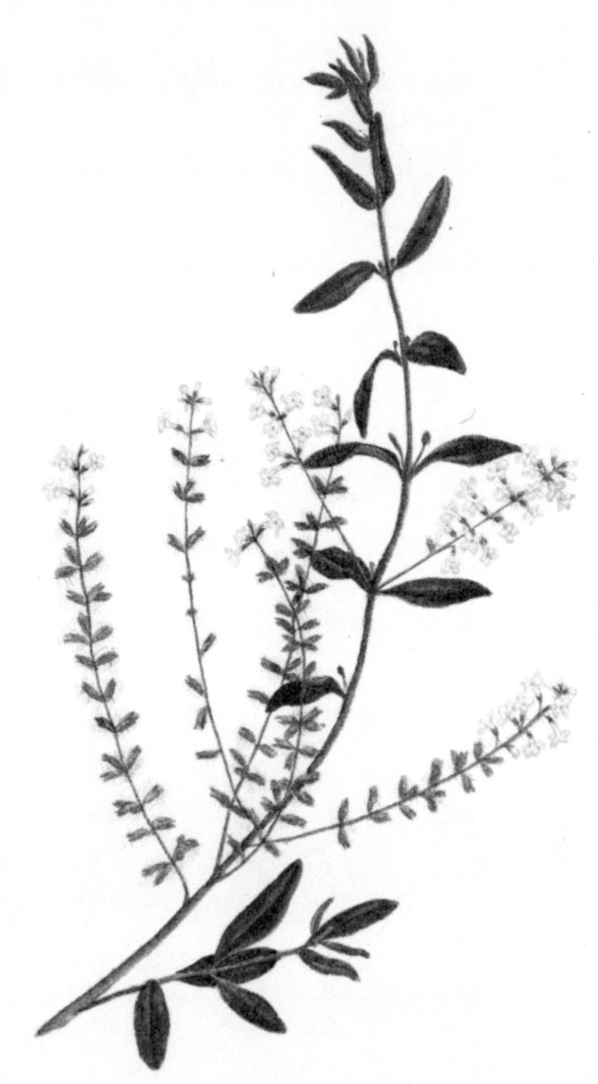

Colorado Myrtle

April 6

A well known plant about 16 inches high, blooms from early in April for about 4 weeks, is found in rich soil.

No. 29

Indian Paintbrush or Scarlet Paintbrush — *Castilleja indivisa* Engelm.

A well known plant about 16 inches high, blooms from early in April for about 4 weeks, is found in rich soil.

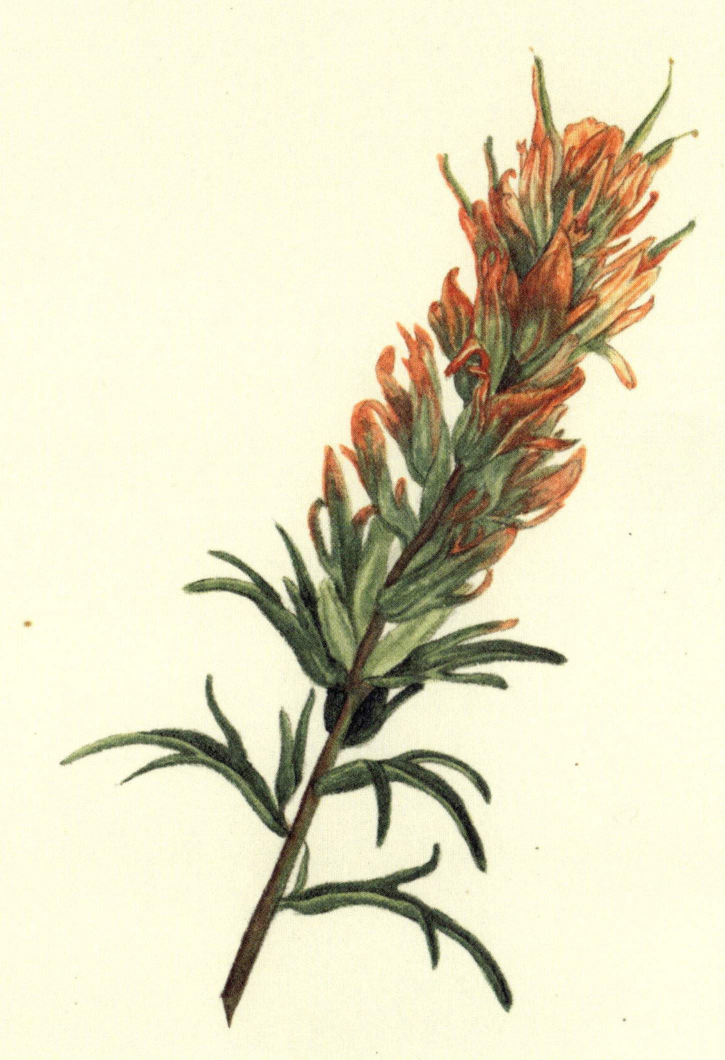

April 5

Grows in moist situations, in sandy soils, blooms during six or eight weeks from early April.

No. 30

Pink Evening Primrose — *Oenothera speciosa* Nutt.

Grows in moist situations, in sandy soils, blooms during six or eight weeks from early April.

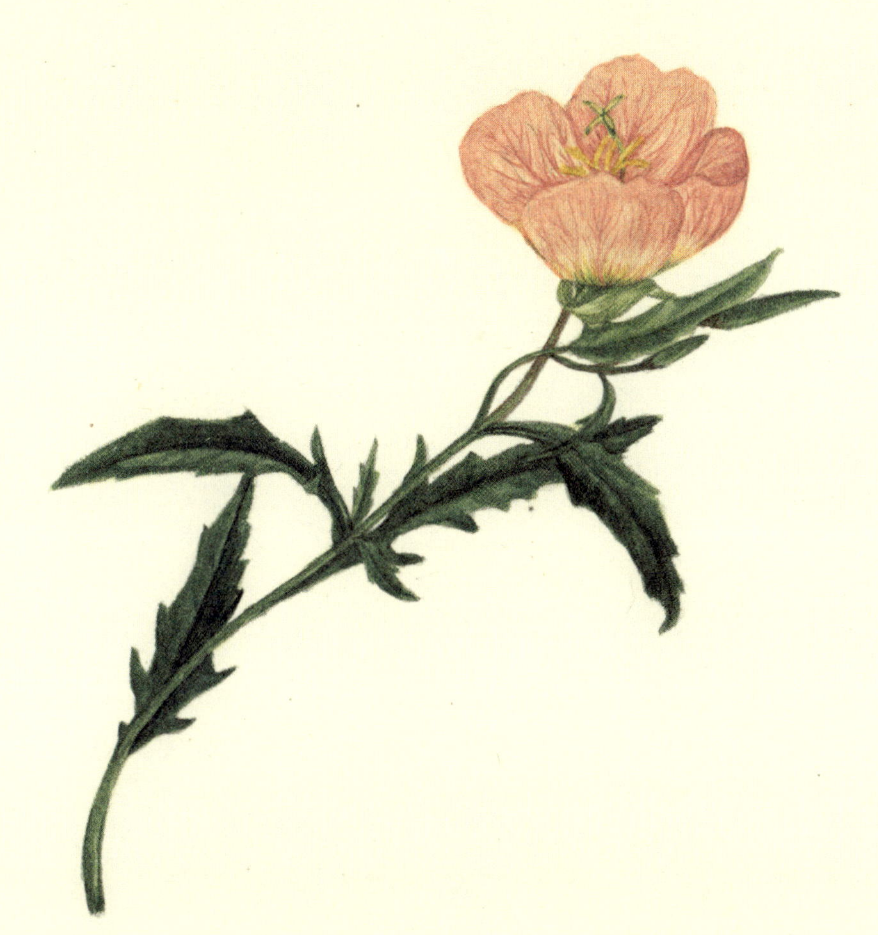

April 6

Sensitive plant, blooms in April, in sandy soil.

No. 31

Partridge Pea or Sensitive Plant — *Cassia fasciculata* Michx.

Sensitive plant, blooms in April, in sandy soil.

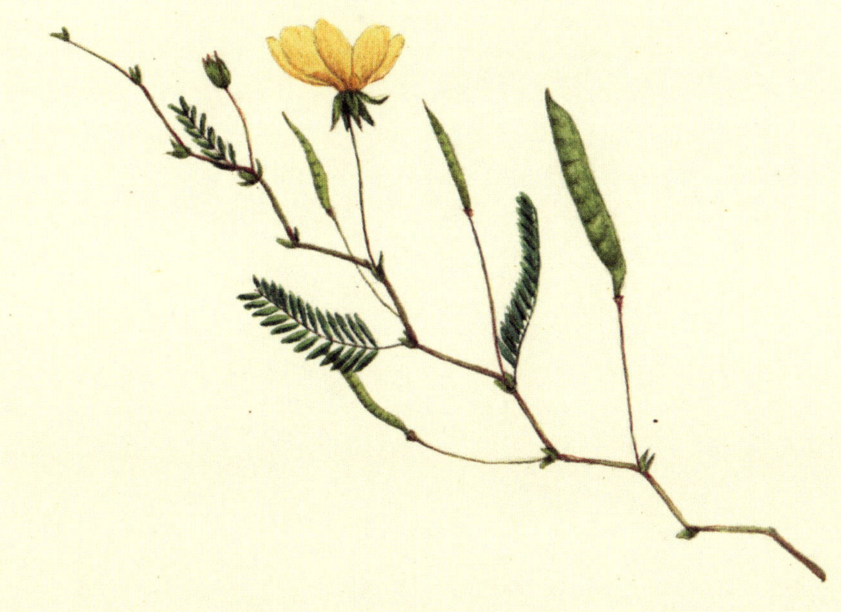

Mountain Honeysuckle, exceedinglingly fragrant, blooms, Spring, and fall, in rich calcareous Soil.

No. 32

White Honeysuckle — *Lonicera albiflora* Torr. and Gray

Mountain Honeysuckle, exceedinglingly fragrant, blooms, Spring, and fall, in rich calcareous Soil.

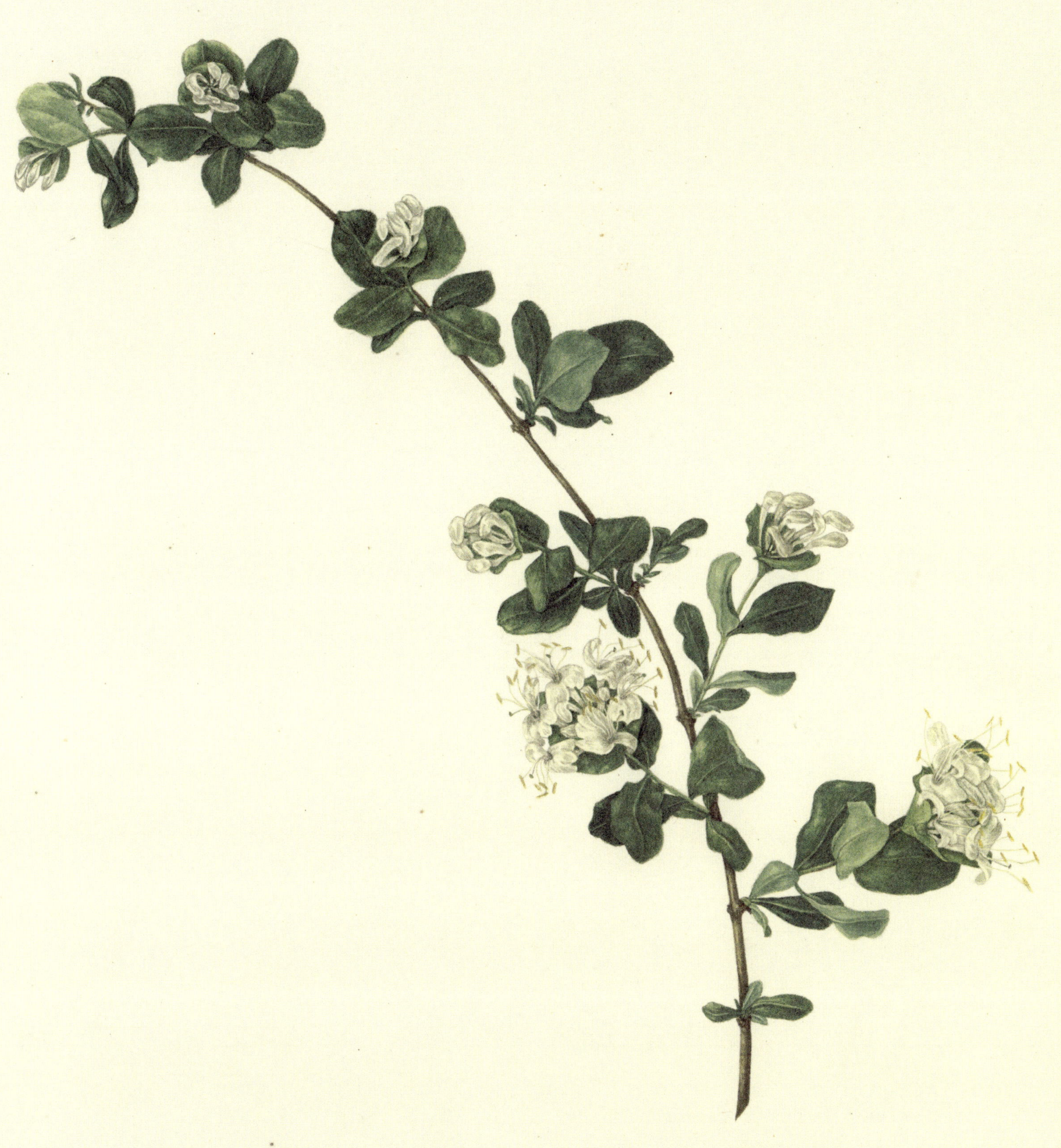

Honey Suckle

April 10th

Very common on the 'table lands' of Texas, there is also a white variety, very pretty, blooms in April and May —

No. 33

Spiderwort — *Tradescantia humilis* Rose

Very common on the 'table lands' of Texas, there is also a white variety, very pretty, blooms in April and May—

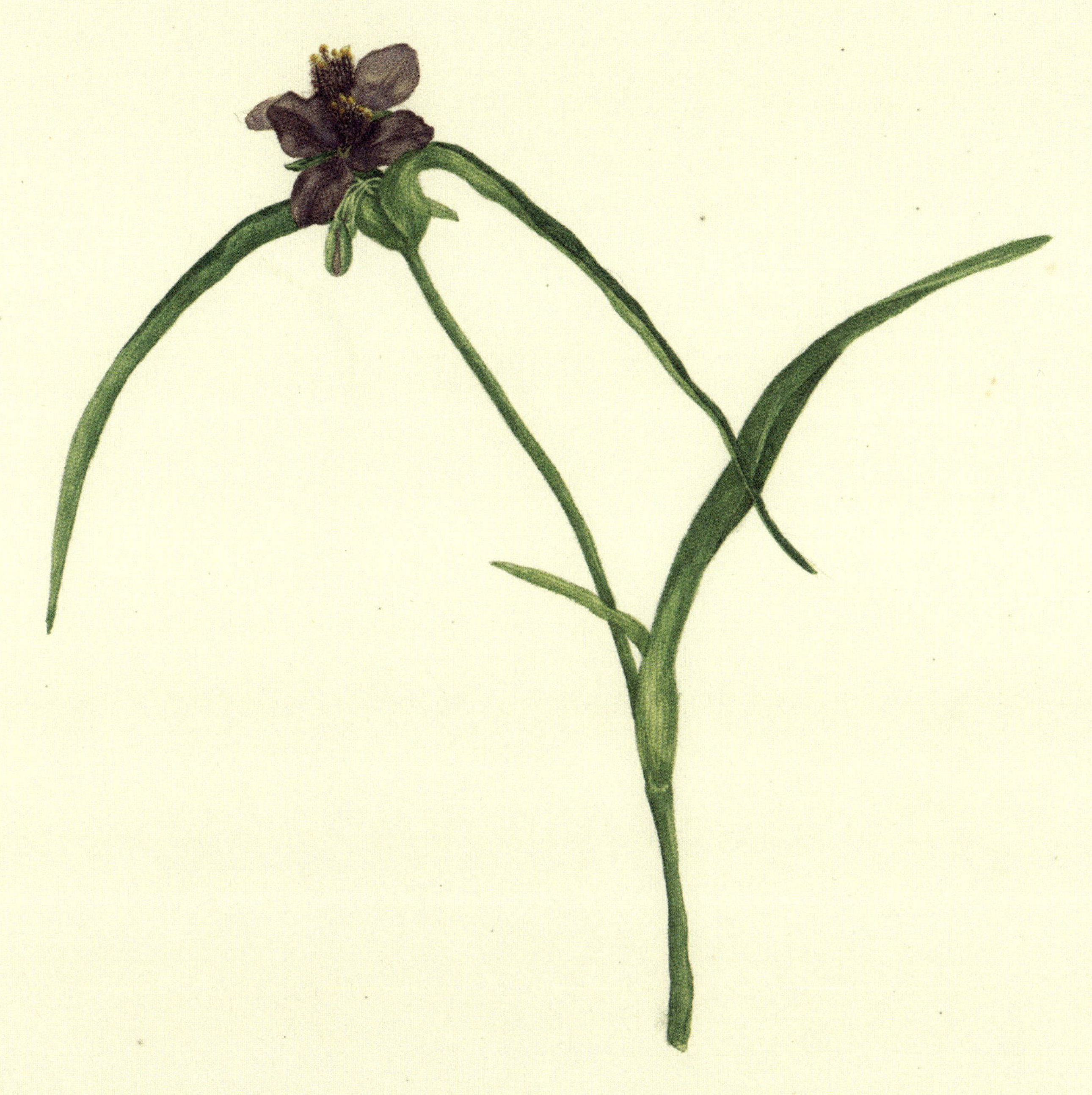

April 16

Argemone Mexicana. Prickly Poppy.
Grows about three feet high, and blooms
in April on rich soil, has the odour of cucumbers

No. 34

Texas Prickly Poppy — *Argemone albiflora* Hornem.

Aremone Mexicana, Prickly Poppy. Grows about three feet high, and blooms in April on rich soil, has the odour of cucumbers.

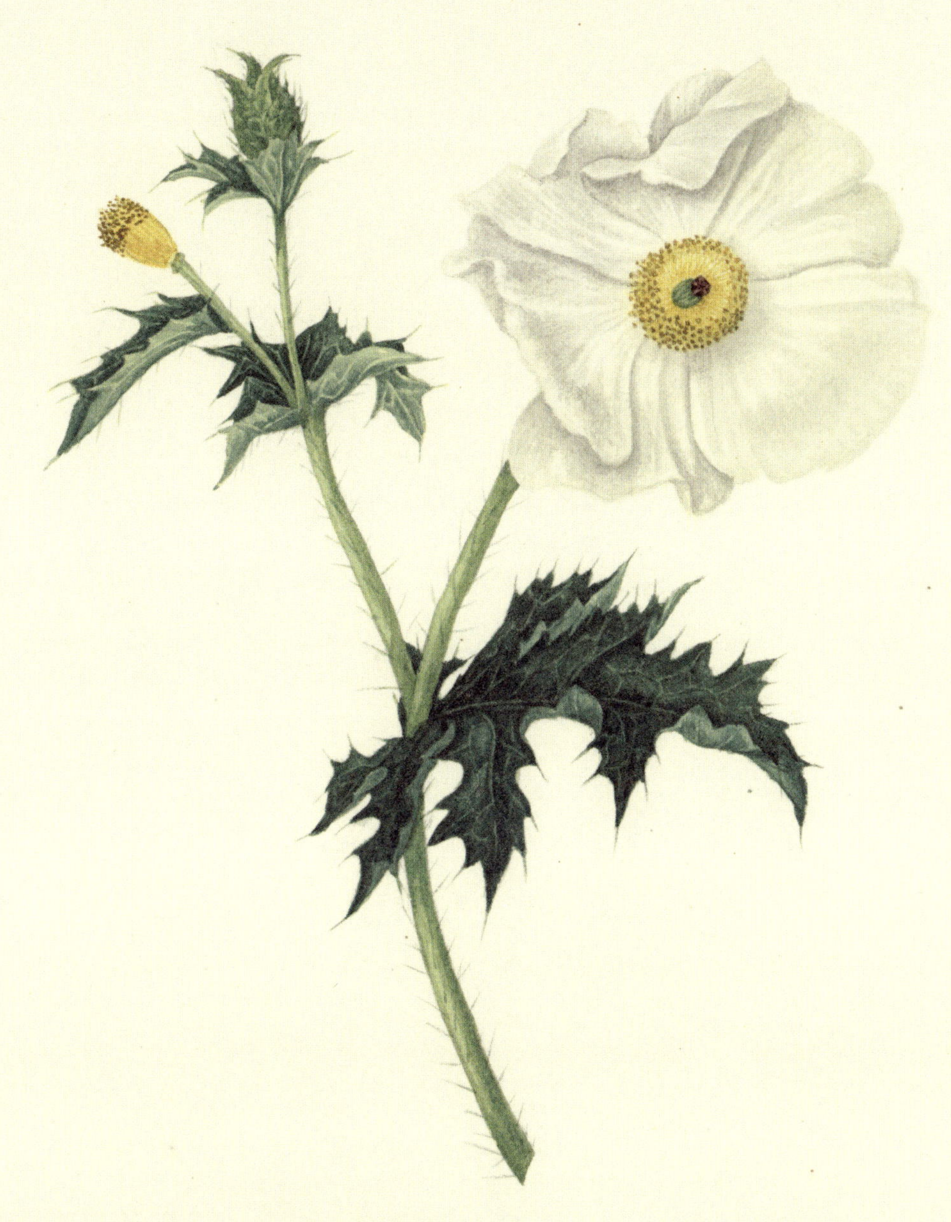

Nettle

April 12

Digitalis Is found in forests, on rich sandy land, blooms in April, and is usually about two feet high.

No. 35

Beard-tongue or Wild Foxglove — *Penstemon cobaea* Nutt.

Digitalis Is found in forests, on rich sandy land, blooms in April, and is usually about two feet high.

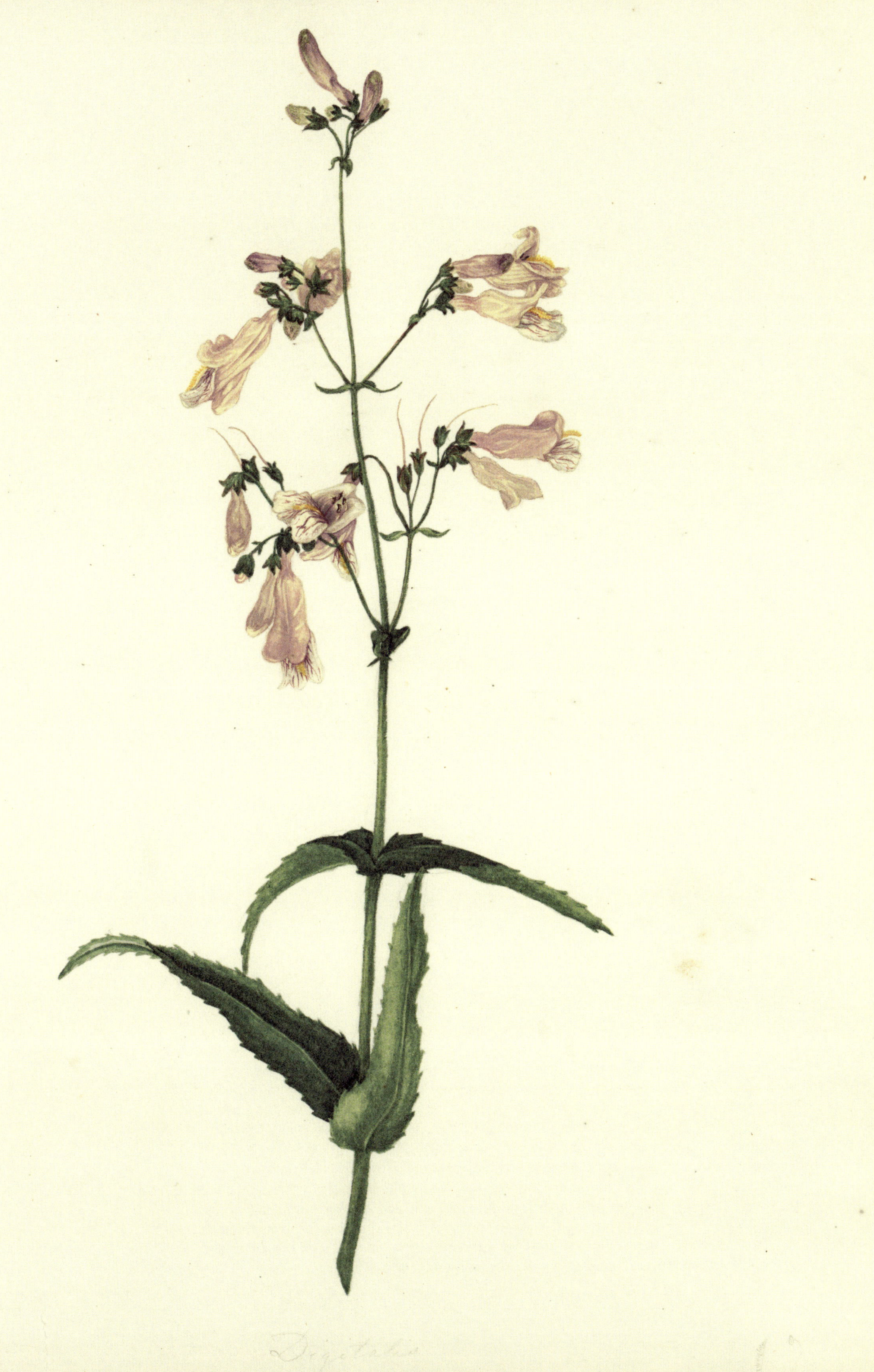
Digitalis

A very rich and profuse bloomer, growing about 18 inches high, it bears flowers in April and May. on all varieties of soil, in the greatest perfection in calcareous loam.— Of this flower is related a very pretty tradition by the Mexicans—The flower originally was of a bright golden hue, and the favourite of the unfortunate Aztec. the young maidens delighted in decorating their jetty hair with a diadem of its golden discs, and the lithe limbs of the little children, were caressed by its sunny petals, as they sported on the glorious Prairies, of their happy land; but it was the will of the Almighty, that this should not last. Cortez came! and the lovely land was deluged with the blood of its innocent, and confiding inhabitants; the loved flower in pity caught the sanguinary stream, as it fell, and to this day has remained stained a deep red, and now when the tiny butterfly of its own colour is seen flitting around it, they say "tis the spirit of the Aztec watching in gratitude his favourite flower.

No. 36

Firewheel — *Gaillardia pulchella* Foug.

A very rich and profuse bloomer, growing about 18 inches high, it bears flowers in April and May, on all varieties of soil, in the greatest perfection in calcareous loam.—Of this flower is related a very pretty tradition by the Mexicans—The flower originally was of a bright golden hue, and the favourite of the unfortunate Aztec. The young maidens delighted in decorating their jetty hair with a diadem of its golden discs, and the lithe limbs of the little children, were caressed by its sunny petals, as they sported on the glorious Prairies, of their happy land; but it was the will of the Almighty, that this should not last. Cortez came! and the lovely land was deluged with the blood of its innocent, and confiding inhabitants; the loved flower in pity caught the sanguinary stream, as it fell, and to this day has remained stained a deep red, and now when the tiny butterfly of its own colour is seen flitting around it, they say "tis the spirit of the Aztec watching in gratitude his favourite flower.

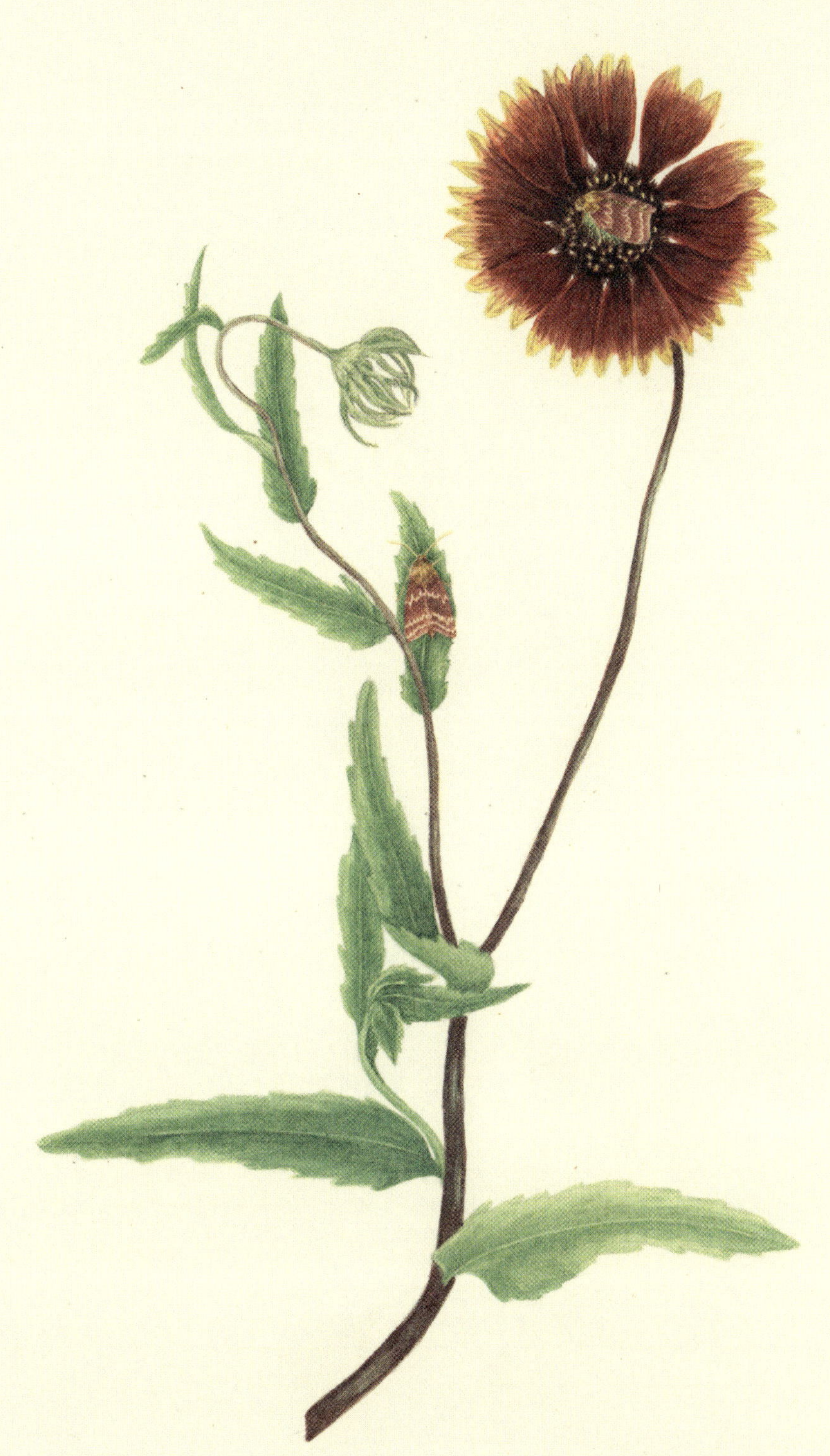

April 27

Lupin, blooms, from early April, through May, and June, the shape of the whole plant is almost round, about a foot in diameter, grows in sand. when dry, it is easily uprooted by the winds and will then be sent rolling over the Prairie with the velocity of the wind, it is for this reason, called by the people "Roll weed", this peculiarity seems a Providential means of scattering its seed over a great extent of country

No. 37

Wild Indigo — *Baptisia leucophaea* Nutt.

Lupin, bloom, from early April, through May, and June, the shape of the whole plant is almost round, about a foot in diameter, grows in sand. When dry, it is easily uprooted by the winds and will then be sent rolling over the Prairie, with the velocity of the wind, it is for this reason, called by the people "Roll Weed," this peculiarity seems a Providential means of scattering its seed over a great extent of country.

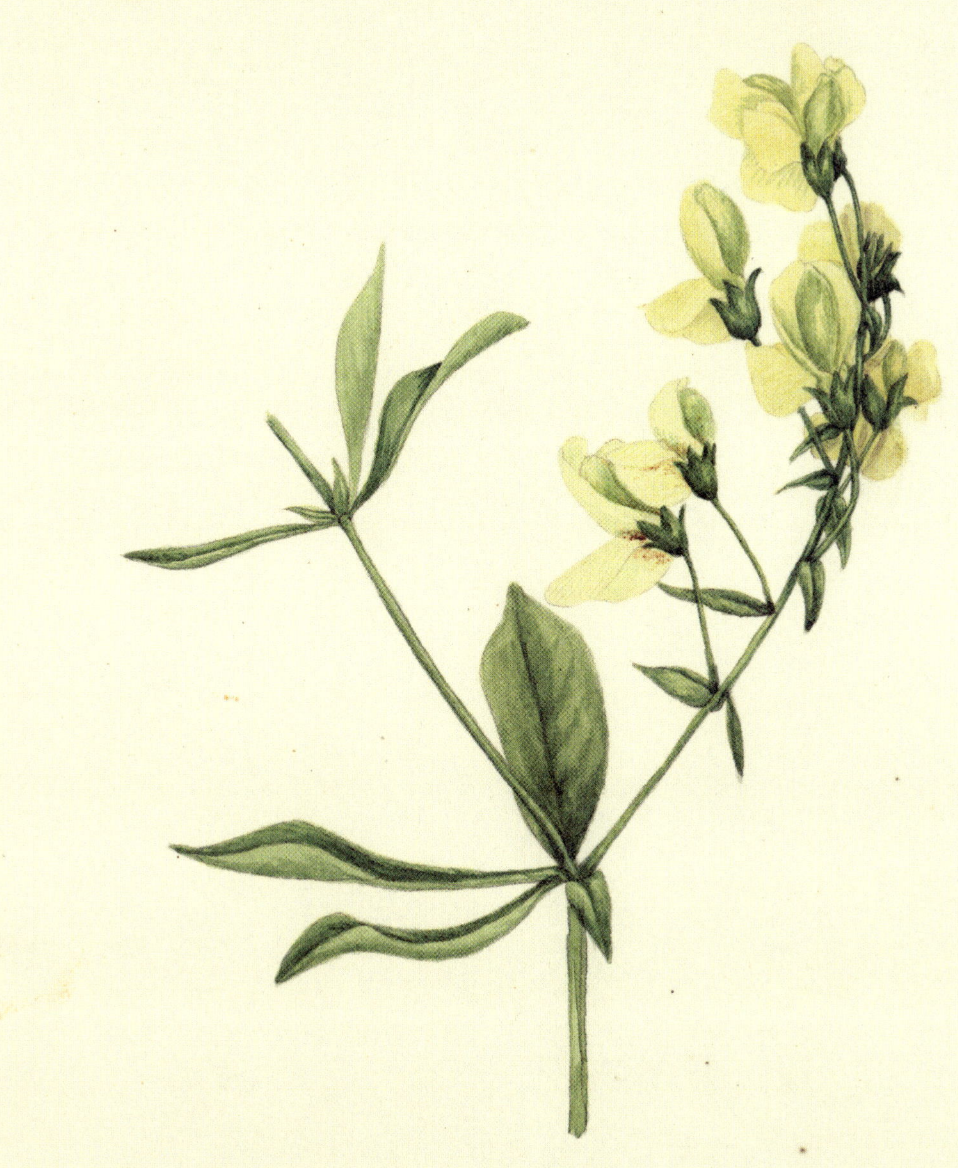
April 27.

Grows in alluvial lands, running over shrubs, blooms in the latter part of April very thick petals.

No. 38

Texas Leather Flower or Scarlet Clematis — *Clematis texensis* Buckl.

Grows in alluvial lands, running over shrubs, blooms in the latter part of April very thick petals.

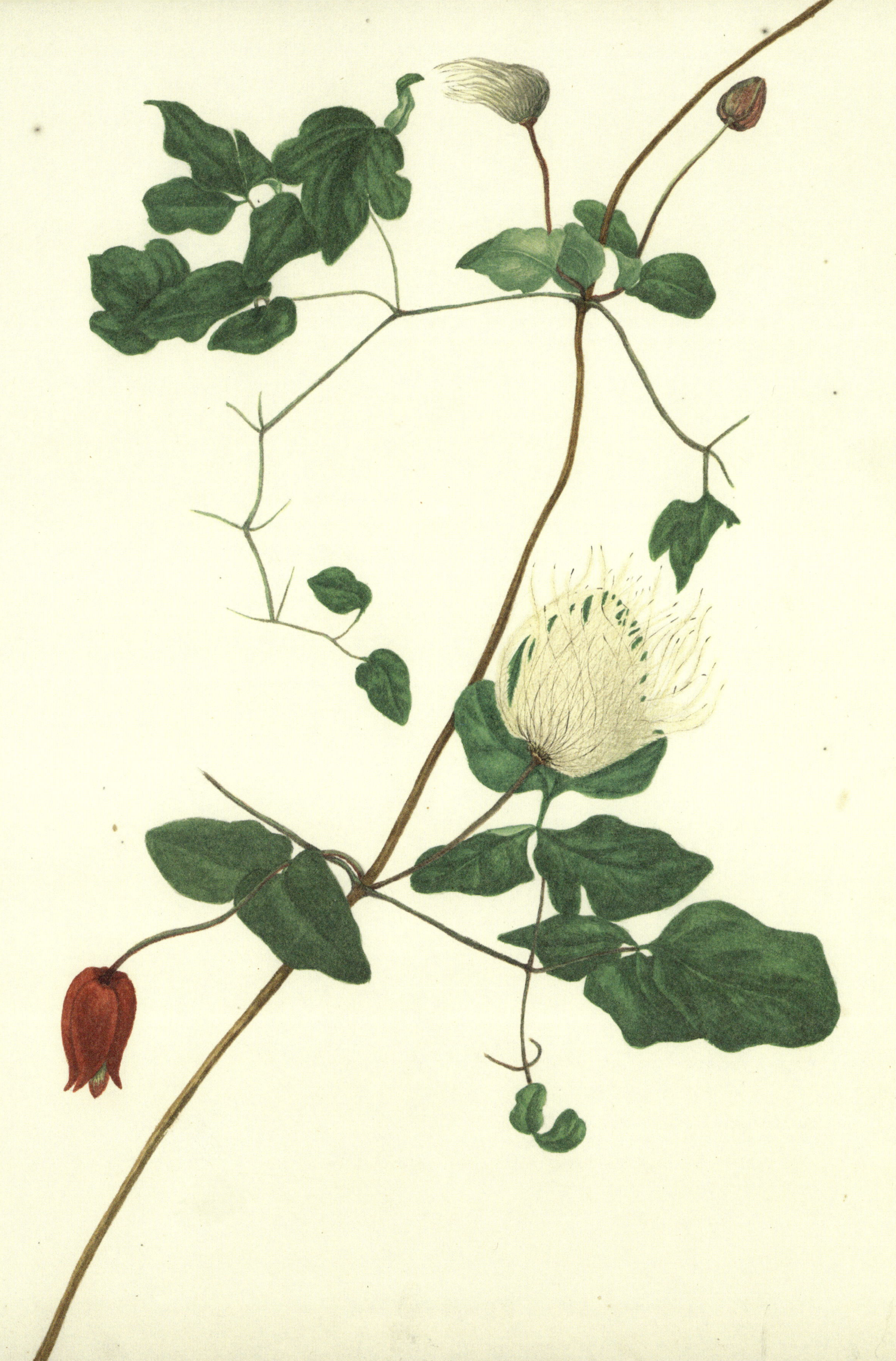

A Bean, a trailing plant, prone upon the grass and sand, blooms towards the end of April.

No. 39

Goat's-rue — *Tephrosia lindheimeri* Gray

A Bean, a trailing plant, prone upon the grass and sand, blooms towards the end of April.

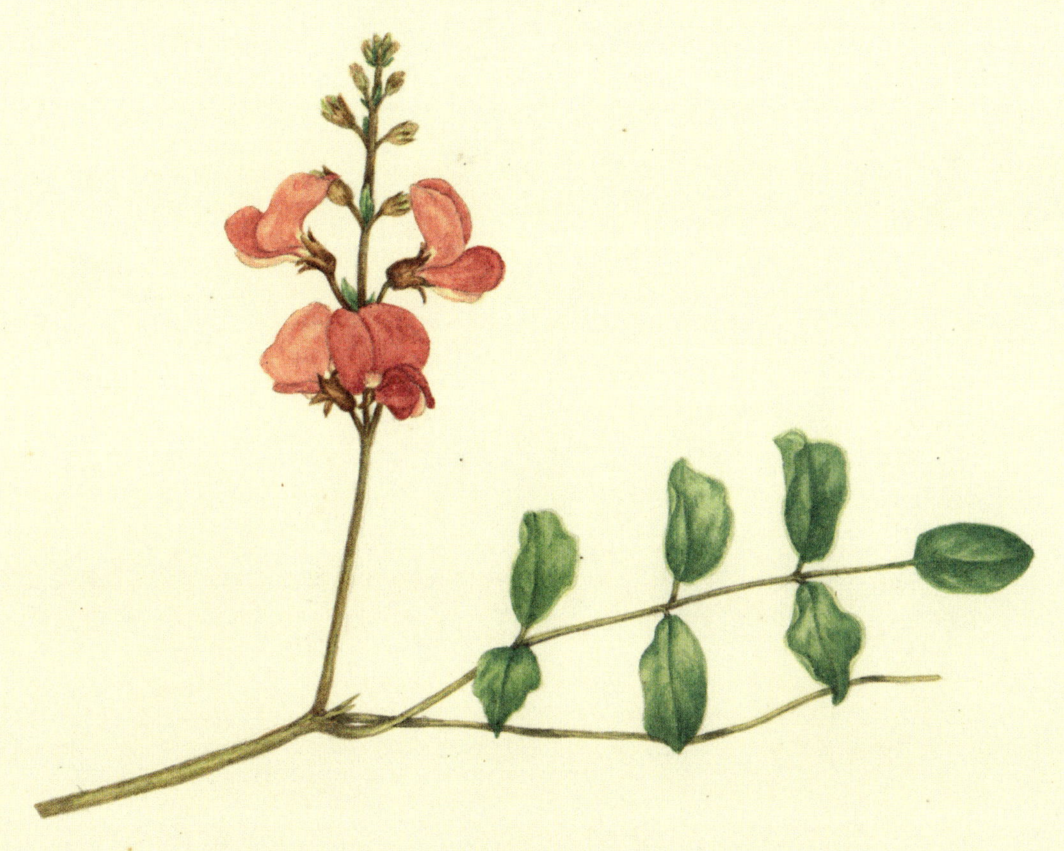

April 26th

10 Stamens

A rich Salvia, a very prolific bloomer, Biennial, easily propagated from the seed, grows freely in alluvials, somewhat sheltered from the sun, blooms from early April throughout the summer and Fall.

No. 40

Scarlet Sage — *Salvia coccinea* L.

A rich Salvia, a very prolific bloomer, Biennial, easily propagated from the seed, grows freely in alluvials, somewhat sheltered from the sun, blooms from early April throughout the Summer and Fall.

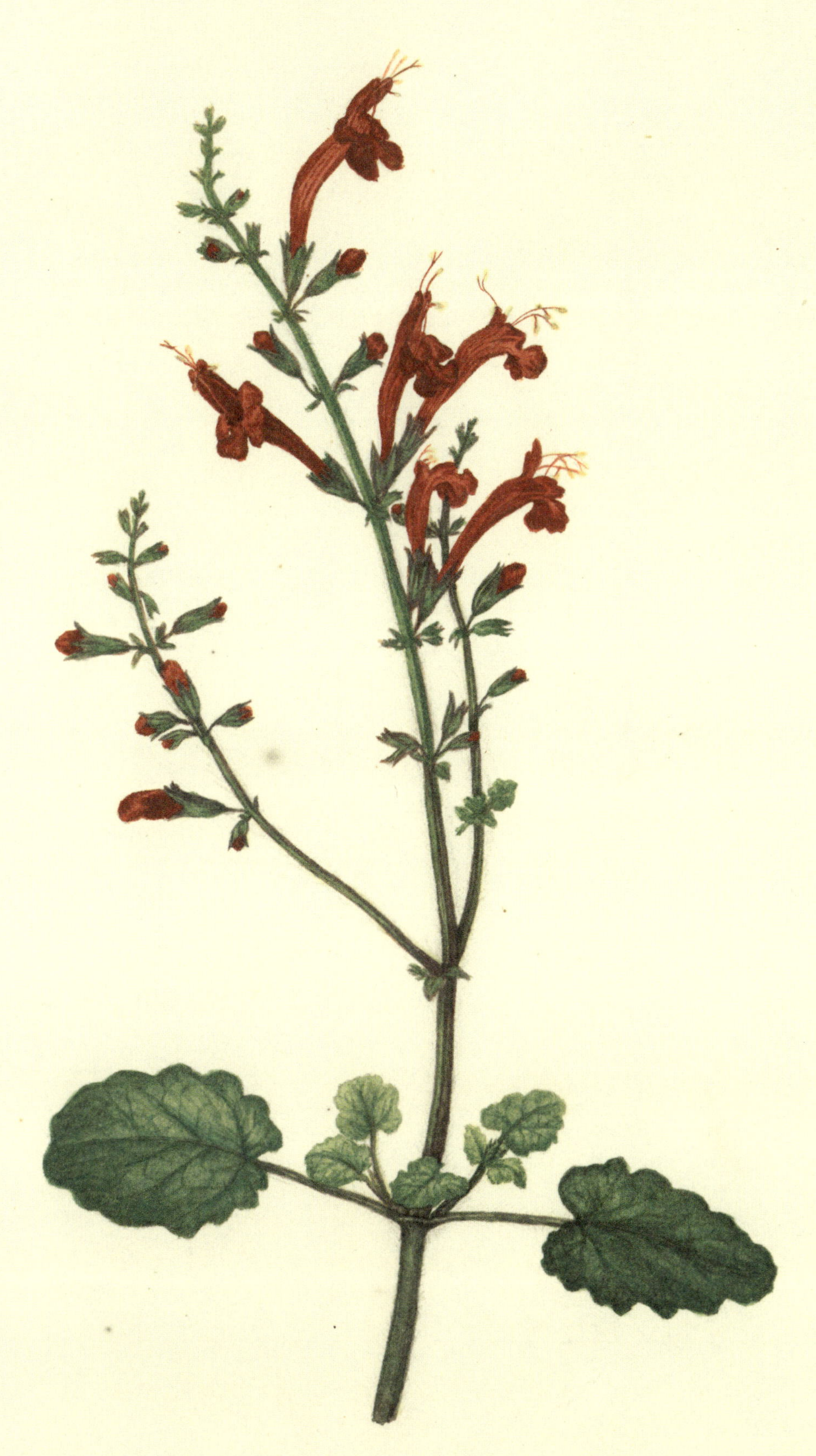

Lentana. A shrub, from 8 to 10 feet high, blooms in April and May, and flourishes in sandy soil.

No. 41

Lantana — *Lantana horrida* H. B. K.

Lentana. A shrub, from 8 to 10 feet high, blooms in April and May, and flourishes in sandy soil.

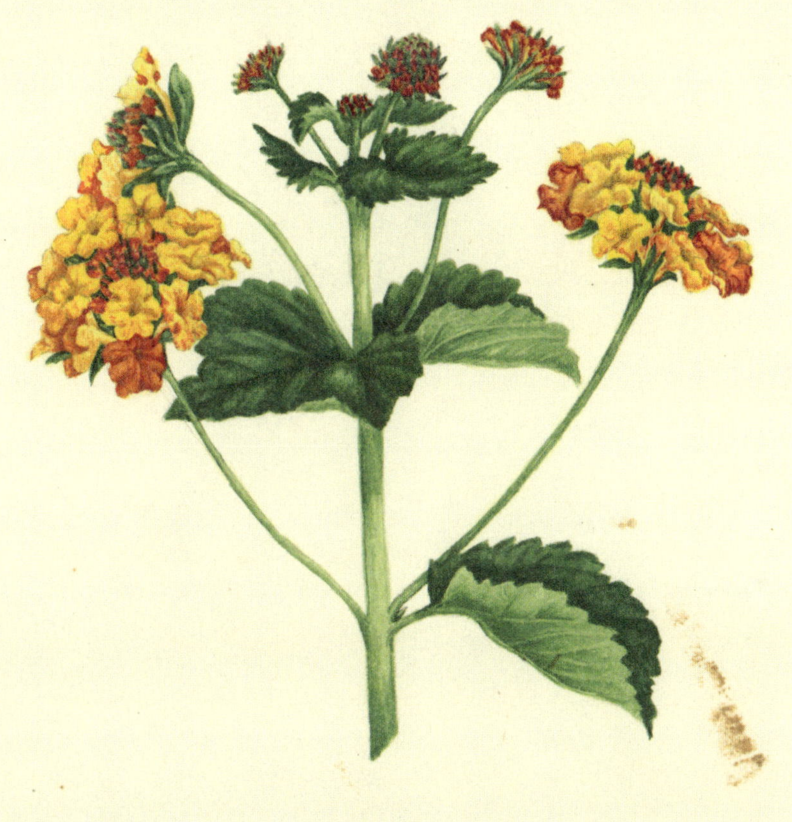

April 23rd 1855

Camp on the Chato

Lotus. very fragrant, both flower and leaf recumbent upon the water, blooms in April and May, bears a seed pod somewhat resembling a wasps nest, filled with nuts, in shape like a small acorn, which are edible, and are commonly called "Monocco nuts."

No. 42

Lotus — *Nelumbo luteum* Willd.

Lotus, very fragrant, both flower and leaf recumbent upon the water, blooms in April and May, bears a seed pod somewhat resembling a wasps nest, filled with nuts, in shape like a small acorn, which are edible, and are commonly called "Monocco nuts."

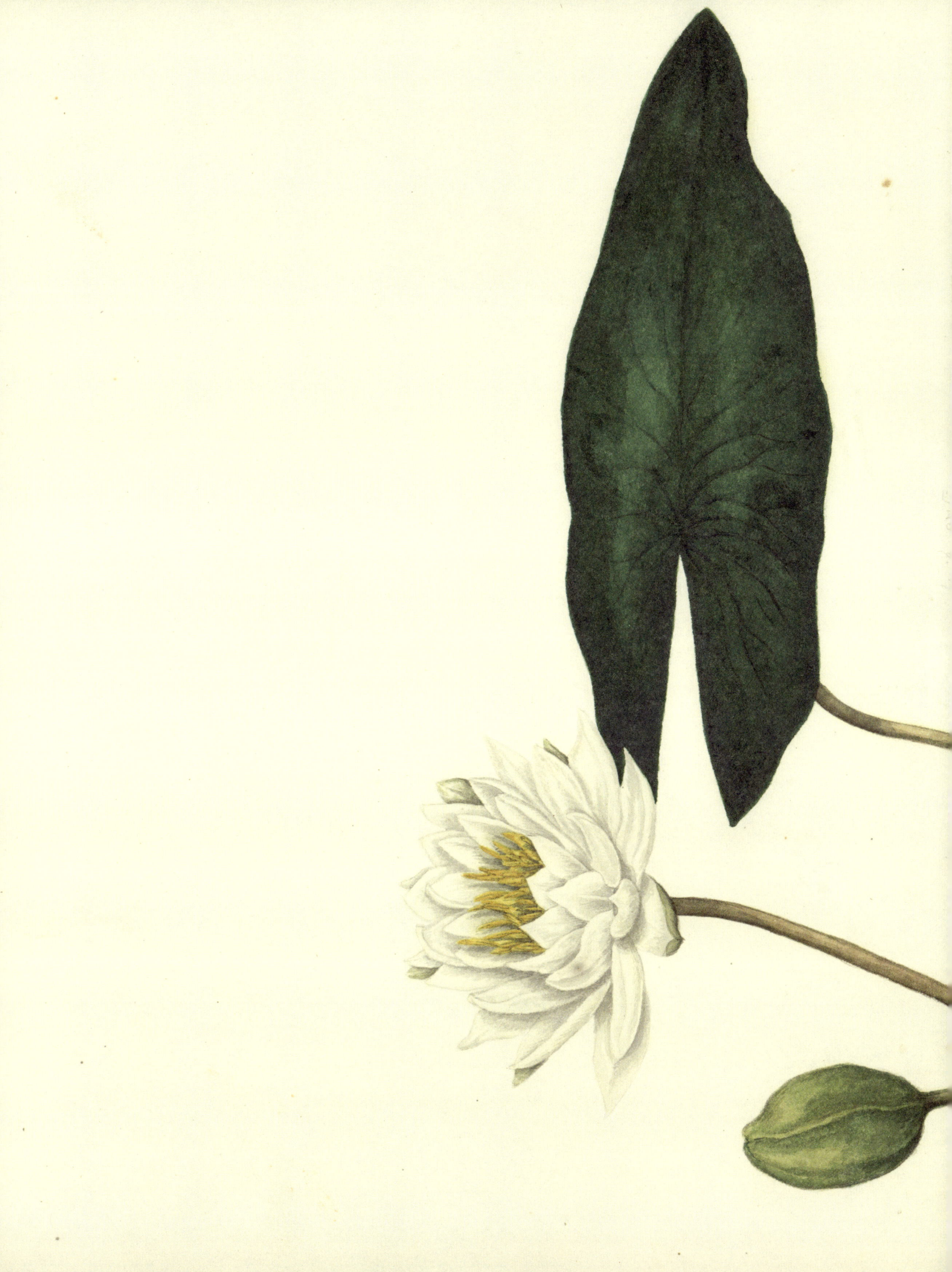

A showy plant, stands about 2½ feet high, in a single plume, is found in very sandy soil, and blooms in April.

No. 43

Scarlet Penstemon — *Penstemon murrayanus* Hook.

A showy plant, stands about 2½ feet high, in a single plume, is found in very sandy soil, and blooms in April.

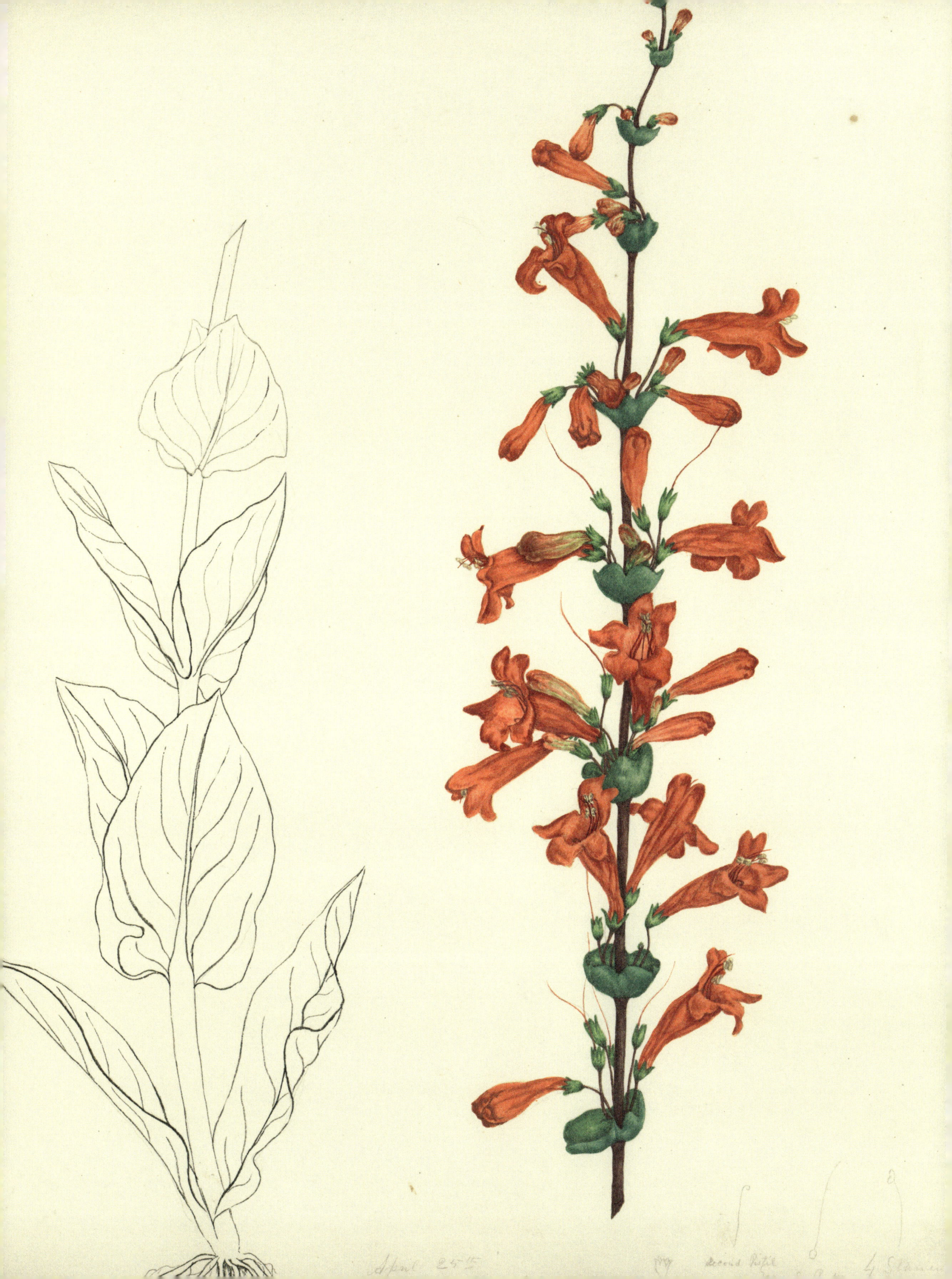
April 25
Second Pistil

Phlox. grows in rich soil, well intermixed with sand, and prefers the open woodland, to the sunny Prairie. blooms through April and May.

No. 44

Annual Phlox — *Phlox drummondii* Hook.

Phlox, grows in rich soil, well intermixed with sand, and prefers the open woodland, to the sunny Prairie. blooms through April and May.

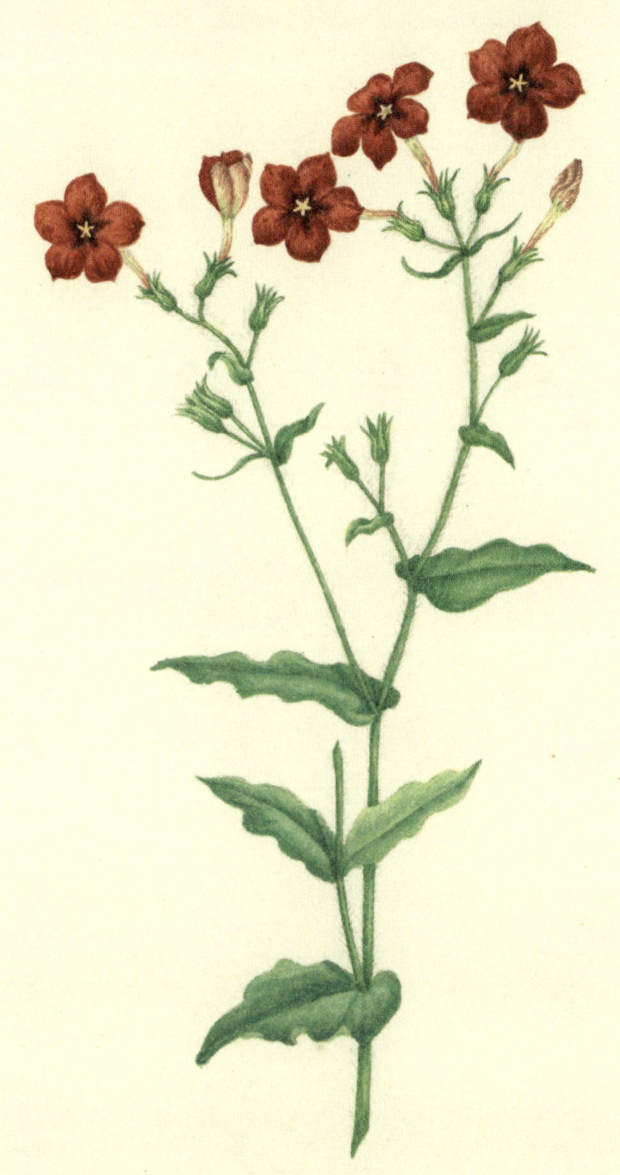

April 25

5 stamens

A plant about 18 inches high, it is found on
rich prairie lands, as well as hill sides, blooms in
April, some times three stalks spring from the same
root, but most frequently a single flower bearing stem.

No. 45

Western Paintbrush — *Castilleja latebracteata* Pennell.

A plant about 18 inches high, it is found on rich prairie lands, as well as hill sides, blooms in April, sometimes three stalks spring from the same root, but most frequently a single flower bearing stem.

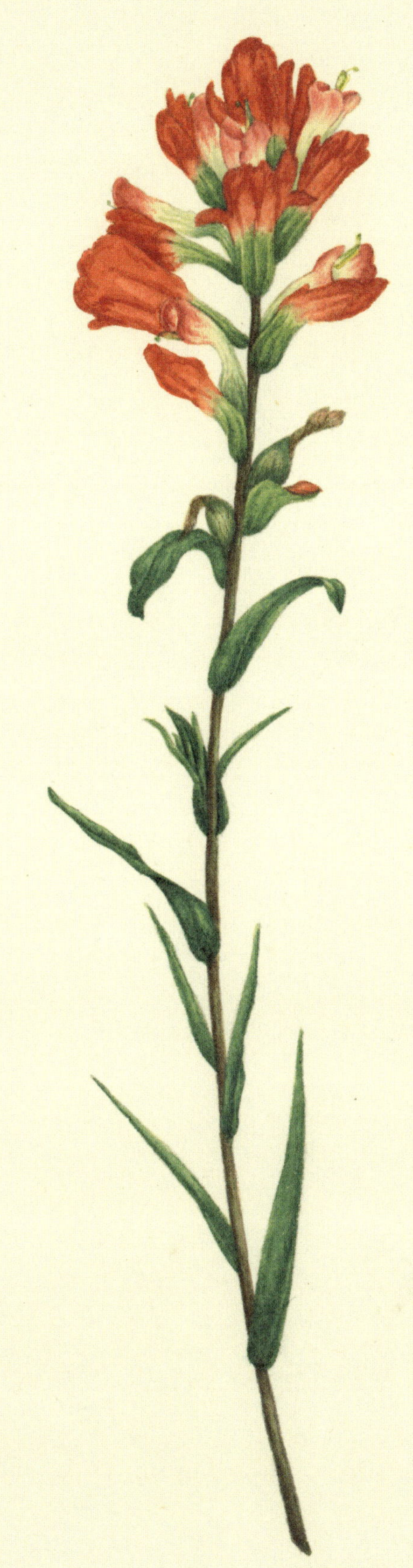

April 21st

Pistil

4 Stamens

A very showy cactus, the flower with stiff wax like petals, blooms in April and May upon a poor soil

No. 47

Claret Cup Cactus — *Echinocereus triglochidiatus* var. *triglochidiatus* Engelm.

A very showy cactus, the flower with stiff wax like petals, blooms in April and May upon a poor soil.

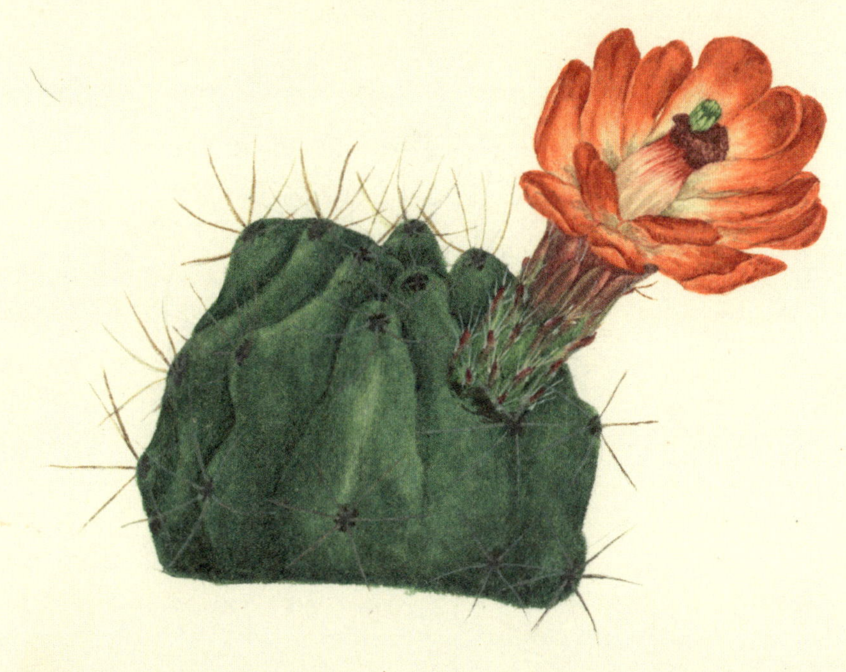

April 14th

Rattama. A small ornamental tree, of about 25 feet in height, native of the Rio Grande blooms from April till November, flowers very fragrant, growth very rapid in sandy soil.

No. 48

Paloverde or Retama — *Parkinsonia aculeata* L.

Rattama. A small ornamental tree, of about 25 feet in height, native of the Rio Grande blooms from April till November, flowers very fragrant, growth very rapid in sandy soil.

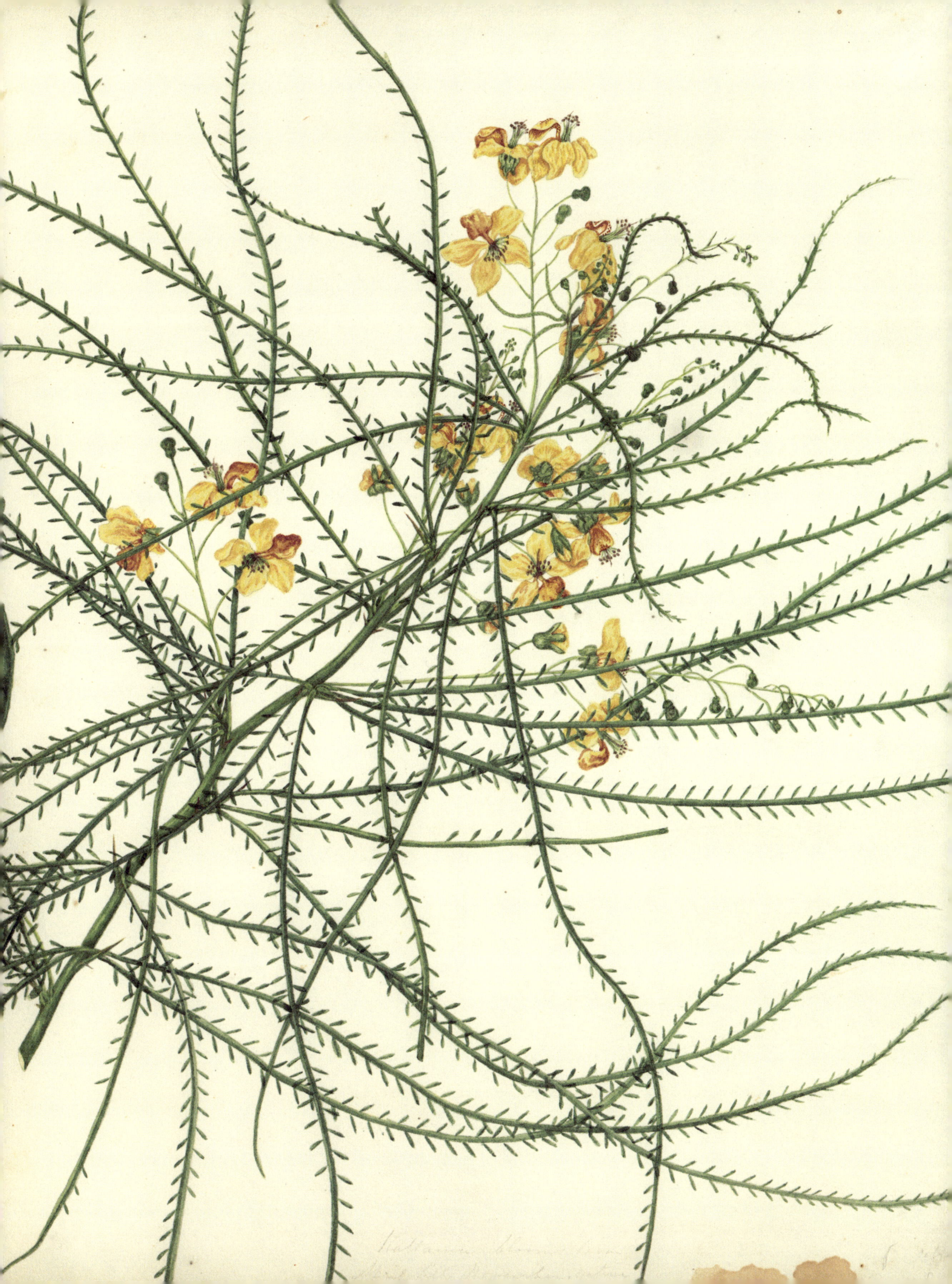

A plant about a foot high, which grows in bunches upon poor hill sides, blooms in April

No. 49

Texas Toad-flax — *Linaria texana* Scheele

A plant about a foot high, which grows in bunches upon poor hill sides, blooms in April.

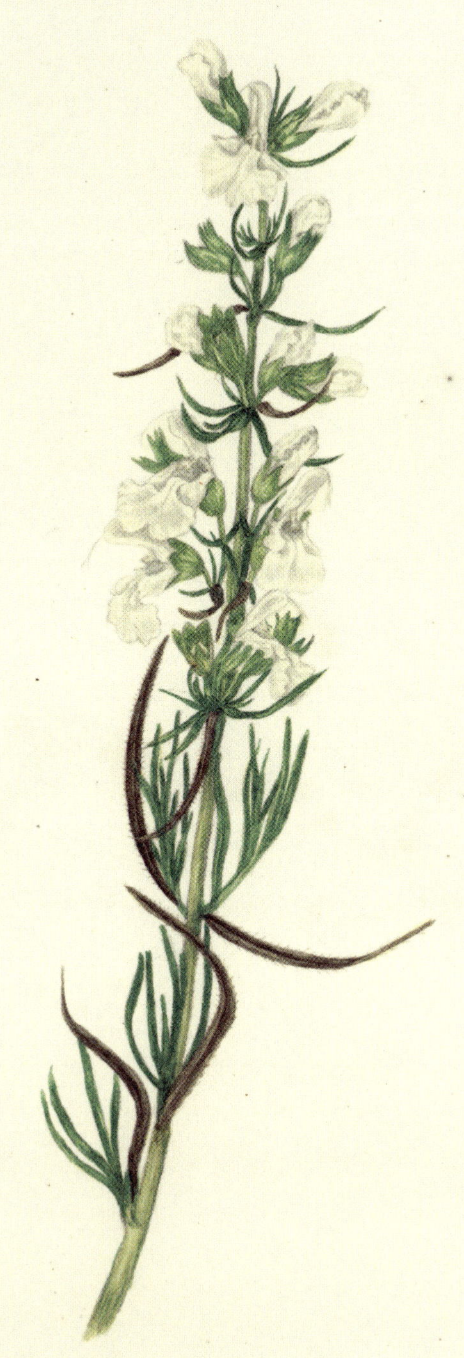

April 30

Mesquite. This has been known in Texas for many years to yield a gum, not distinguishable from the Gum Arabic of Commerce, and has been much used in medicine. It is a tree of low stature, but in favourable localities it reaches the size of the black locust of 15 or 20 years growth, its blossoms have a delightful odour, and throughout a wet summer the blooms are seen at the same with the bean of which some persons are fond, the pod contains a honey somewhat resembling that of the Honey Locust.

No. 50

Mesquite — *Prosopis juliflora* Swartz, D. C. (= *P. glanduloso* Torr.)

Mesquite. This has been known in Texas for many years to yield a gum, not distinguishable from the Gum Arabic of Commerce, and has been much used in medicine. It is a tree of low stature, but in favourable localities it reaches the size of the black locust of 15 or 20 years growth, its blossoms have a delightful odour, and throughout a wet summer the blooms are seen at the same with the bean of which some persons are fond, the pod contains a honey somewhat resembling that of the Honey Locust.

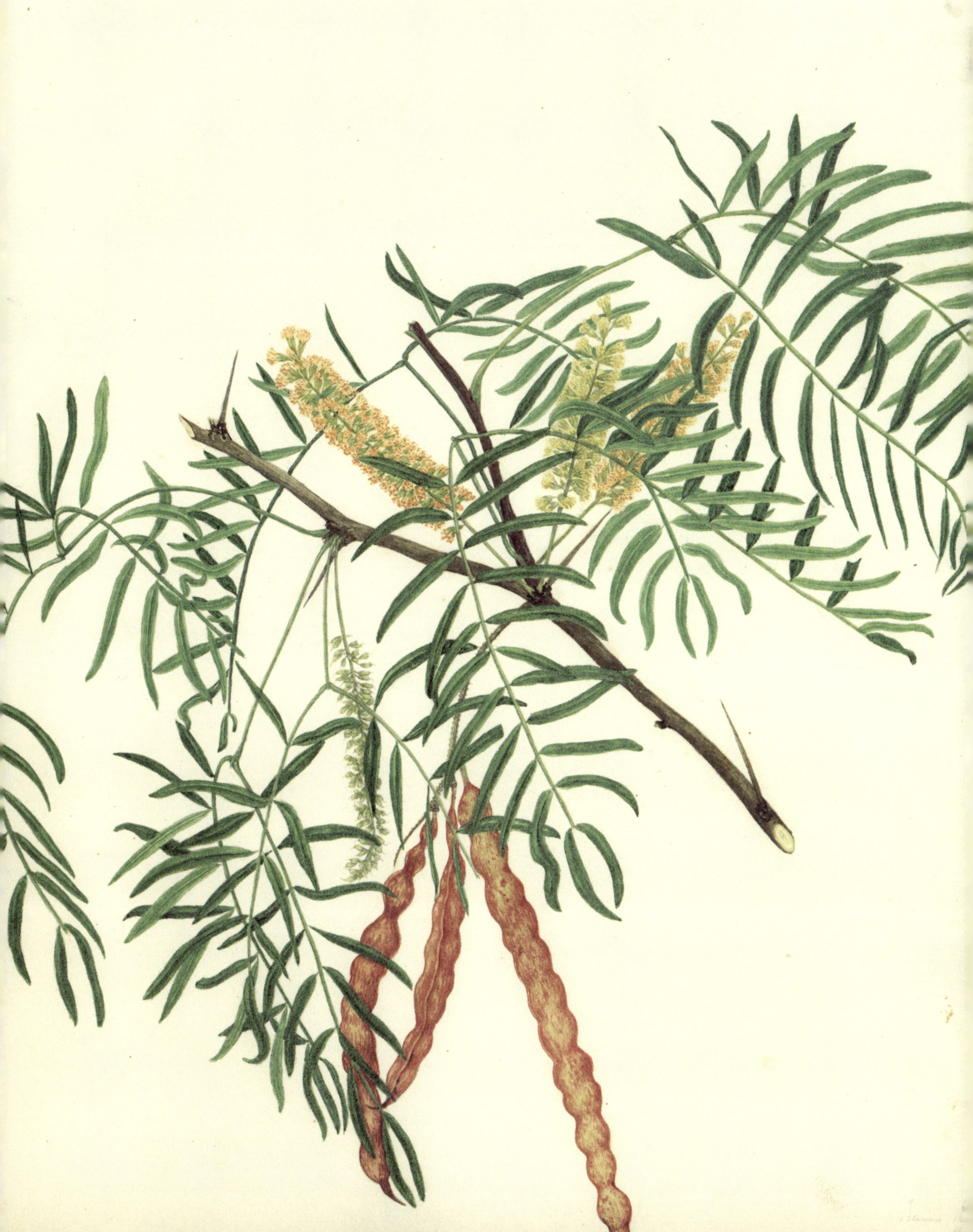

Digitalis, A plant about 14 inches high, blooms early in May on sandy soil.

No. 51

False Dragon-head or Lion's Heart — *Physostegia digitalis* Small.

Digitalis. A plant about 14 inches high, blooms early in May on sandy soil.

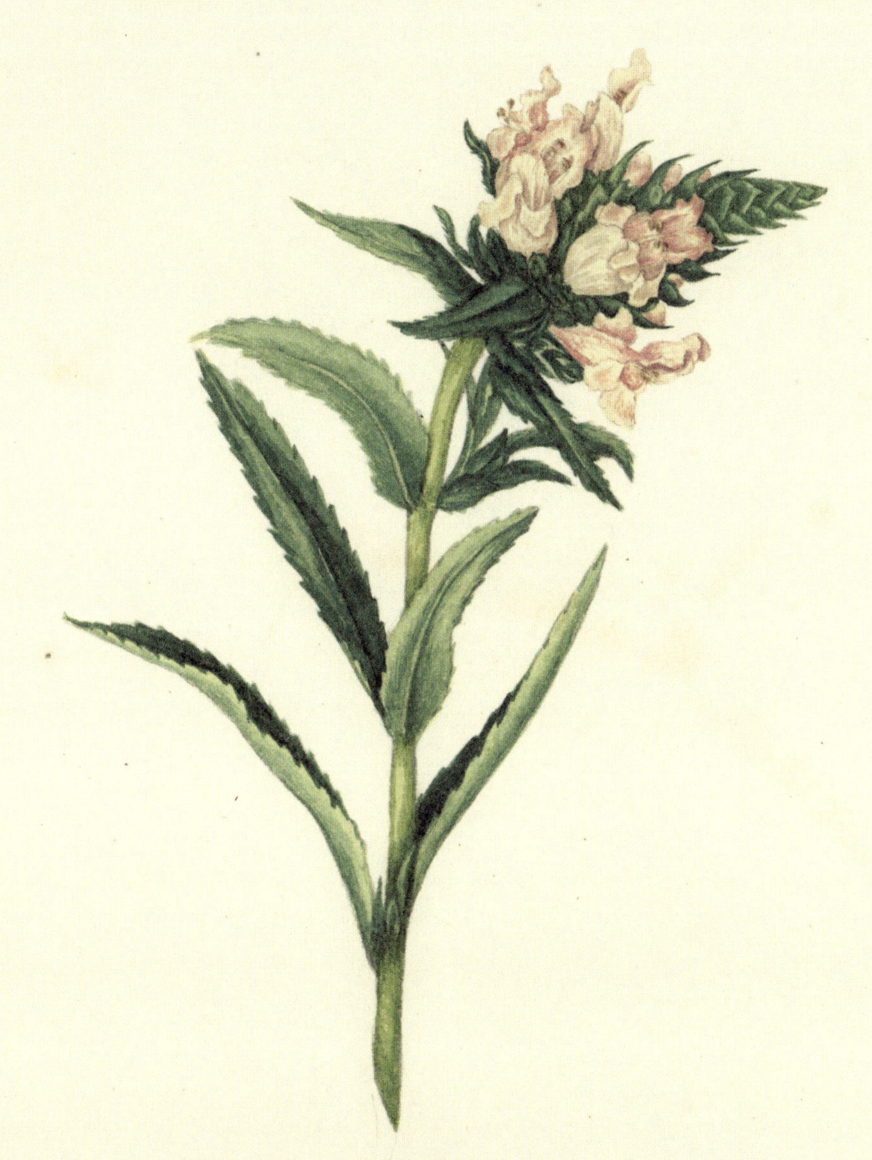

May 1st

A plant about 12 inches in height, blooms in April upon very poor soil

No. 52

Texas Sage — *Salvia texana* Scheele and Torr.

A plant about 12 inches in height, blooms in April upon very poor soil.

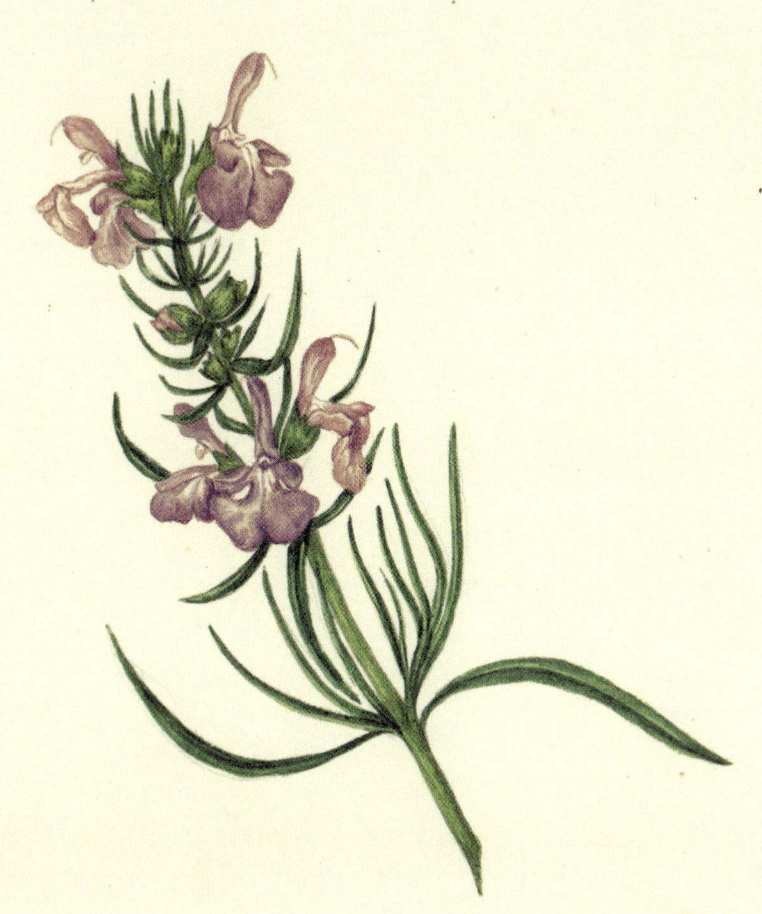

Cactus Flourishes in moderately rich soil, blooms during May and June, has a pleasant odour

No. 53

Barrel Cactus or Viznaga — *Ferocactus wislizeni* Engelm.

Cactus Flourishes in moderately rich soil, blooms during May and June, has a pleasant odour.

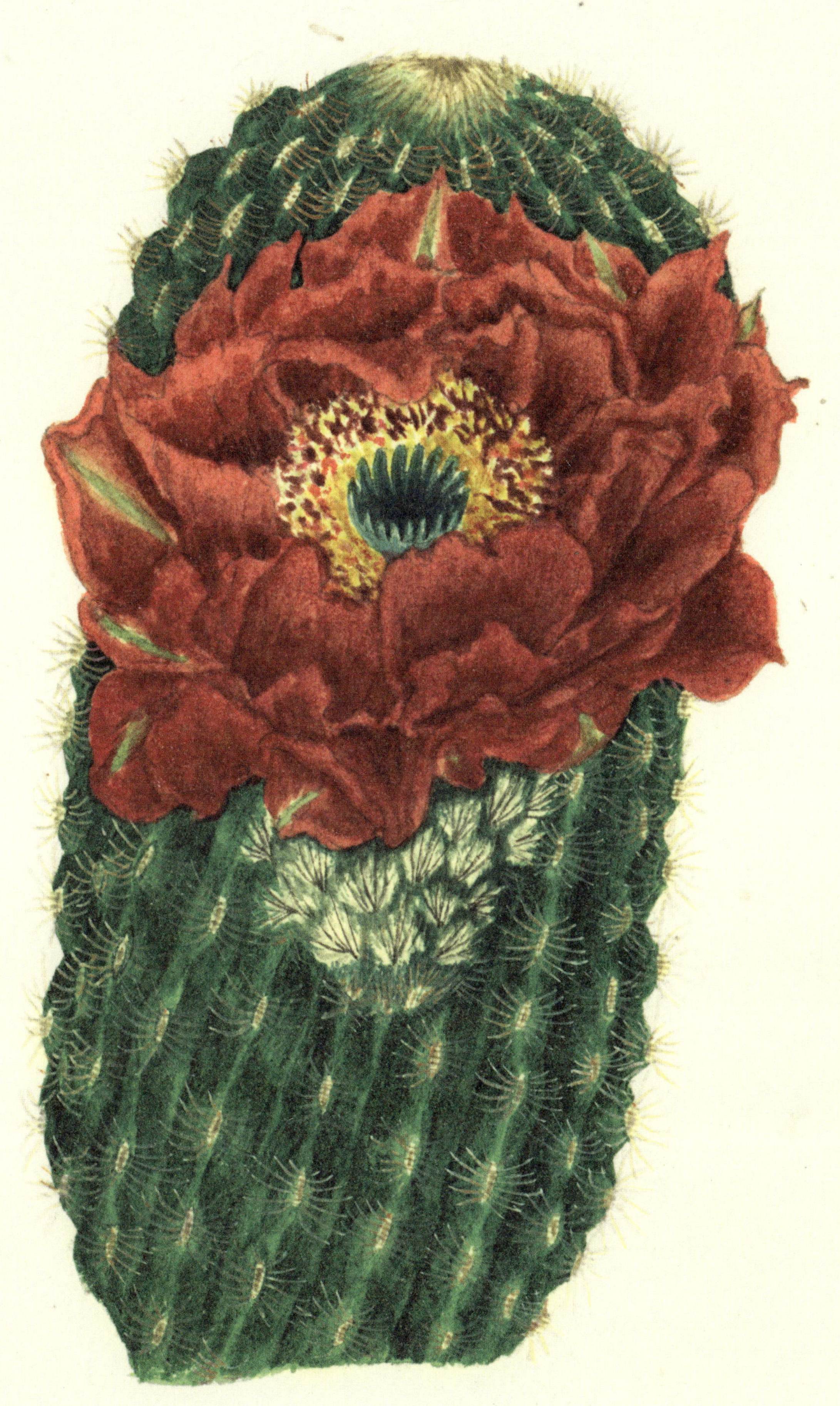

A pretty plant four feet in height, with a profusion of flowers in May, continuing to bloom through June, its native soil is alluvial.

No. 54

Black-eyed Susan — *Rudbeckia serotina* Nutt (= *R. bicolor* Nutt.)

A pretty plant four feet in height, with a profusion of flowers in May, continuing to bloom through June, its native soil is alluvial.

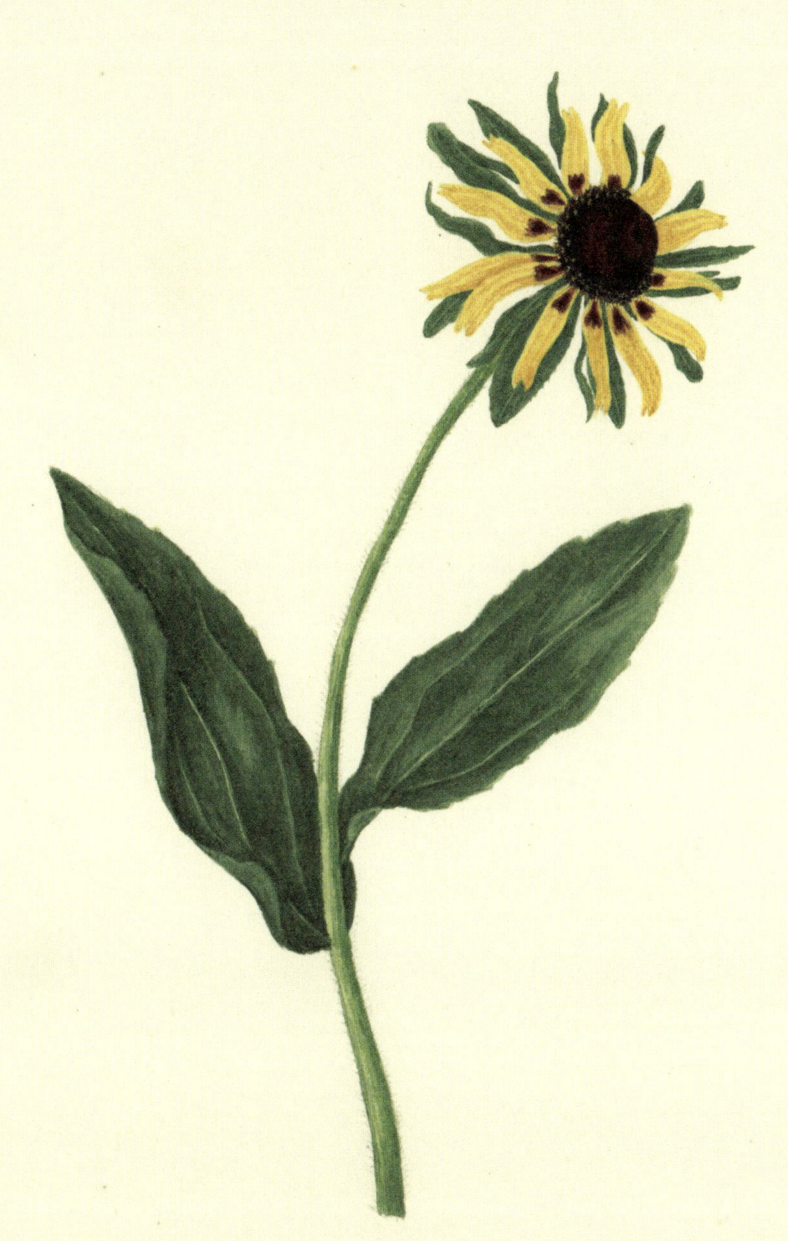

A modest little flower of the family of Lupin, seldom has more than two flowers on a stem and lies hid in the grass until a passing footstep exposes it to view.

No. 55

Scarlet Pea or Indigo Plant — *Indigofera leptosepala* Nutt.

A modest little flower of the family of Lupin, seldom has more than two flowers on a stem and lies hid in the grass until a passing footstep exposes it to view.

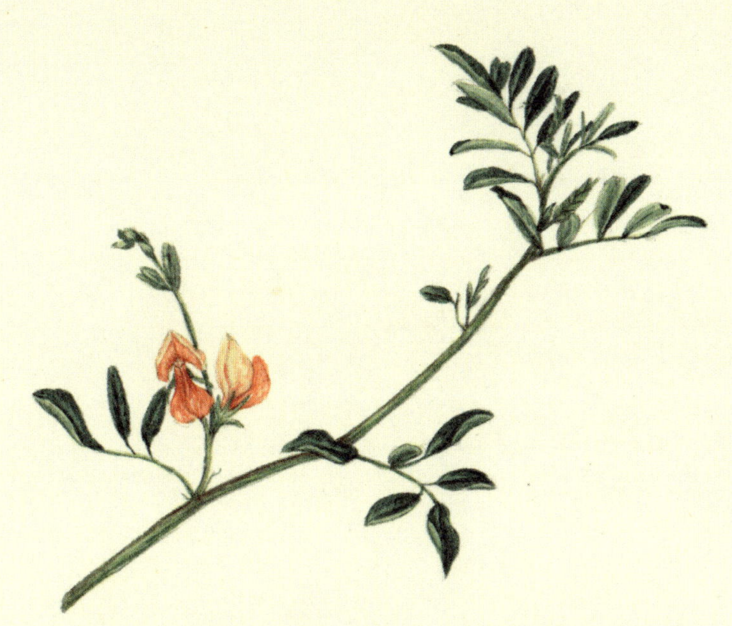

A very delicate and beautiful plant. In the curiously shaped sheath, there is always a good supply of water, in the midst of which, closely lie cradled the young buds, which will develope their beautiful blue petals in succession. As soon as one fades (like the Phoenix from its ashes) from the same sheath, another rises and spreads its petals, like fairy wings, to the Sun, & seems a real little fairy arising from the surrounding verdure. The effect of its bright little face peeping at one, above the grass is most cheering. — It varies in size according to the richness of the soil, blooms from May through the whole summer and fall, after every rain.

No. 56

Dayflower or Widow's Tears — *Commelina augustifolia* Michx.

A very delicate and beautiful plant. In the curiously shaped sheath, there is always a good supply of water, in the midst of which, closely lie cradled the young buds, which will develope their beautiful blue petals in succession. As soon as one fades, (like the Phoenix from its ashes) from the same sheath, another rises and spreads its petals, like fairy wings, to the Sun & seems a real little fairy arising from the surrounding verdure. The effect of its bright little face peeping at one, above the grass is most cheering. —It varies in size according to the richness of the soil, blooms from May through the whole summer and fall, after every rain.

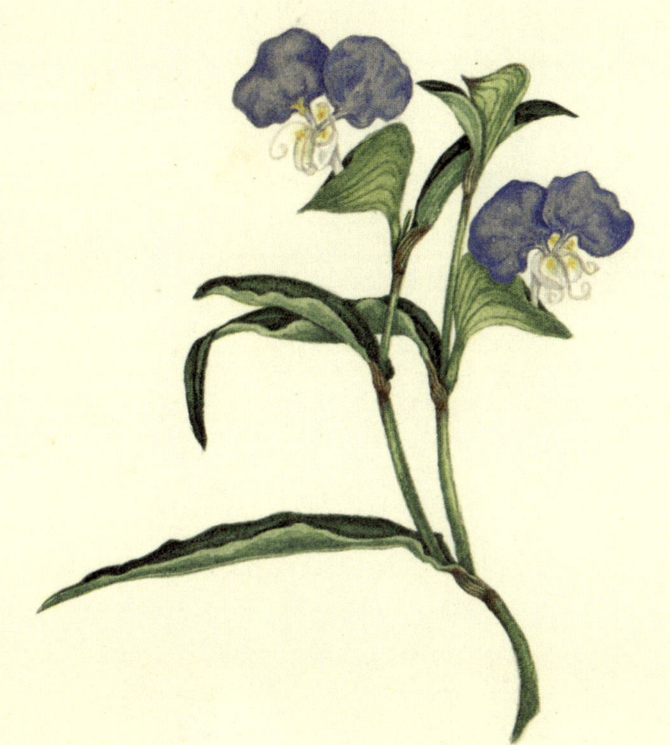

These are varieties of the same plant, the Indians make use of the leaves as a cure for the bite of a snake, pounding them and applying to the wound. giving whisky to drink. Blooms in May and June.

No. 57

Mexican Hat — *Ratibida columnaris* (Pursh) Raf.

These are varieties of the same plant, the Indians make use of the leaves as a cure for the bite of a snake, pounding them and applying to the wound giving whisky to drink. Blooms in May and June.

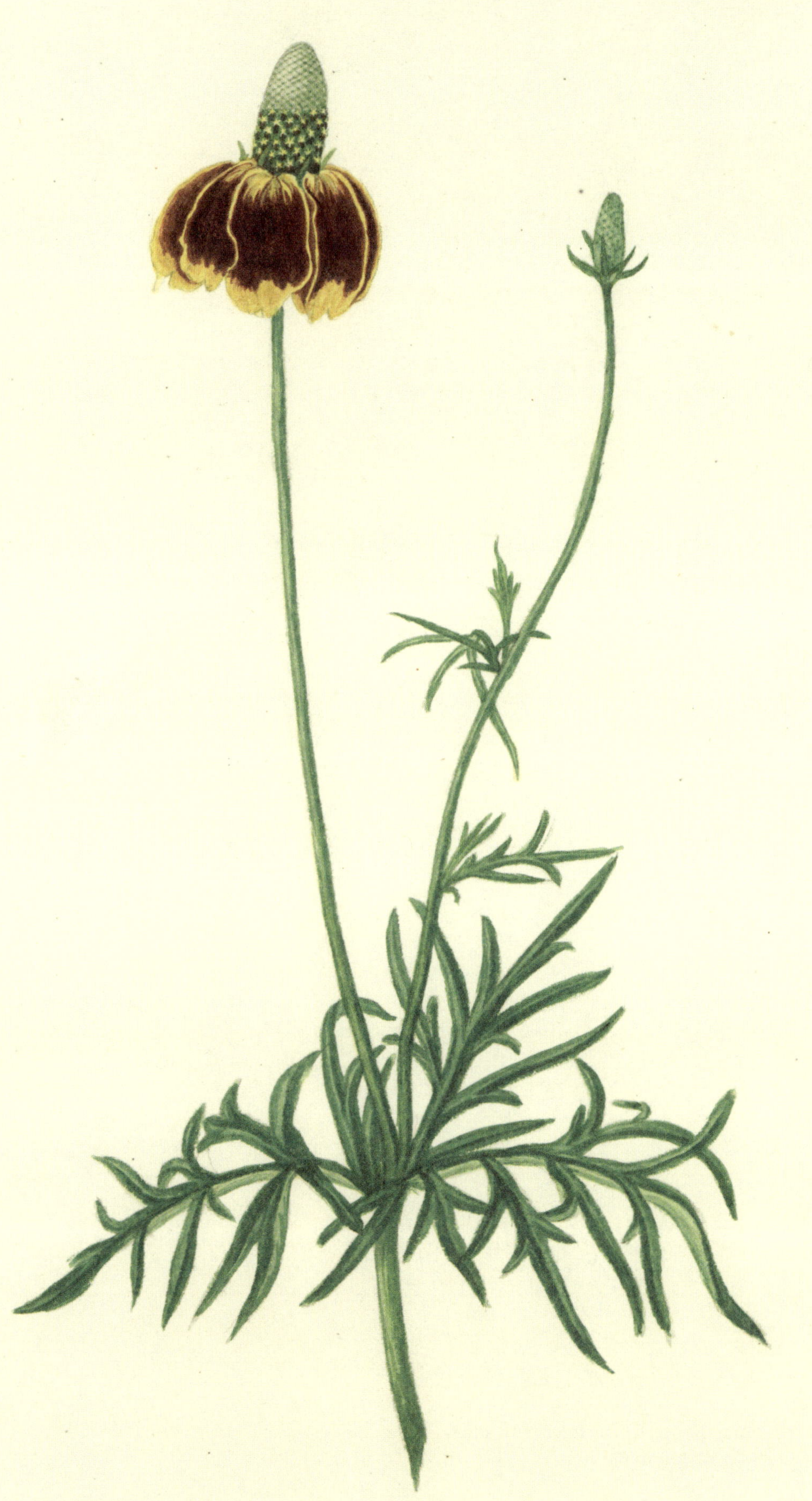

These are varieties of the same plant, the Indians make use of the leaves as a cure for the bite of a snake, pounding them and applying to the wound. giving whisky to drink. Blooms in May and June.

No. 58

Mexican Hat — *Ratibida columnaris* (Pursh) Raf.

These are varieties of the same plant, the Indians make use of the leaves as a cure for the bite of a snake, pounding them and applying to the wound giving whisky to drink. Blooms in May and June.

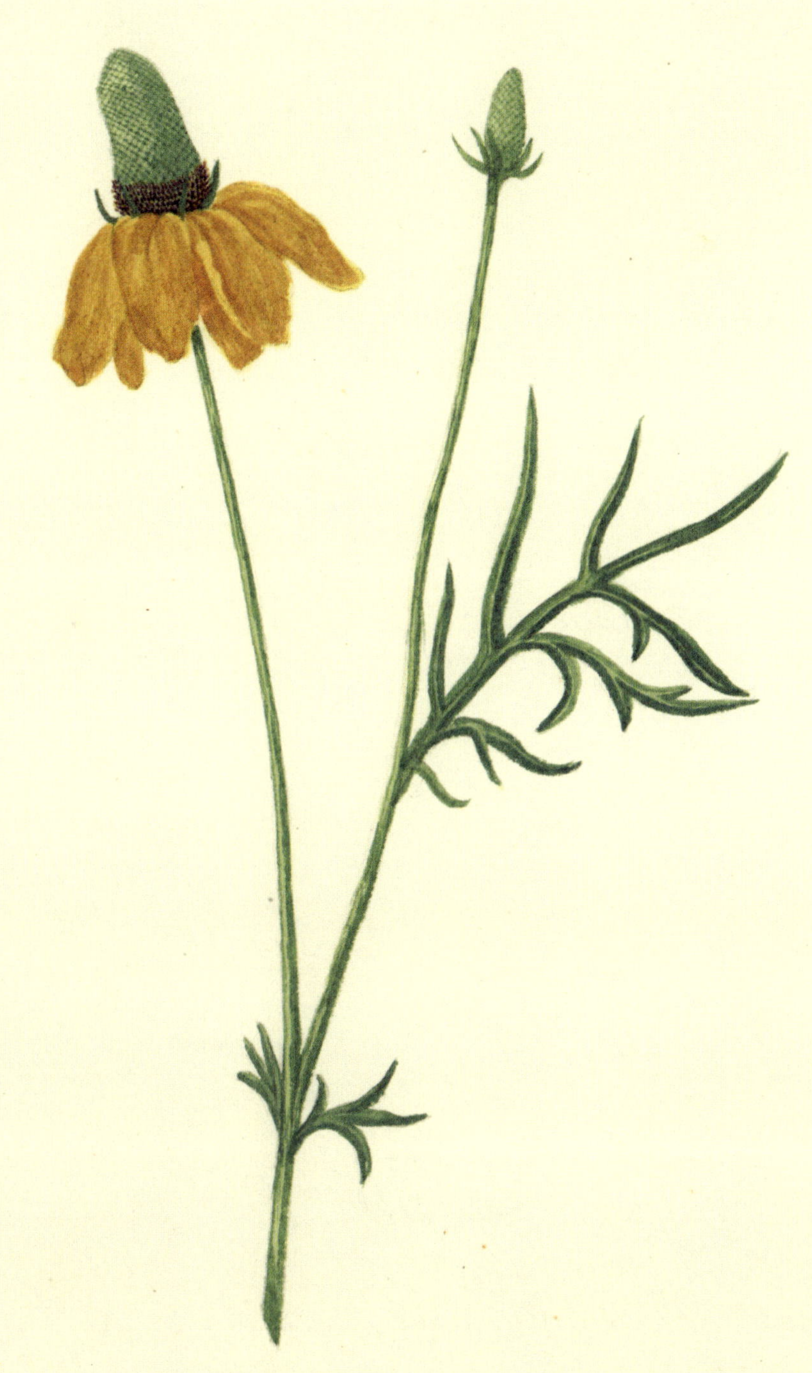

May 16

A milk weed, grows 2 feet high in rich, sandy woodlands, blooms in May and June.

No. 59

Milkweed or Butterfly-weed — *Asclepias tuberosa* L.

A milk weed, grows 2 feet high in rich, sandy woodlands, blooms in May and June.

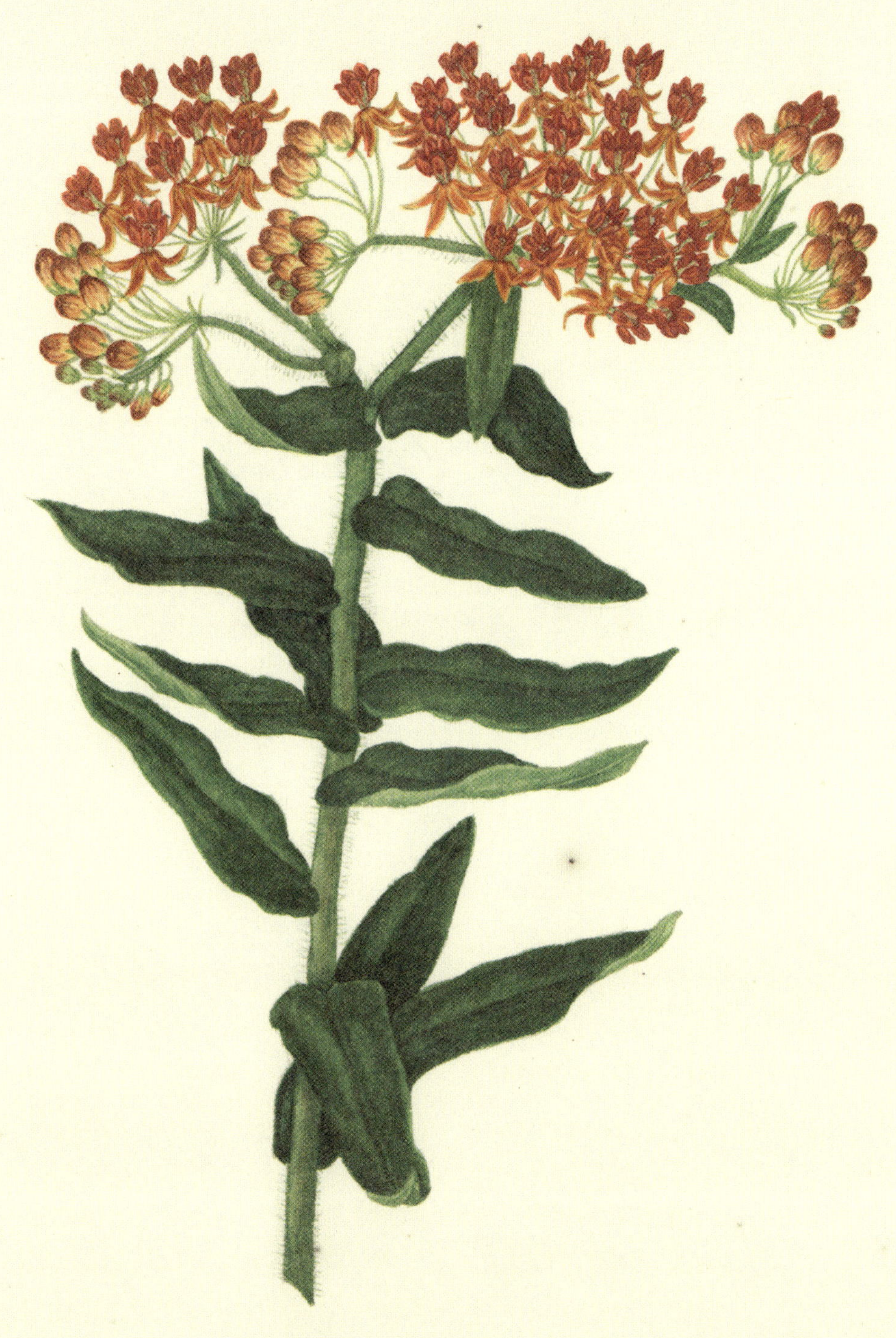

Asclepias

Cactus, Common Prickly Pear, blooms in May on thin soil, bears a purple pear shaped fruit, covered with small thorns.

No. 60

Cactus Texas Prickly Pear — *Opuntia lindheimeri* Engelm.

Cactus, Common Prickly Pear, blooms in May on thin soil, bears a purple pear shaped fruit, covered with small thorns.

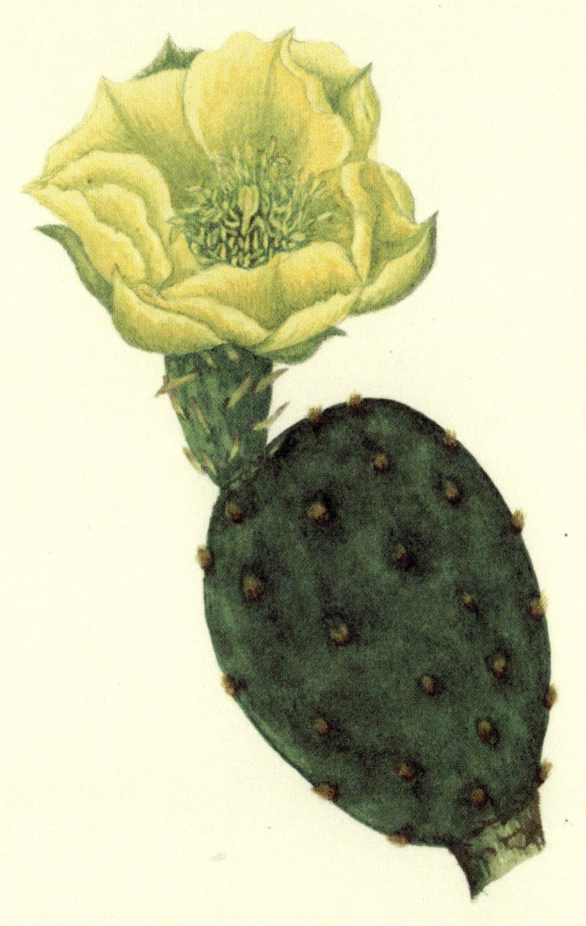

May 9

One of the most exquisitely beautitiful varieties of the Mimosa sensitiva, has an agreeable fragrance, blooms in May, its seeds are encased in small bean pods, arranged upon the stems in whorls.

No. 61

Sensitive-briar or Catclaw — *Schrankia uncinata* Nutt.

One of the most exquisitely beautitiful varieties of the Mimosa sensitiva, has an agreeable fragrance, blooms in May, its seeds are encased in small bean pods, arranged upon the stems in whorls.

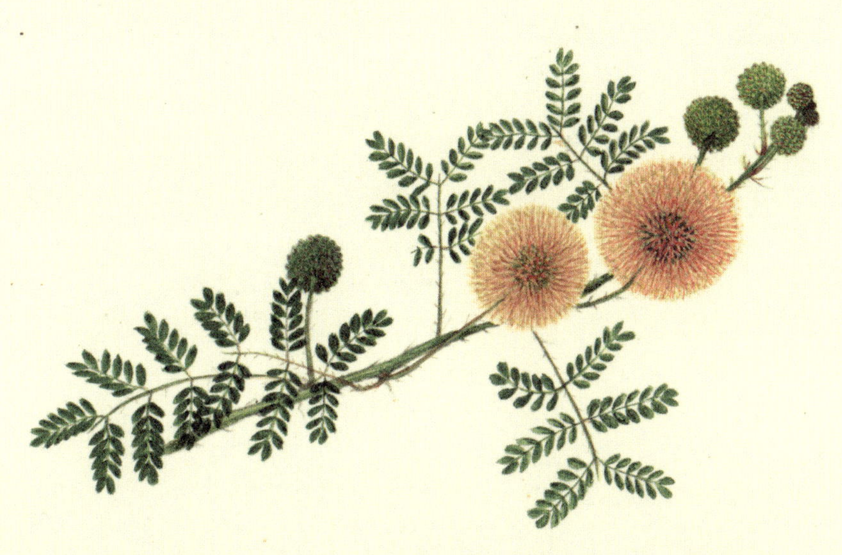

A variety of the sensitive plant with yellow blossoms. Found at the same season & locality as the pink kind.

No. 62

Yellow Sensitive-briar — *Neptunia lutea* Benth.

A variety of the sensitive plant with yellow blossoms, found at the same season & locality as the pink kind.

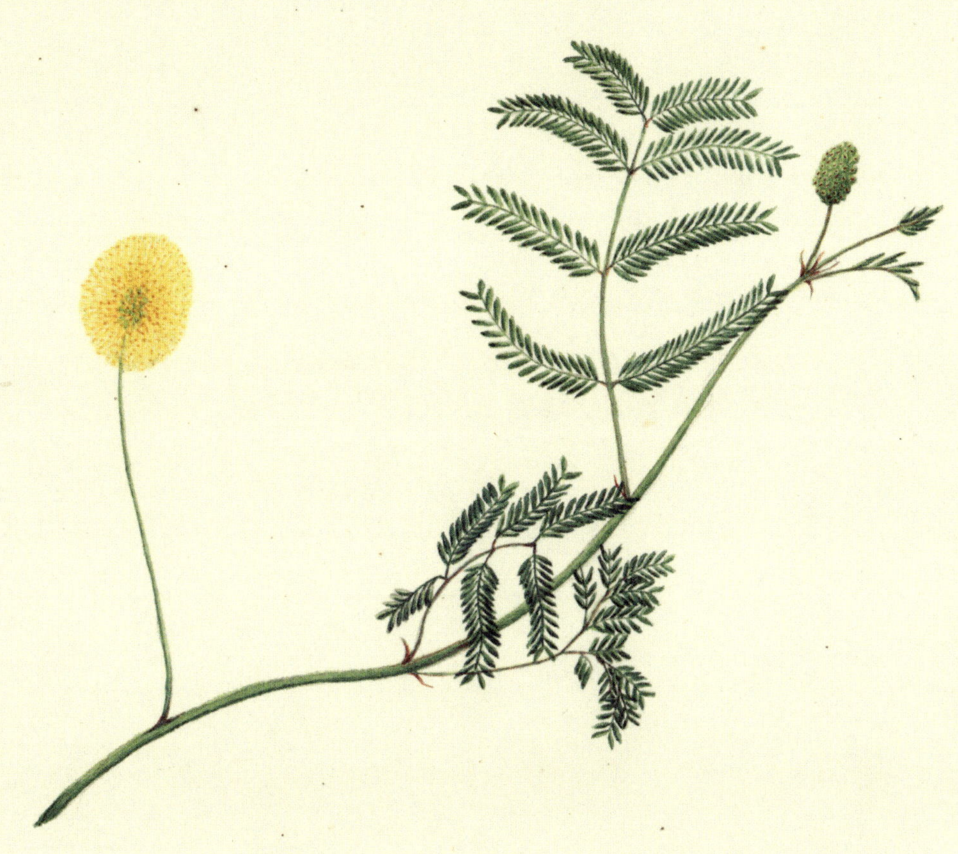

May 7th

Is a plant from three to four feet high; in passing through north western Texas, the traveller will frequently find his path bordered for miles, by this flower mingled with the sunflower. the seed, falling from a single cluster of each will stock many acres; by being caught up, by passing wheels, or clinging to horses feet, they are planted, and thus become ornaments for the roadside. It blooms from the middle of May till the last of August.

No. 63

Star-thistle — *Centaurea americana* Nutt.

Is a plant from three to four feet high; in passing through north western Texas, the traveller will frequently find his path bordered for miles, by this flower mingled with the sunflower, the seed, falling from a single cluster of each will stock many acres, by being caught up, by passing wheels, or clinging to horses feet, they are planted, and thus become ornaments for the roadside. It blooms from the middle of May till the last of August.

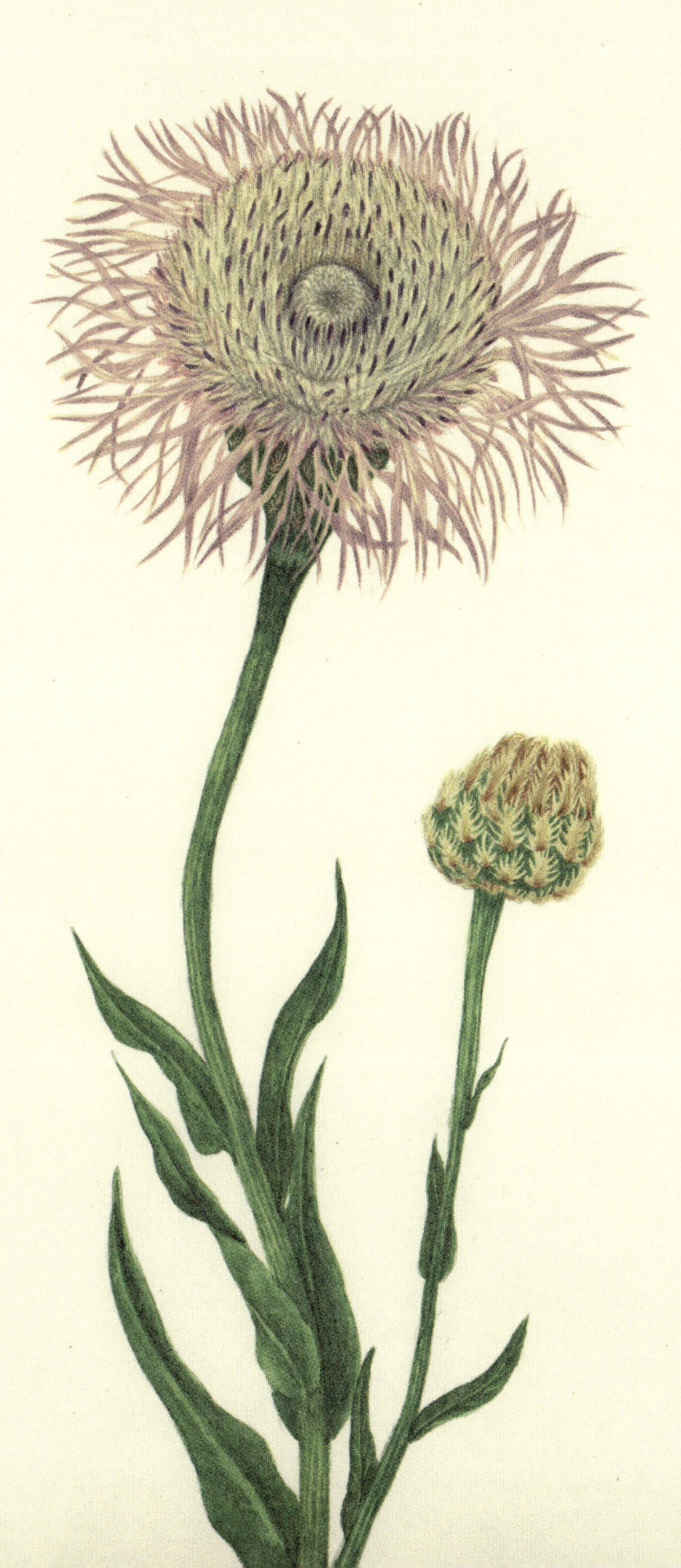

A pretty little prostrate vine growing in sandy districts, the flowers are glossy and have the appearance of Garnets glittering in the grass. it blooms in May.

No. 64

Prairie Sand-bur or Linear-leaved Krameria –

*Krameria lanceolat*a D. C.

A pretty little prostrate vine growing in sandy districts, the flowers are glossy and have the appearance of Garnets glittering in the grass. It blooms in May.

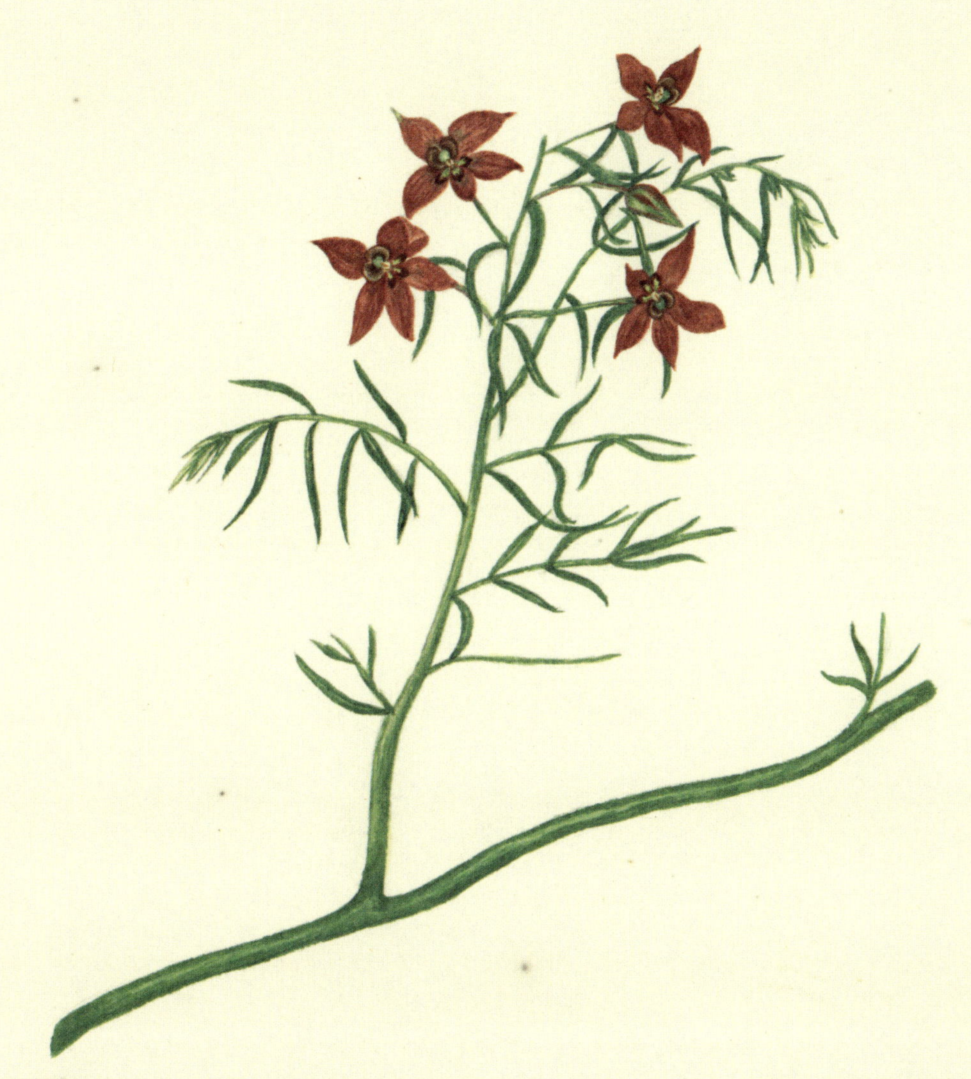

A white flowered milk weed, found on rich Prairies, blooms in May.

No. 65

White-flowered Milkweek — *Asclepias verticillata* L.

A white flowered milk week, found on rich Prairies, blooms in May.

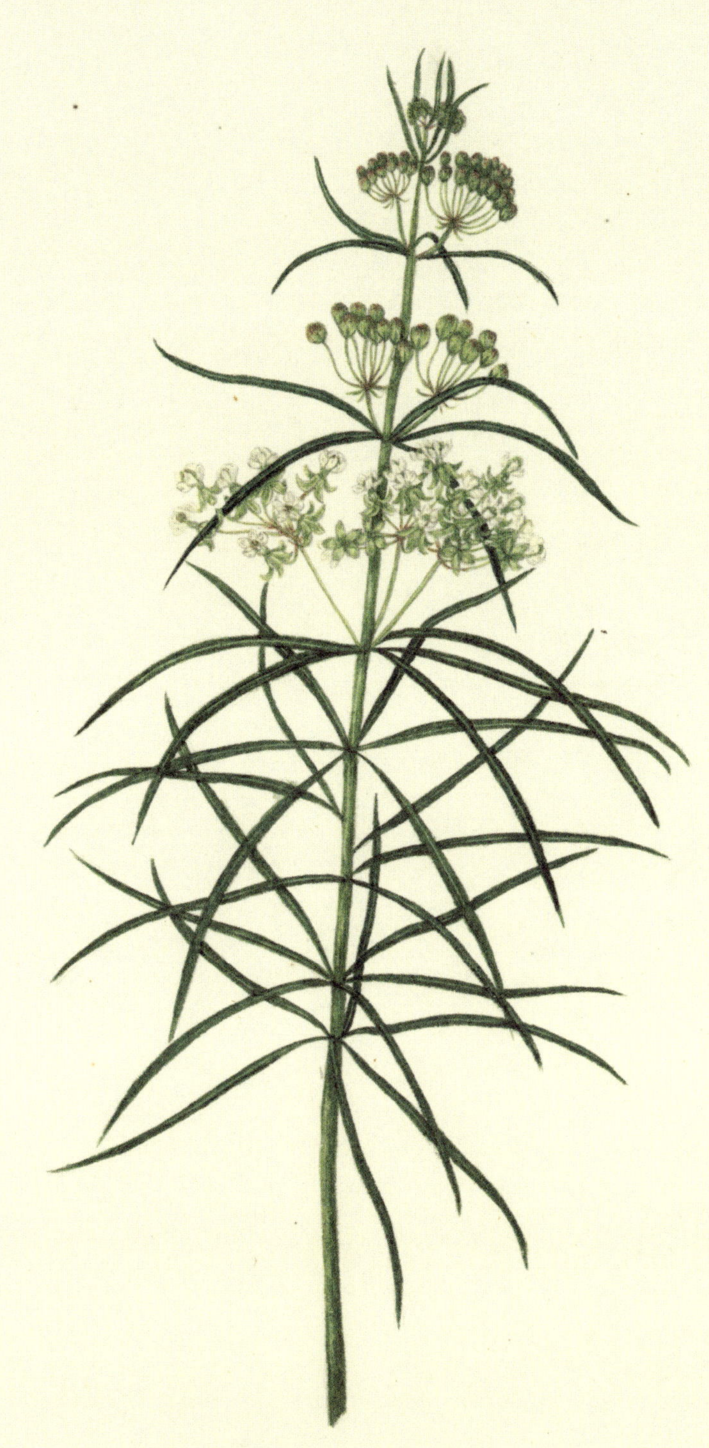

A pretty little flower, from 6 to 8 inches high, blooms in May on rich Prairie lands

No. 66

Hypericum — *Hypericum apocynifolium* Small.

A pretty little flower, from 6 to 8 inches high, blooms in May on rich Prairie lands.

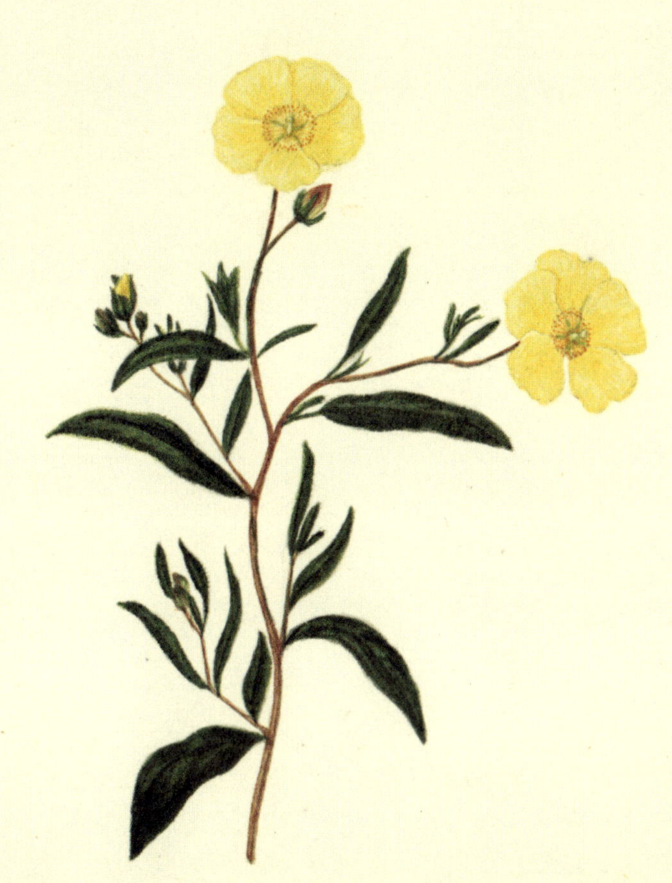

Dwarf Passion flower, a vine growing prostrate on the sands, near the banks of streams, blooms in May and June.

No. 67

Dwarf Passion Flower or May-pop — *Passiflora incarnata* L.

Dwarf Passion flowe, a vine growing prostrate on the sands, near the banks of streams, blooms in May and June.

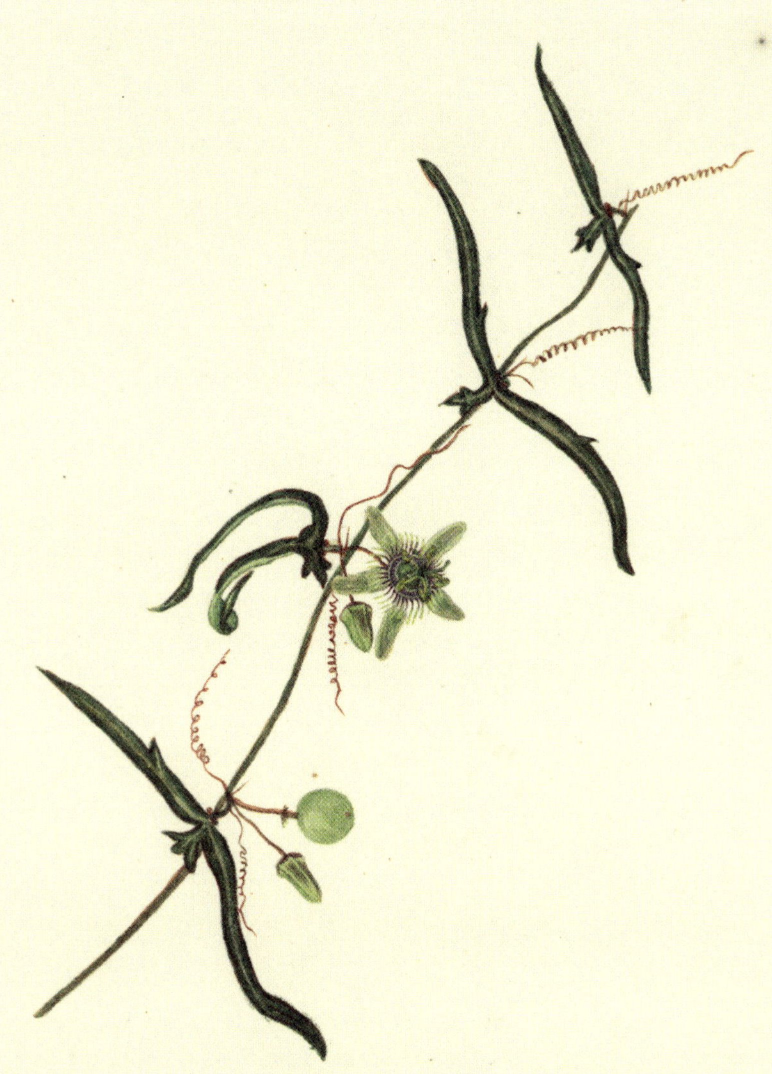

Dwarf Passion Flower

A delicate and attractive little plant, from 4 to 6 inches high, found on the sands near rivers, blooms in May and June.

No. 68

Centaury, Grass-pink or Star Flower — *Erythraea calycosa* Buckl. (= *Centaurium calycosum* Nutt.)

A delicate and attractive little plant, from 4 to 6 inches high, found on the sands near rivers, blooms in May and June.

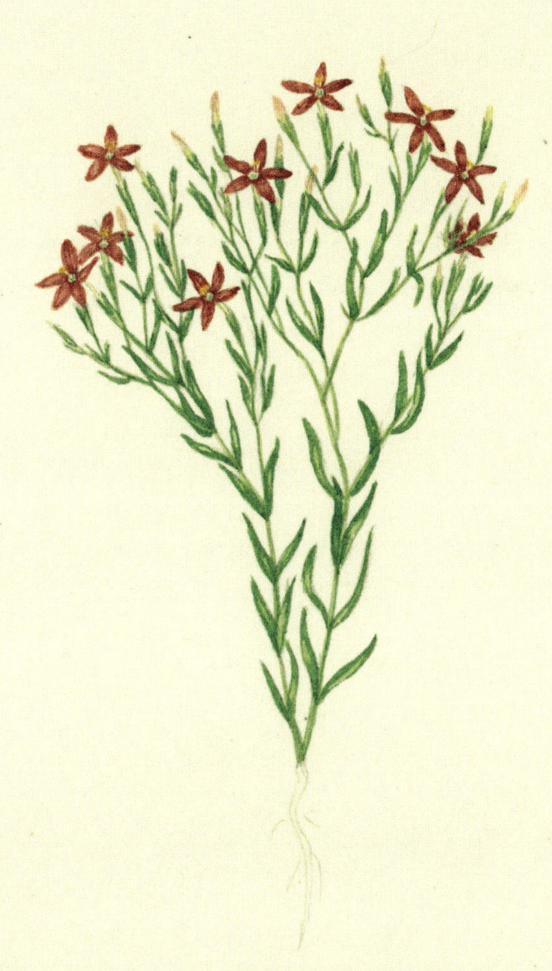

May 17

Pistil & Stem 6 Stam

A small plant with a delightful odour, flourishes in the sandy soil of open forest, blooms in the middle of May.

No. 69

Texas Star or Meadow Pink — *Sabatica campestris* Nutt.

A small plant with a delightful odour, flourishes in the sandy soil of open forests, blooms in the middle of May.

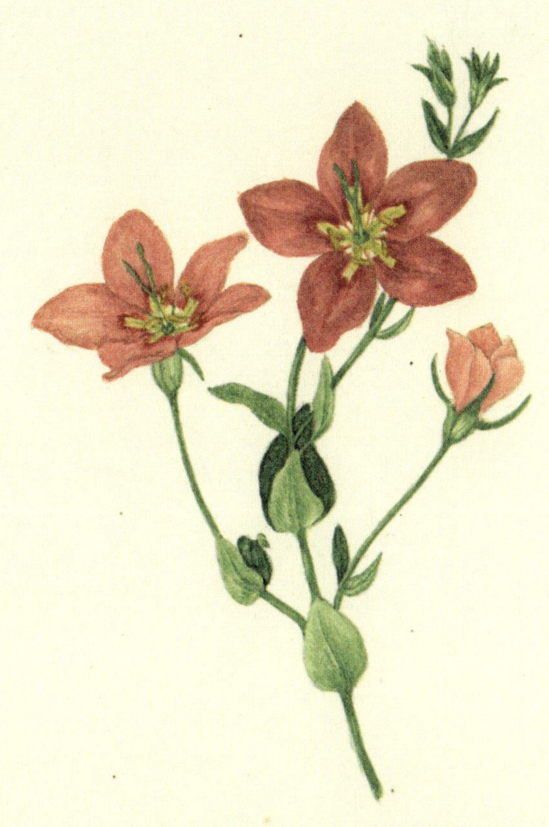

Star of Texas

May 18

Wild Heliotrope, entirely without fragrance, grows from three to four feet high, the whole plant when in bloom, would measure perhaps three feet across, is found upon the sandy banks of rivers, in bloom during May and June.

No. 70

Blue Curls or Wild Heliotrope — *Phacelia congesta* Hook.

Wild Heliotrope, entirely without fragrance, grows from three to four feet high, the whole plant when in bloom, woudl measure perhaps three feet across, is found upon the sandy banks of rivers, in bloom during May and June.

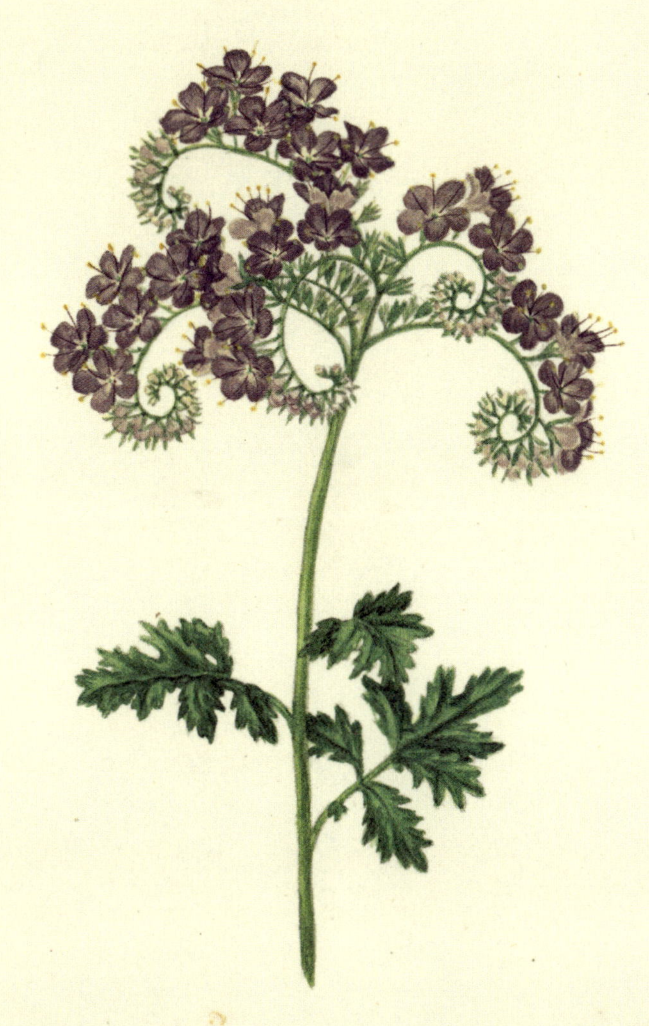

Wild Heliotrope

May 19

Grows luxuriantly in sandy soil, from May throughout the summer, after wet seasons.

No. 71

Wild Petunia — *Ruellia occidentalis* A. Gray

Grows luxuriantly in sandy soil, from May throughout the summer, after wet seasons.

11

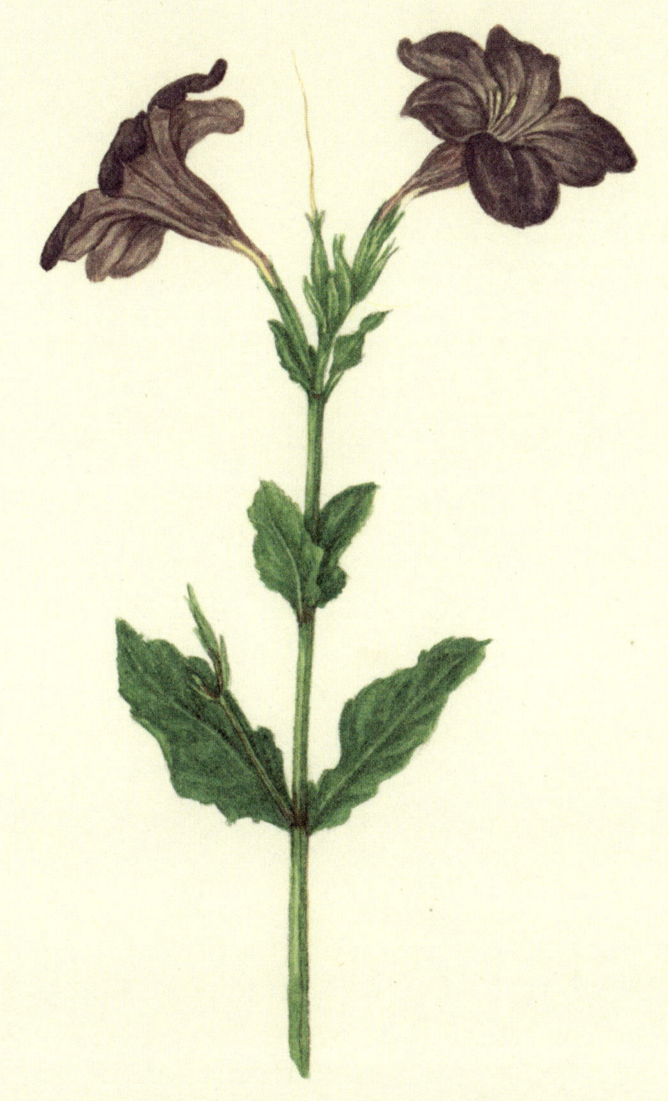

Petunia

May 20

A small plant from 6 to 8 inches high, blooms in May on rich soil.

No. 72

Wild Shasta Daisy or Lazy Daisy — *Aphanostephus skirhobasis* D. C., Trel.

A small plant from 6 to 8 inches high, blooms in May on rich soil.

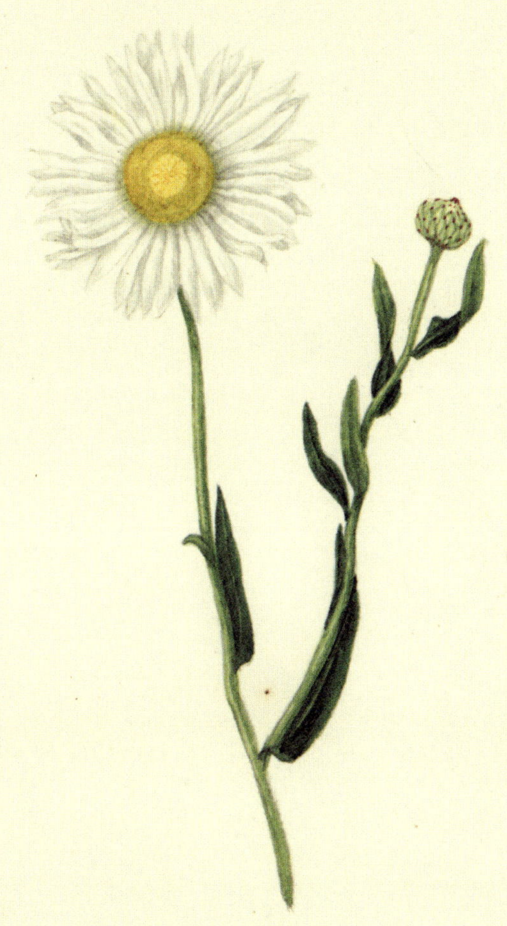

May 20

A pretty, but frail flower, blooms about three weeks in May, the plant, from 10 to 12 inches high, is found on rich soil.

No. 73

False Honeysuckle — *Siphonoglossa pilosella* Nees., Torr.

A pretty, but frail flower, blooms about three weeks in May, the plant, from 10 to 12 inches high, is found on rich soil.

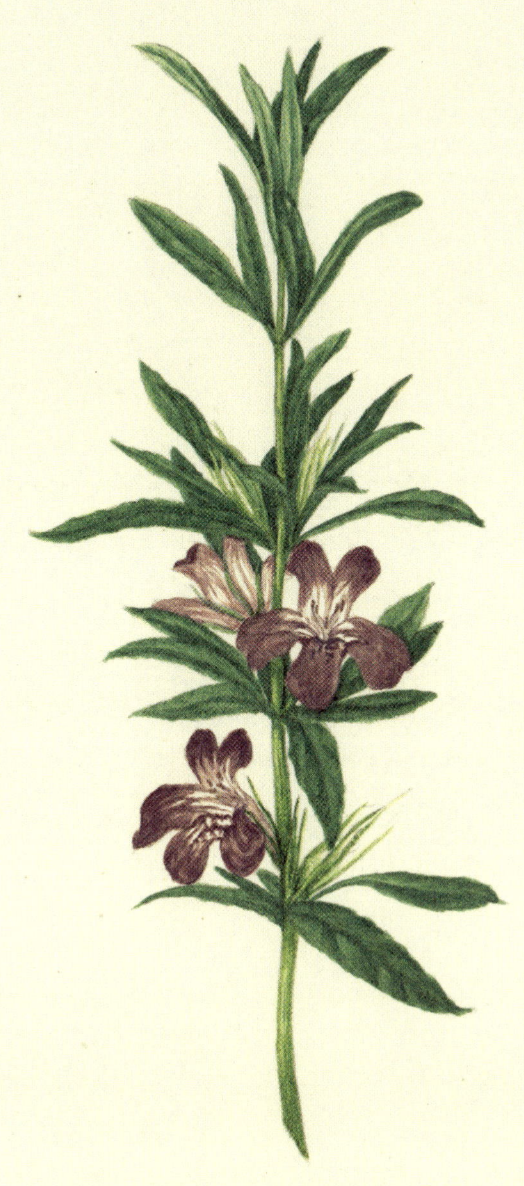

May 26

4 Stamens

"Polar Plant or North and South Weed." Morning and evening the points of its leaves are directed North and South, at midday, they point in no particular direction, the plant is resinous, and delights in spreading the surface of its leaves to the sun. there is also a white flowered variety, blooms freely from May till the end of Summer on rich land.

No. 74

Englemann Daisy or Cut-leaved Daisy — *Engelmannia pinnatifida* Nutt.

"Polar Plant or North and South Weed." Morning and evening the points of its leaves are directed north and south, at midday, they point in no particular direction, the plant is resinous, and delights in spreading the surface of its leaves to the sun. There is also a white flowered variety, blooms freely from May till the end of Summer on rich land.

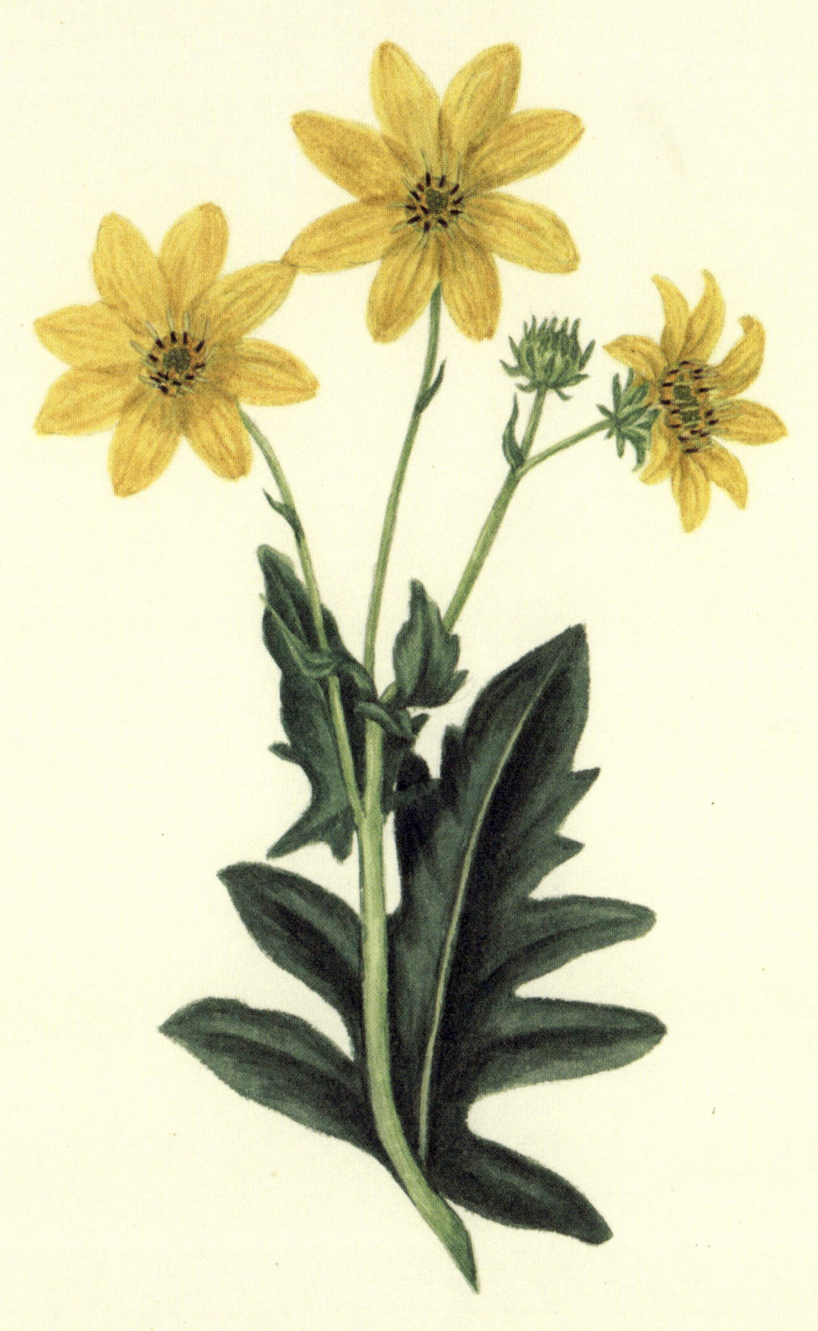

Polar Plant

May 21st

The small petals of this plant have the appearance of Butterflies hovring round the flower. The sheath encloses buds in different stages of developement, each one as it arrives at maturity escaping from its protection, expands its rich petals to light and life, and leaves its unperfected fellows snugly wrapped in their envelope, until the season of their perfection arrives. Its bulb is found in the alluvial lands of the Yegua. it blooms during the six weeks after the middle of May.

No. 75

Wild Iris or Celestial — *Nemastylis purpurea* Herb.

The small petals of this plant have the appearance of Butterflies hovering round the flower. The sheath encloses buds in different stages of developement, each one as it arrives at maturity escaping from its protection, expands its rich petals to light and life, and leaves its unperfected fellows snugly wrapped in their envelope, until the season of their perfection arrives. Its bulb is found in the alluvial lands of the Yegua, it blooms during the six weeks after the middle of May.

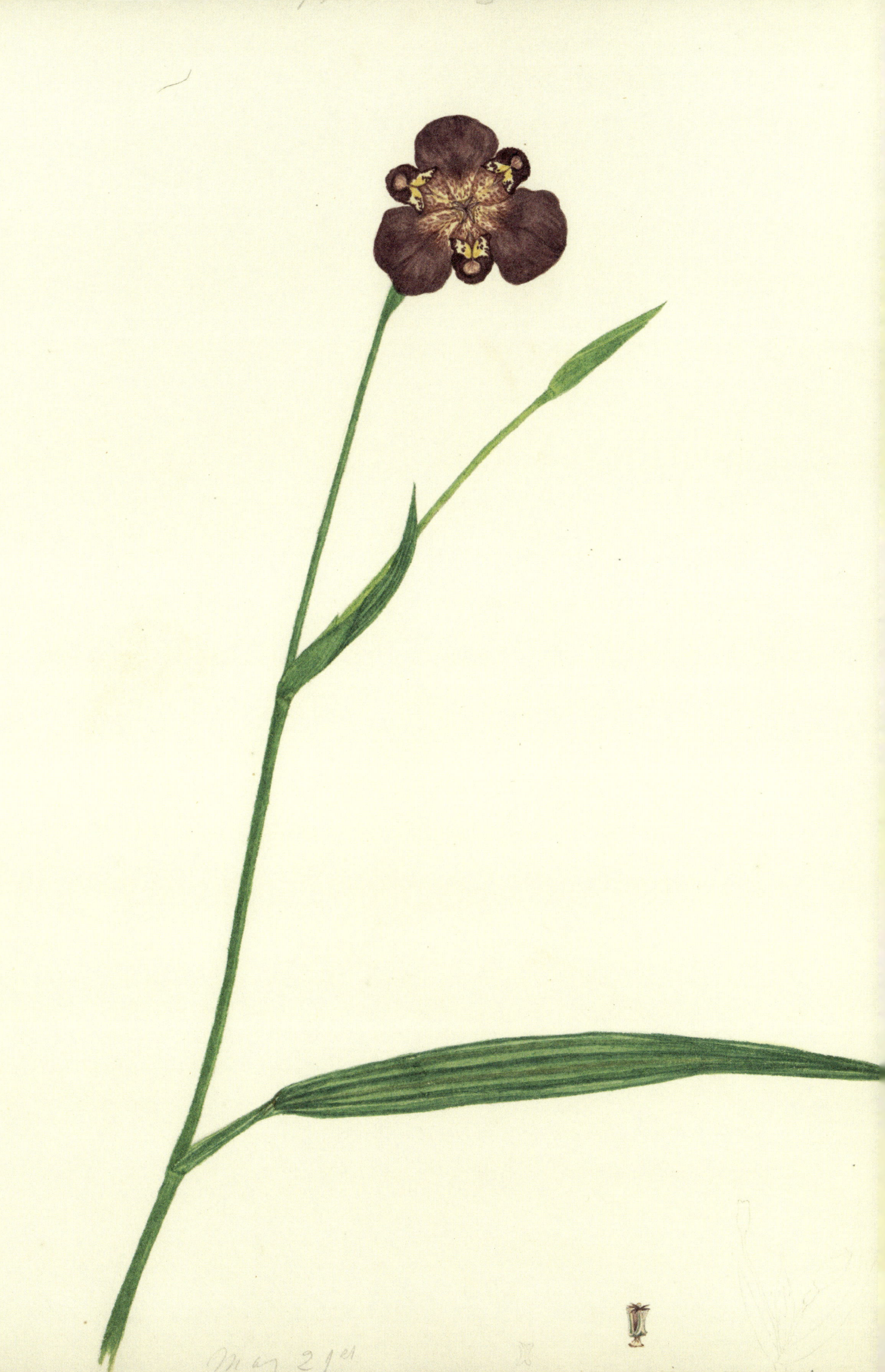
May 21st

A prolific blooming plant two feet high, in perfection in May and June.

No. 76

Two-leaved Senna — *Cassia roemeriana* Scheele.

A prolific blooming plant two feet high, in perfection in May and June.

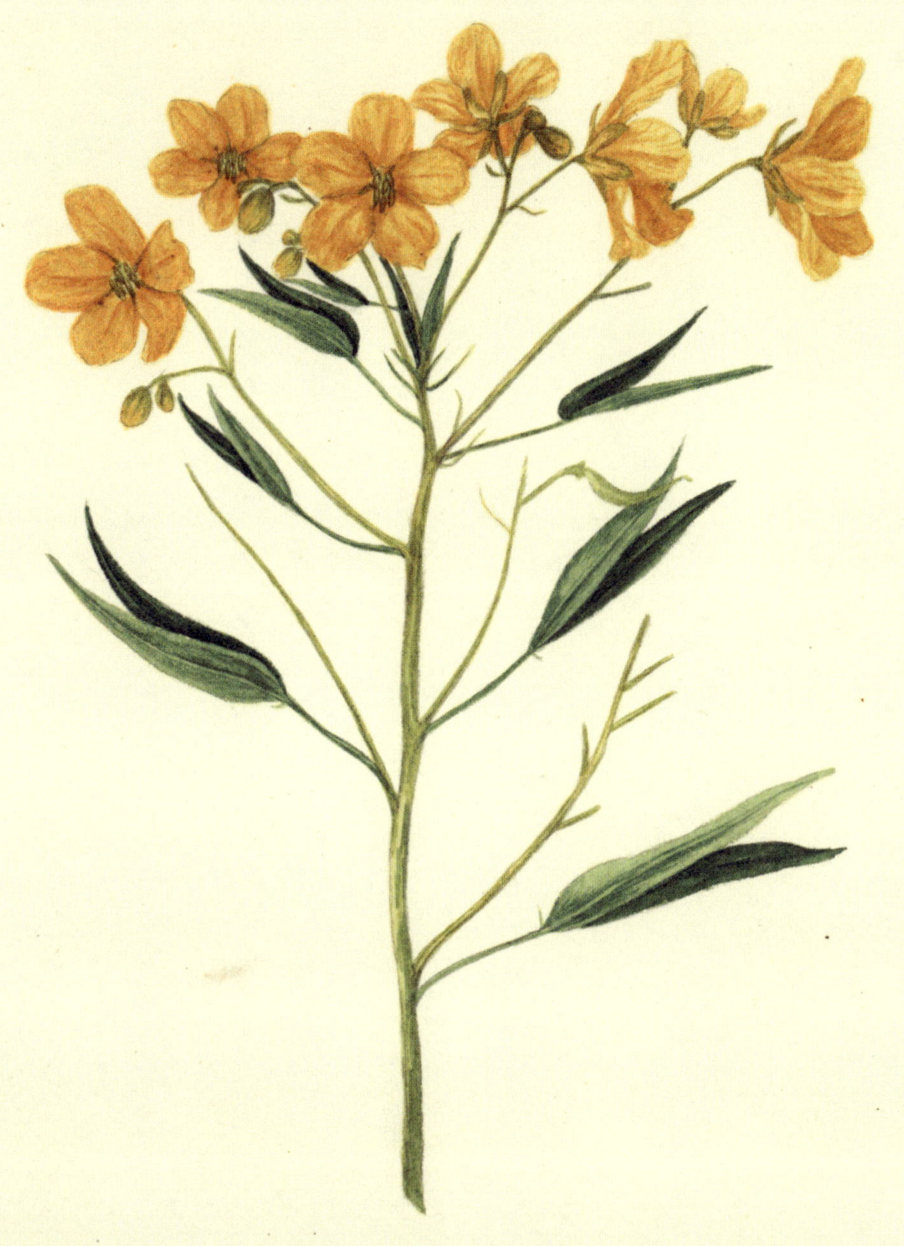

May 22

10 Stamens 1 Pistil

Commonly known as "Bear Grass", it rears its wealth of bell like blossoms to the height of 6 or 8 feet, a single stalk covered with many branches, a part of one of these branches is represented in the plate. it blooms in May, and flourishes on high land and in calcarious soil.

No. 77

Yucca or Bear Grass — *Yucca rupicola* Scheele.

Commonly known as "Bear Grass," it rears its wealth of bell like blossoms to the height of 6 to 8 feet, a single stalk covered with many branches, a part of one of these branches is represented in the plate. It blooms in May, and flourishes on high land and in calcarious soil.

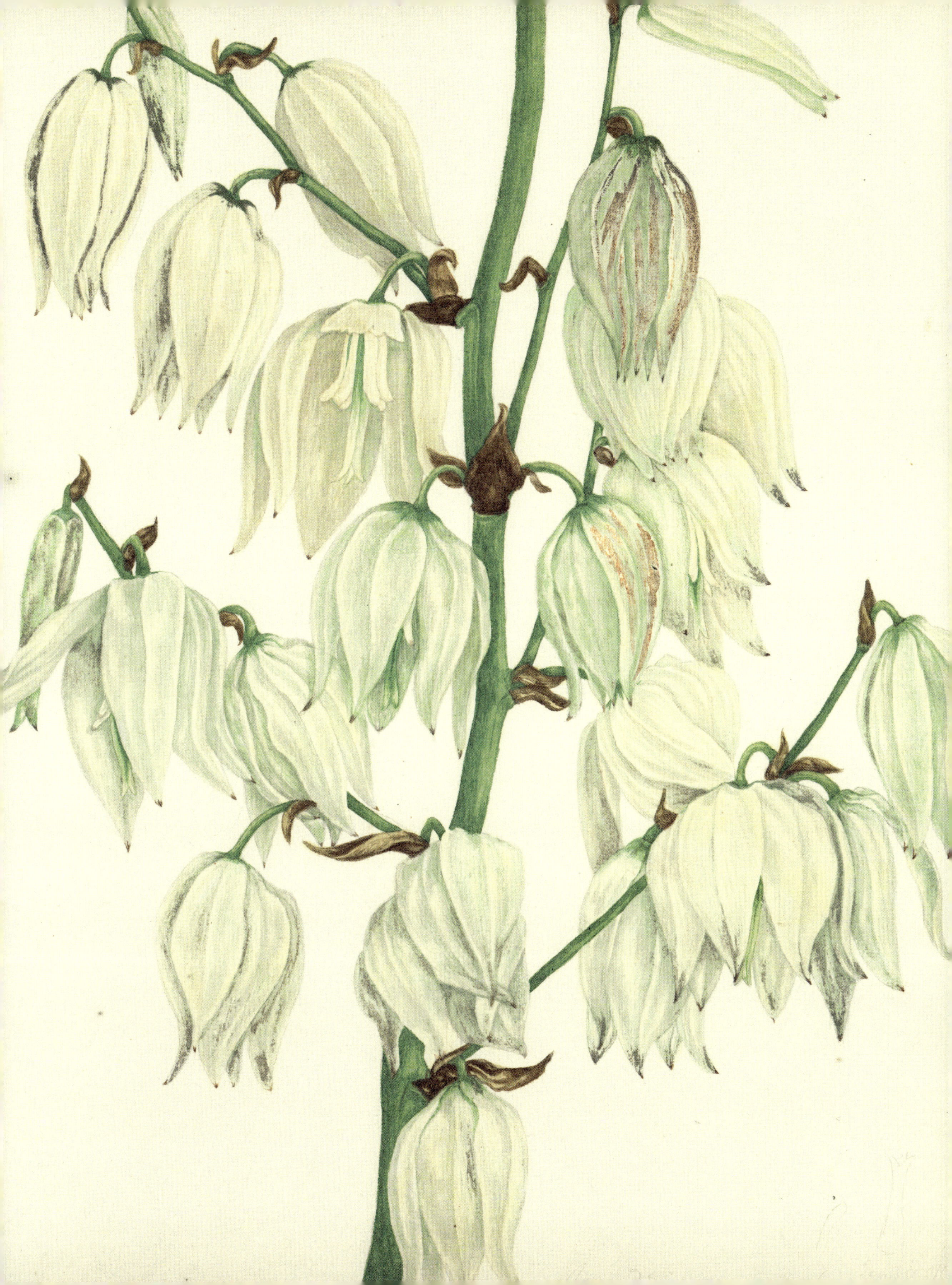

Is found in great profusion on rich soil, blooms from May through the summer and part of the fall.

No. 78

Purple Horsemint or Lemon-scented Horsemint –

Monarda citriodora Cerv. ex Lag. (=*M. dispersa* Small)

Is found in great profusion on rich soil, blooms from May through the summer and part of the fall.

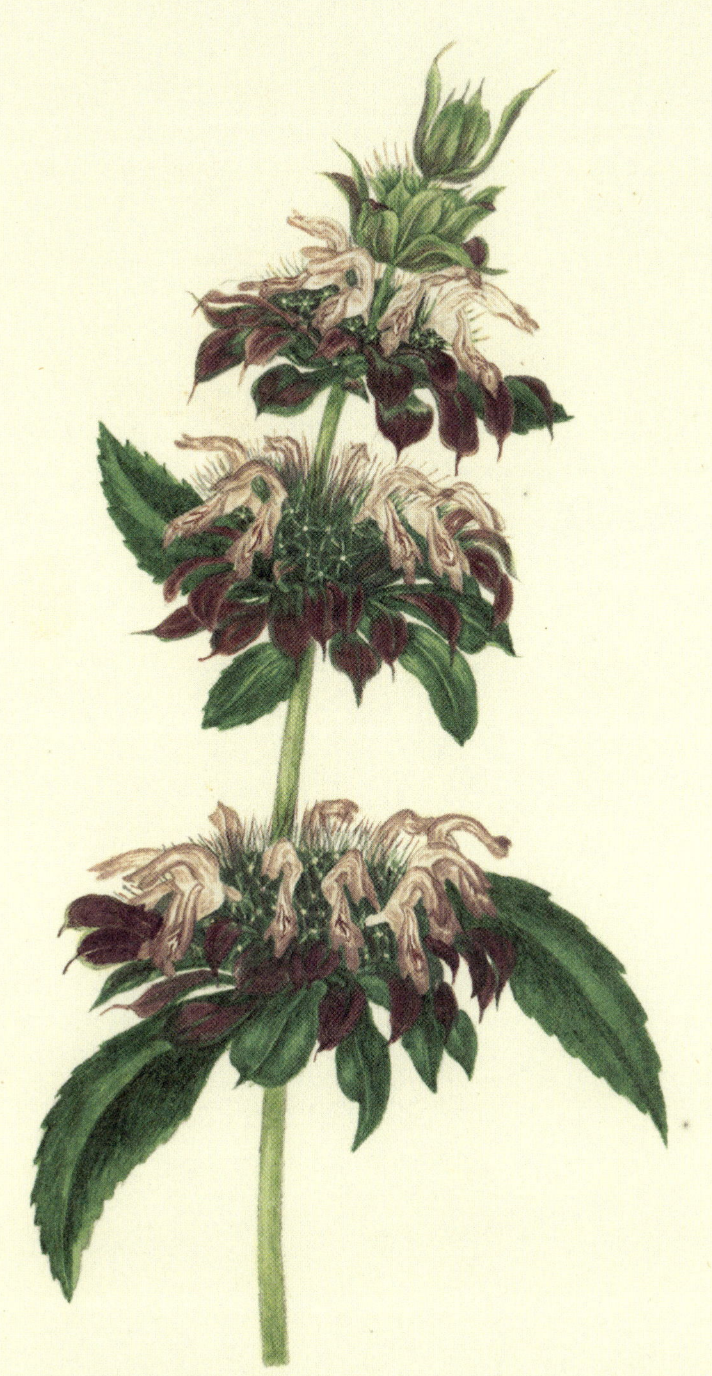

'Coreopsis,' blooms in May, in such profusions, that the surface of the Prairie, seems of a bright golden hue.

No. 79

Coreopsis or Golden Wave — *Coreopsis tinctoria* L.

'Coreopsis,' blooms in May, in such profusions, that the surface of the Prairie, seems of a bright golden hue.

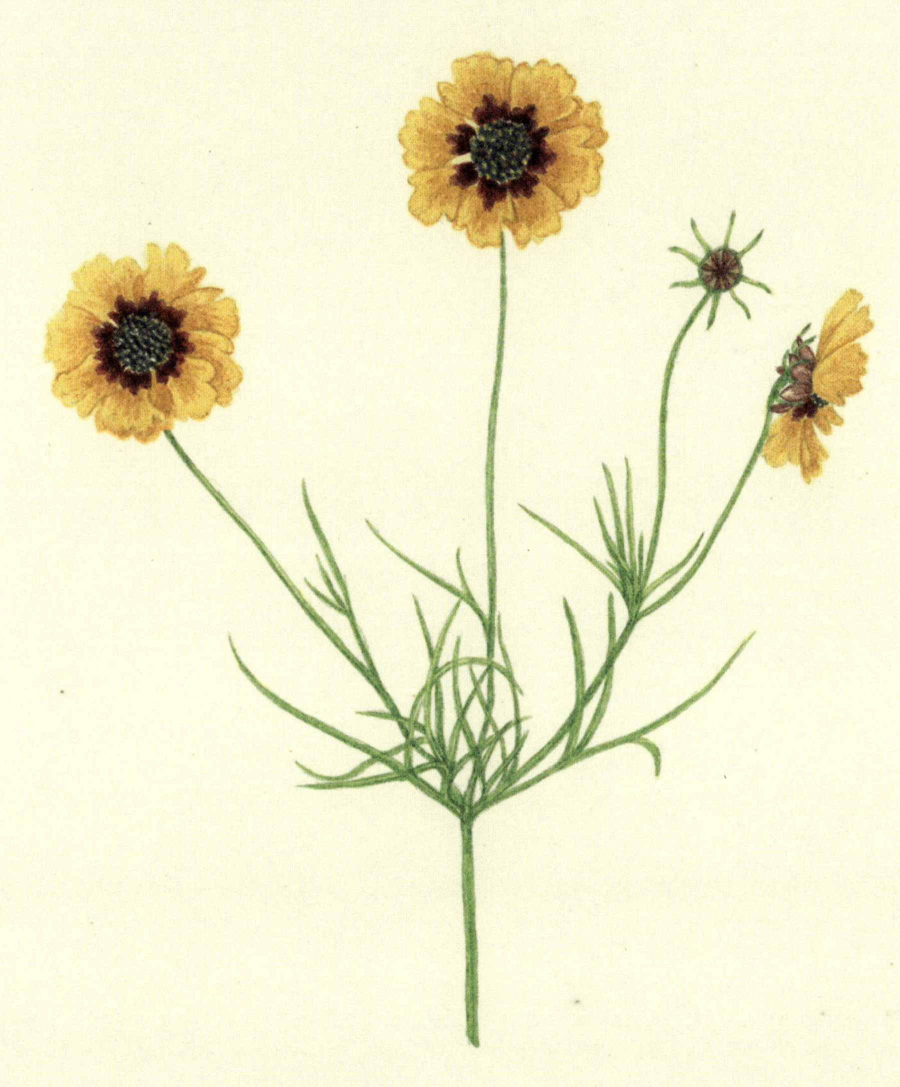

"White Verbena" blooms early in June on rich table land Prairies.

No. 80

White Verbena — *Verbena pumila* Rydb.

"White Verbena" blooms early in June on rich table land Prairies.

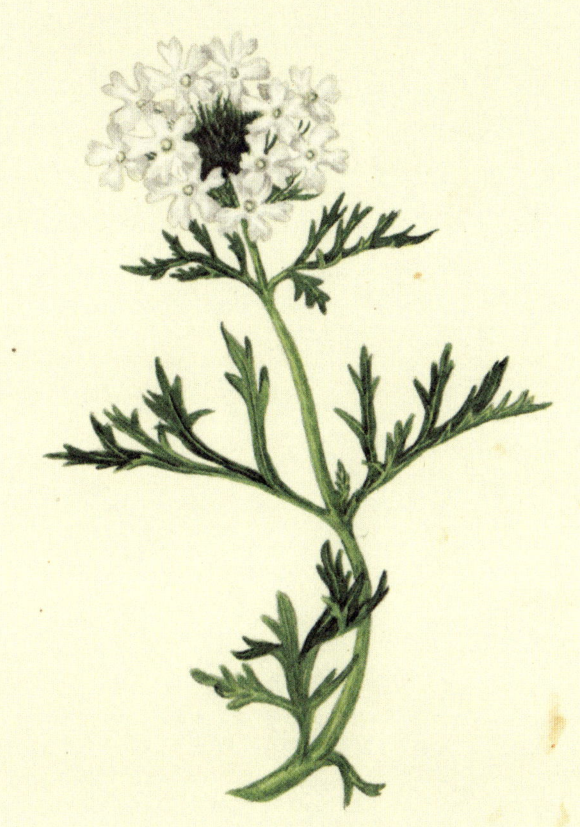

White Verbena

June 3d

"Standing Cypress" or "Indian Plume." Biennial.
many plumes clustered round a single stalk, blooms
from early May till October on rich table lands.

No. 81

Standing Cypress or Indian Plume — *Ipomopsis rubra* L., Wherry (= *Gilia rubra* L. Heller)

"Standing Cypress" or "Indian Plume." Biennial, many plumes clustered round a single stalk, blooms from early May till October on rich table lands.

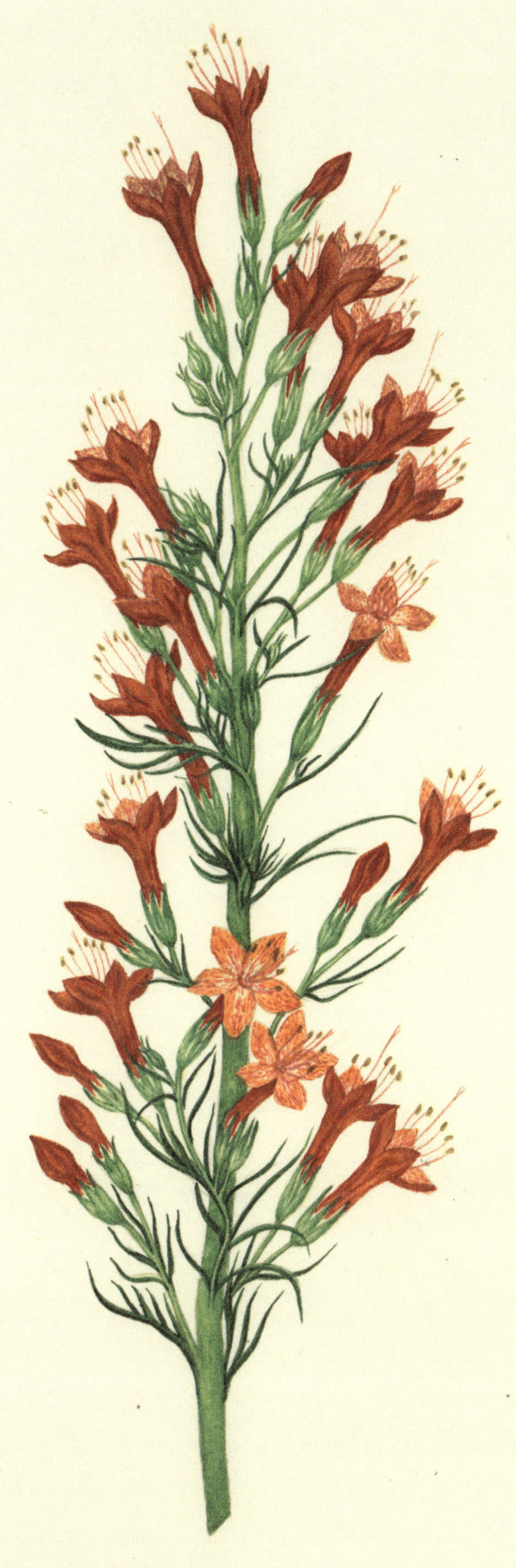

June 5

5 Stamens 1 Germ & Pis

A troublesome weed, blooms in June and July,
there is another variety with a briar on the sta

No. 82

Purple Nightshade or Trompillo — *Solanum eleagnifolium* Cav.

A troublesome weed, blooms in June and July, there is another variety with a briar on the sta[lk]

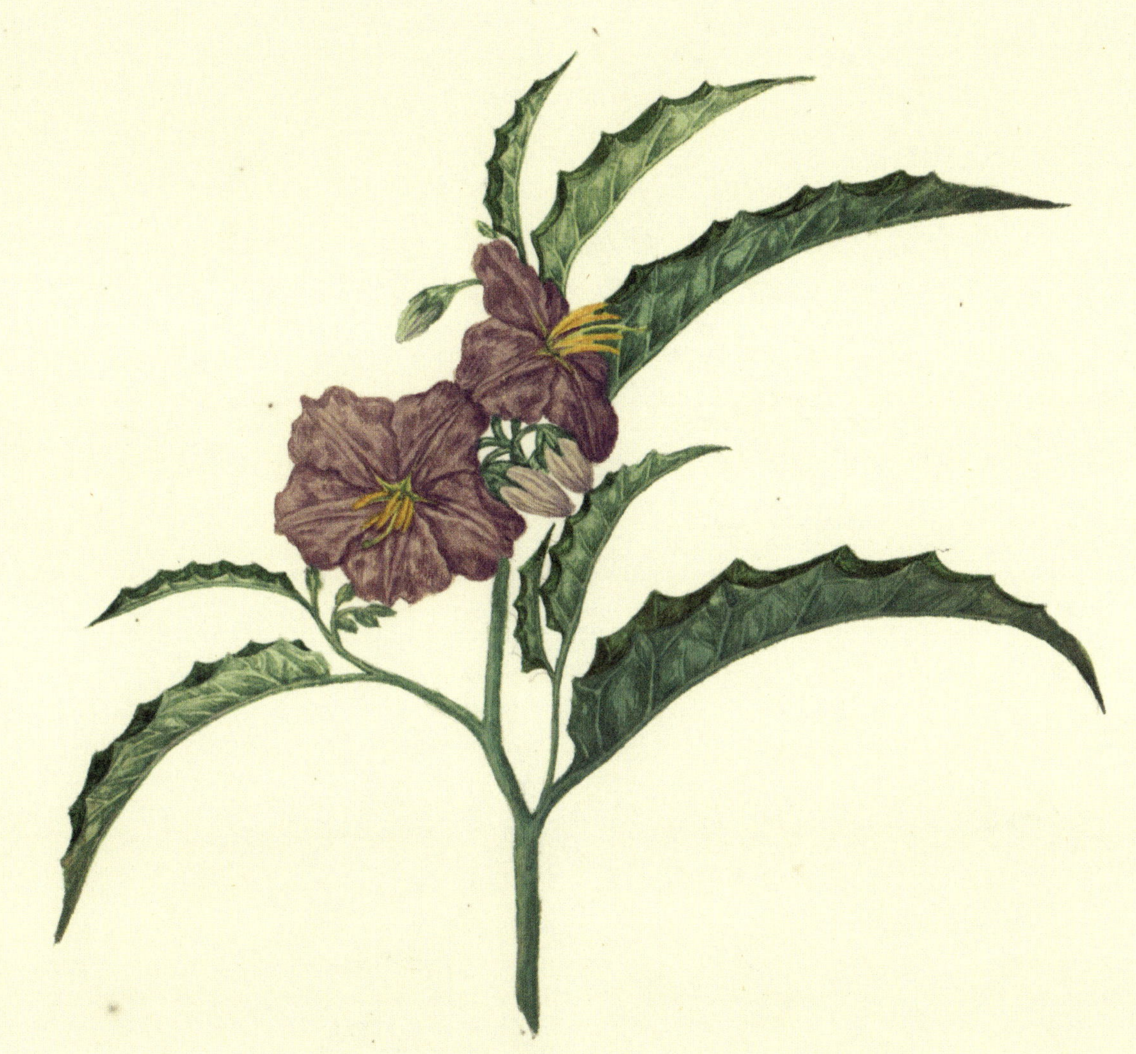

June 9th

5 Stamens 1 Sem

'Wild Balsam Apple' a vine. clinging to the undergrowth of the forests, its scarlet fruit forms a gorgeous decoration. it is found in perfection about the middle of June in open forests, with sandy soil.

No. 83

Balsam Gourd — Ibervillea lindheimeri A. Gray, Greene

'Wild Balsam Apple' a vine, clinging to the undergrowth of the forests, its scarlet fruit forms a gorgeous decoration. It is found in perfection about the middle of June in open forests, with sandy soil.

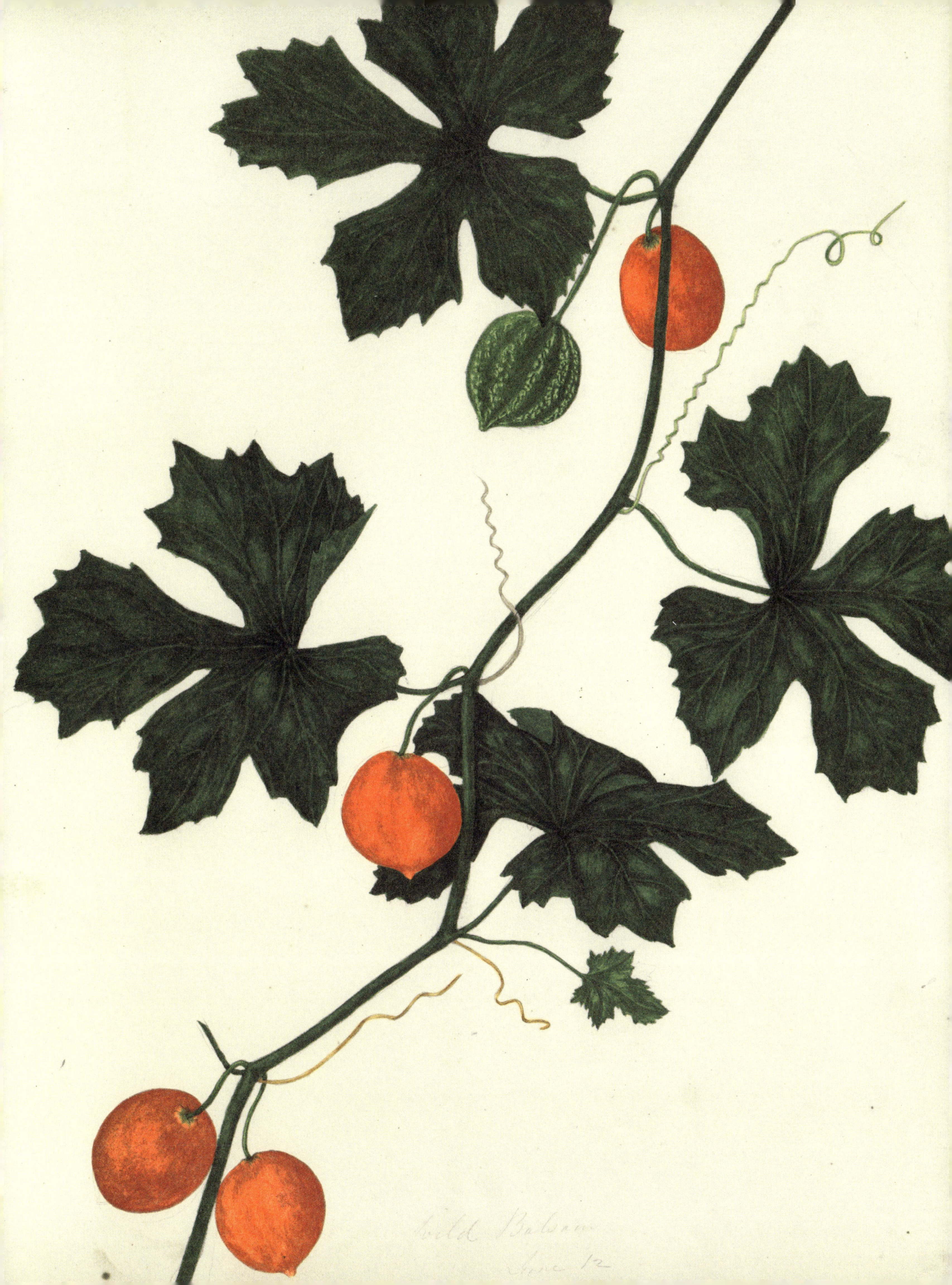
Wild Balsam
June 12

A noxious Nettle, which takes possession of cultivated land, and is not eradicated without great trouble, blooms in June and July.

No. 84

Buffalo-bur — *Solanum rostratum* Dunal.

A noxious Nettle, which takes possession of cultivated land, and is not eradicated without great trouble, blooms in June and July.

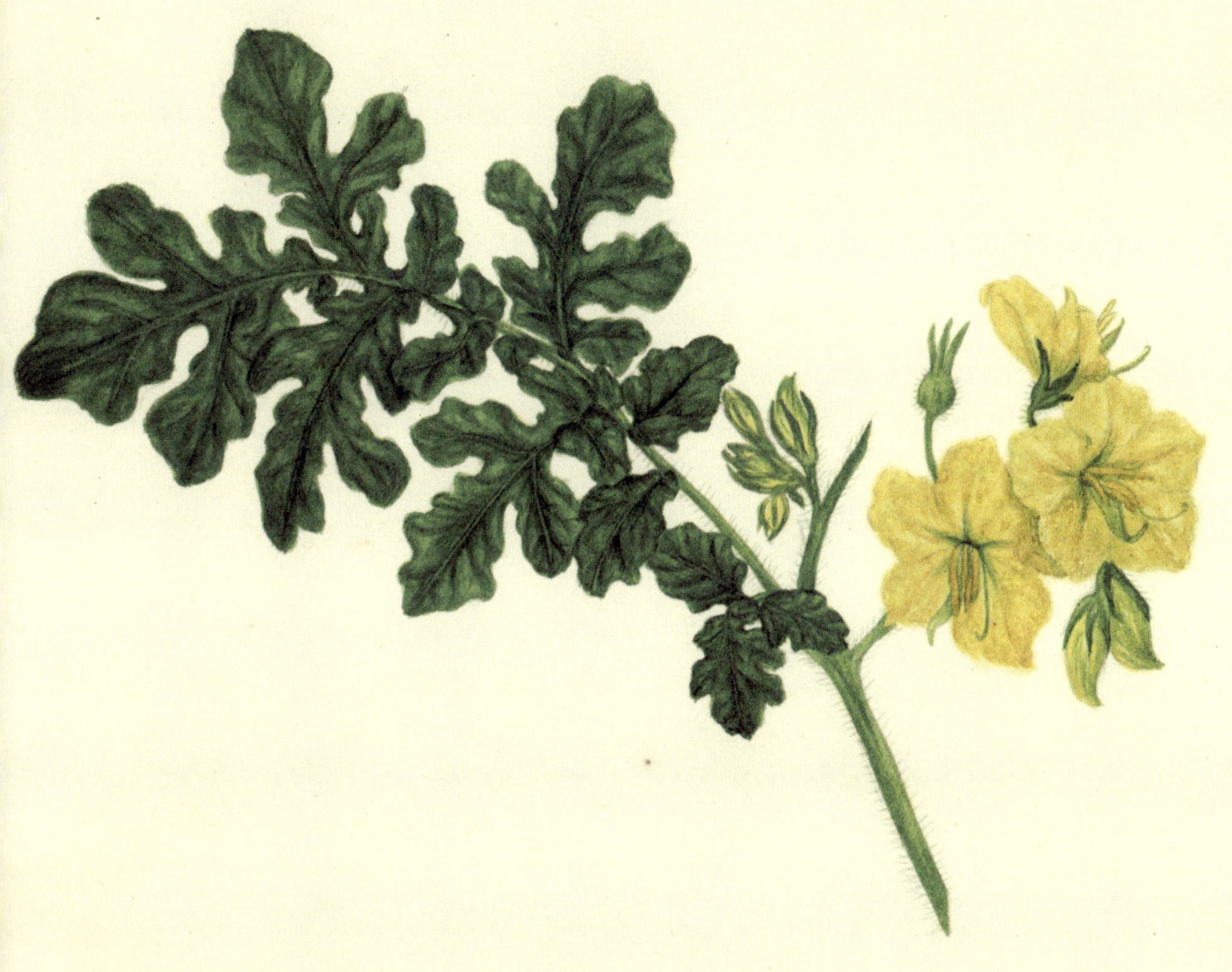

Nettle

Pleasant Odour

June 12

1 large Stamen

4 Small Stamens

A plant which should be cherished by florists, for its exquisite fragrance, and the length of time of its flowering. a single plant will throw out a continued succession of fresh blossoms, for sixteen days, before it shews any indication of withering, it is an annual, there is also a white variety, it blooms three or four weeks in June and grows on moist hill sides.

No 85

Mountain Pink — *Erythraea beyrichii* Torr. and Gray

A plant which should be cherished by florists, for its exquisite fragrance, and the length of time of its flowering. A single plant will throw out a continued succession of fresh blossoms, for sixteen days, before it shews any indication of withering, it is an annual, there is also a white variety, it blooms three or four weeks in June and grows on moist hill sides.

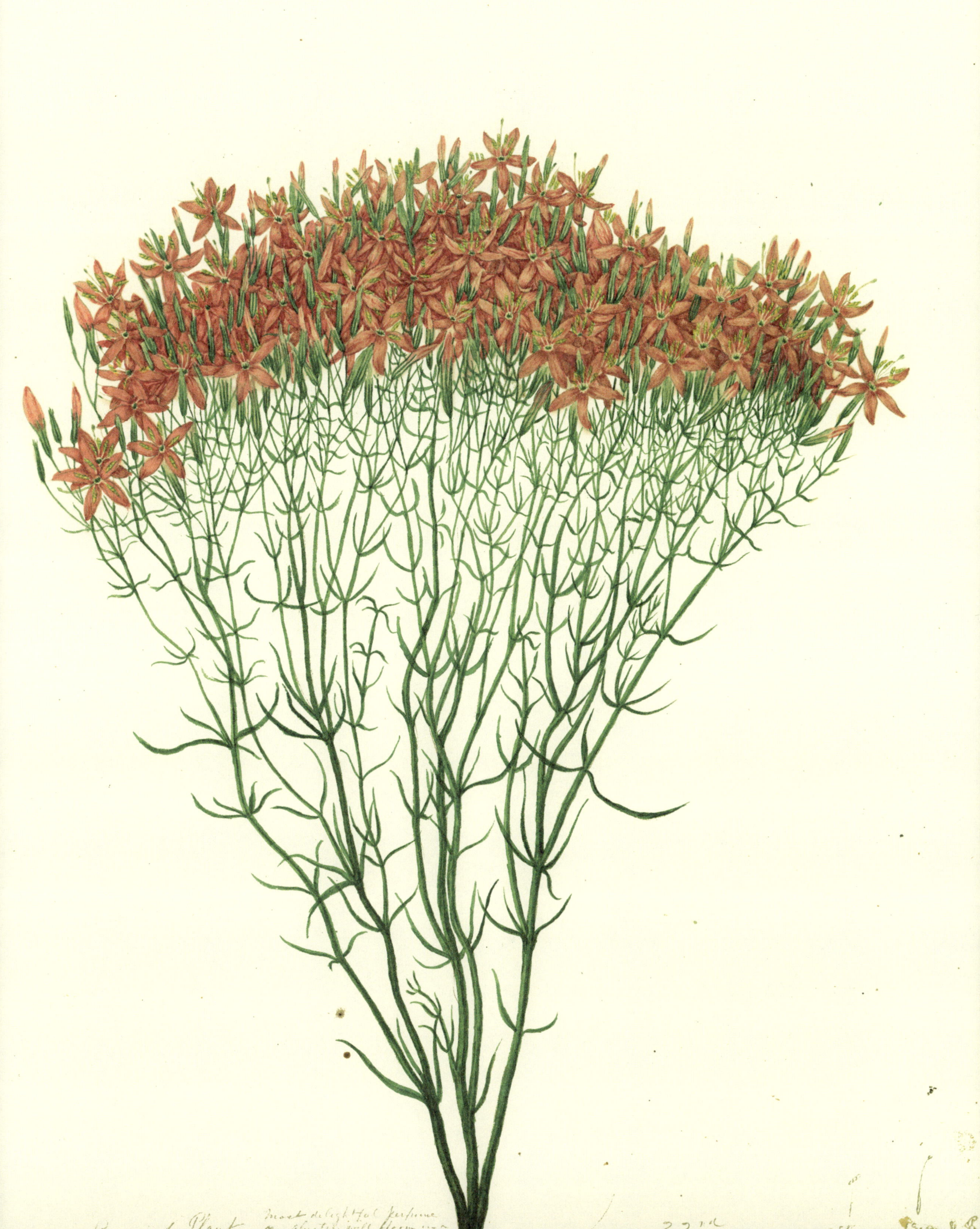
Plant
most delightful perfume

'Petunia' blooms for two or three weeks in July on rich lands.

No. 86

Wild Petunia (white) — *Ruella metzae* Tharp

'Petunia' blooms for two or three weeks in July on rich lands.

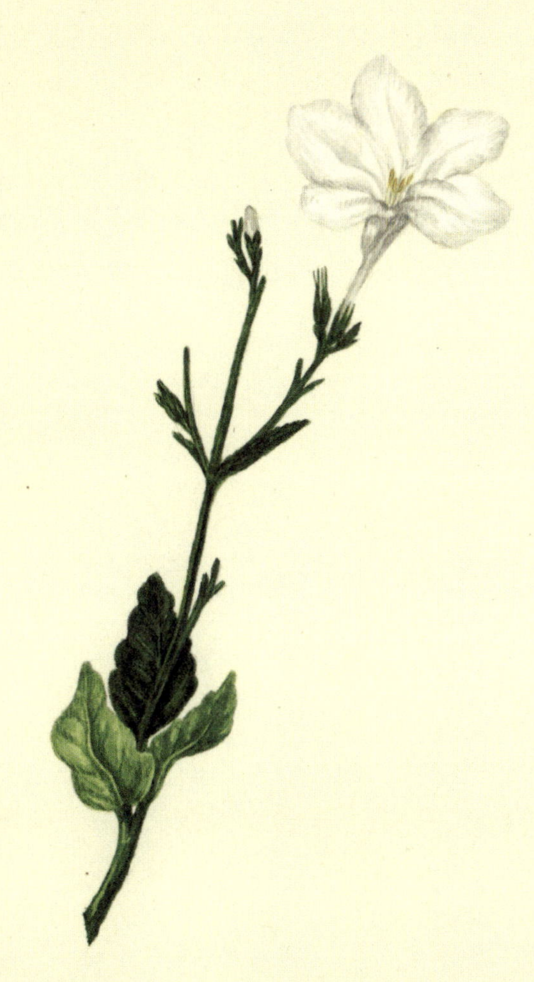

White Petunia

'Cactus.' blooms from early June until the last of July on poor calcarious soil.

No. 87

Nipple Cactus — *Mammillaria similis* Engelm. (= *Neobesseya similis* Engelm., Brit and Rose; = *Mammillaria missouriensis* Sweet; = *M. missouriensis* var. *similis* Schumann)

'Cactus', blooms from early June until the last of July on poor calcarious soil.

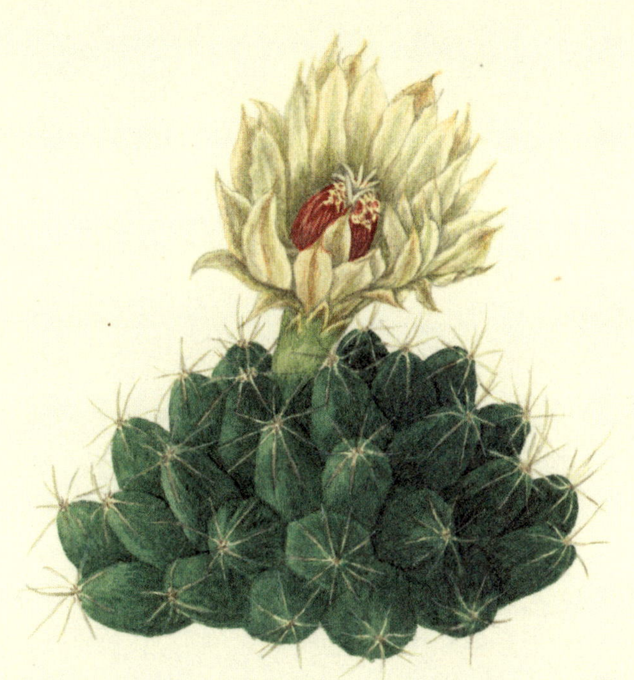

July 8

'Cactus' very fragrant, and a fine bloomer, its flowers burst forth after each spring and summer shower, grows well on thin soil.

No. 88

Twisted-rib Cactus or Hedgehog Cactus — *Hamatacactus setispinus Engelm.* (= *Echinocactus setispinus hamatus* Engelm.)

'Cactus' very fragrant, and a fine bloomer, its flowers burst forth after each spring and summer shower, grows well on thin soil.

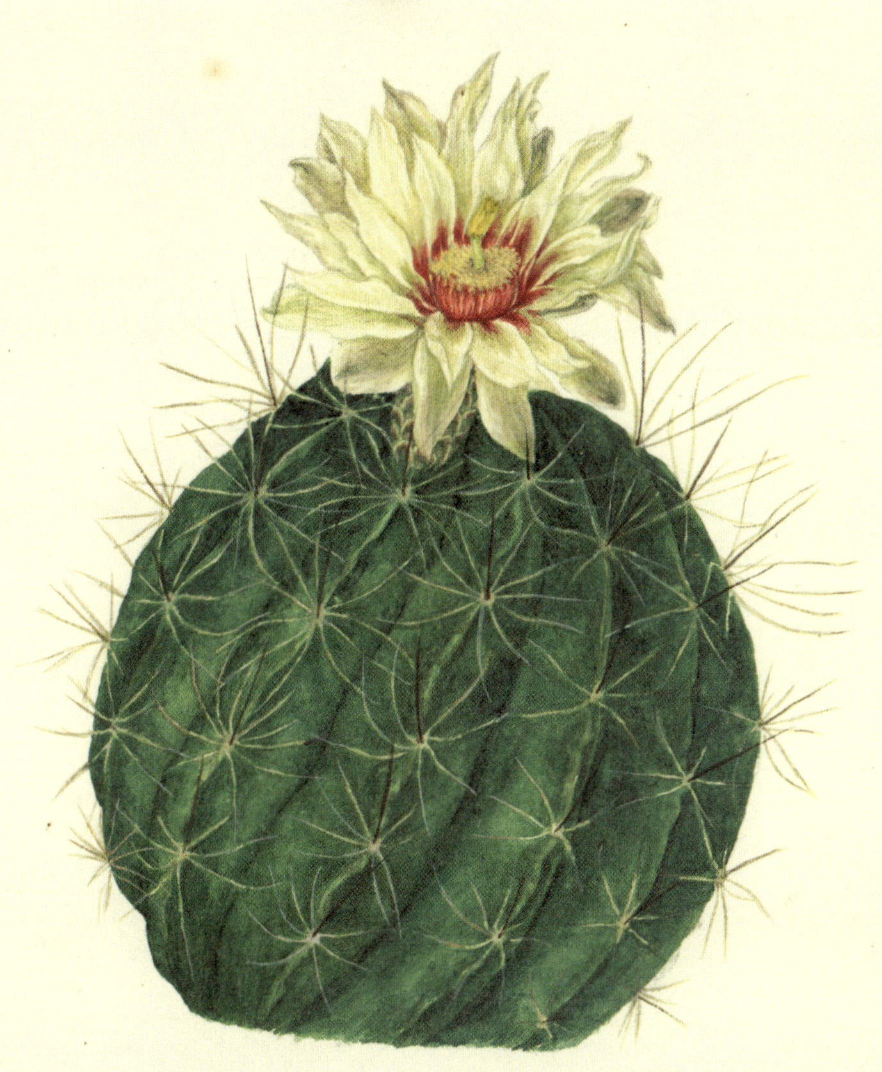

July 12

Clematis, blooms in July and August; trains itself over prairie shrubs in such profusion that it seems a bed of pure down. from the breast of the swan.

No. 89

Old Man's Beard or Texas Virgin's Bower — *Clematis drummondii* Torr. and Gray.

Clematis, blooms in July and August, trains itself over prairie shrubs in such profusion that it seems a bed of pure down, from the breast of a swan.

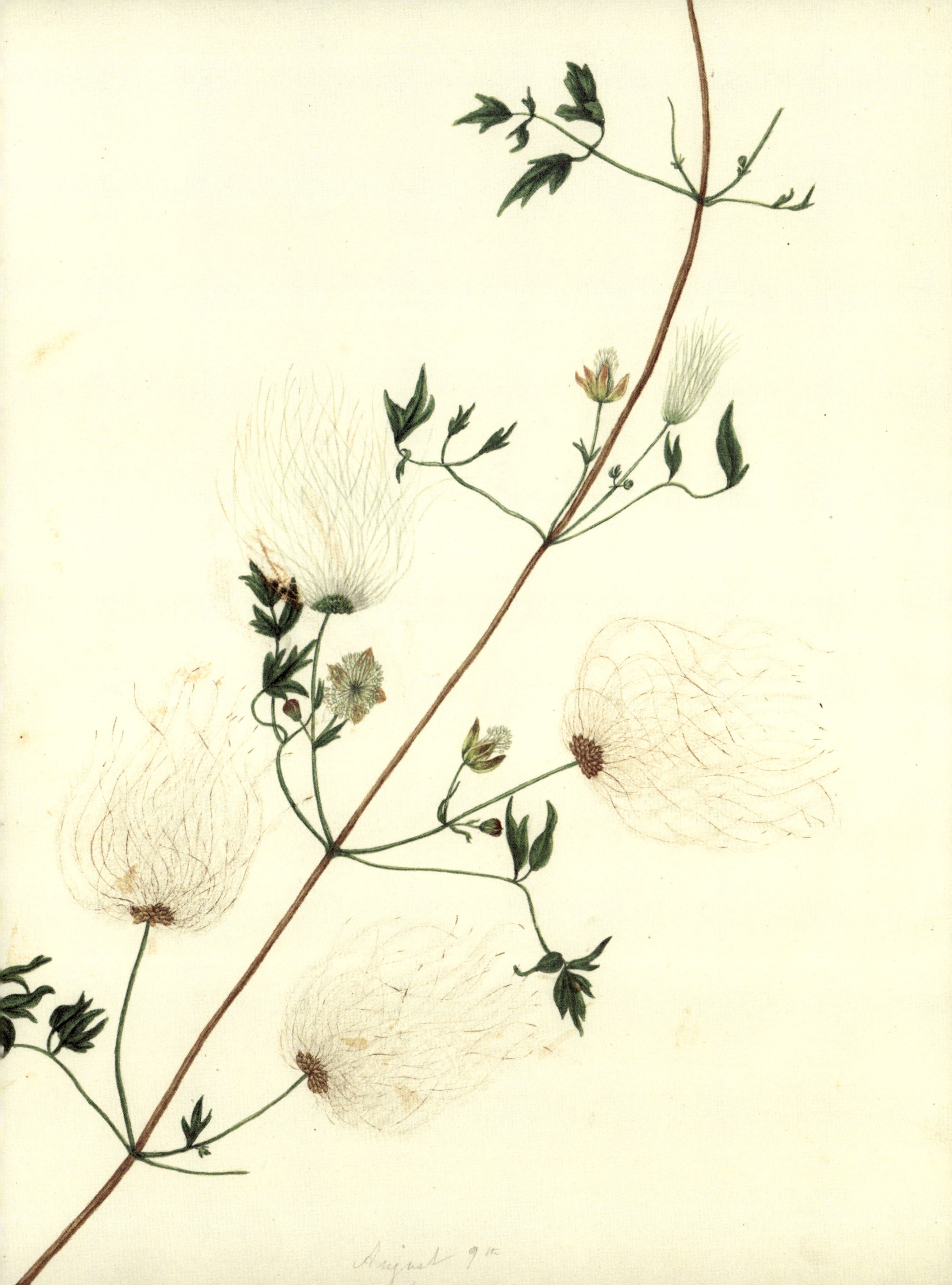
August 9th

A nettle of rich, and brilliant purple colour, grows on rich lands, is from 2 to 3 feet high and blooms in July.

No. 90

Eryngo — *Eryngium leavenworthii* Torr. and Gray.

A nettle of rich, and brilliant purple colour, grows on rich lands, is from 2 to 3 feet high and blooms in July.

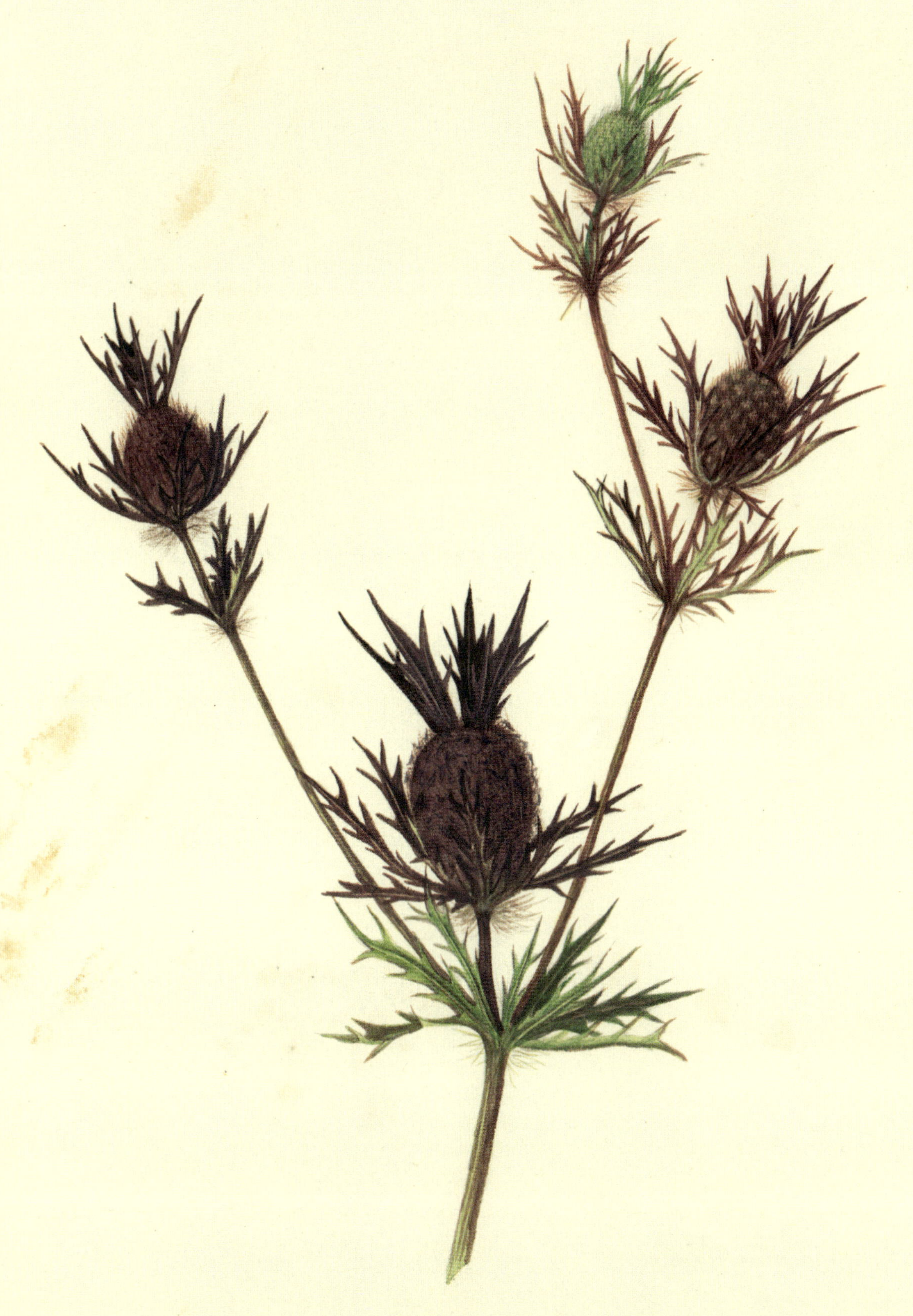

Thistle

August 9th

Clematis, a vine, found on low wet forest lands, it blooms in August.

No. 92

Leather Flower — *Clematis reticulata* Walt. (= *Viorna reticulata Walt.*, Small)

Clematis, a vine, found on low wet forest lands, it blooms in August.

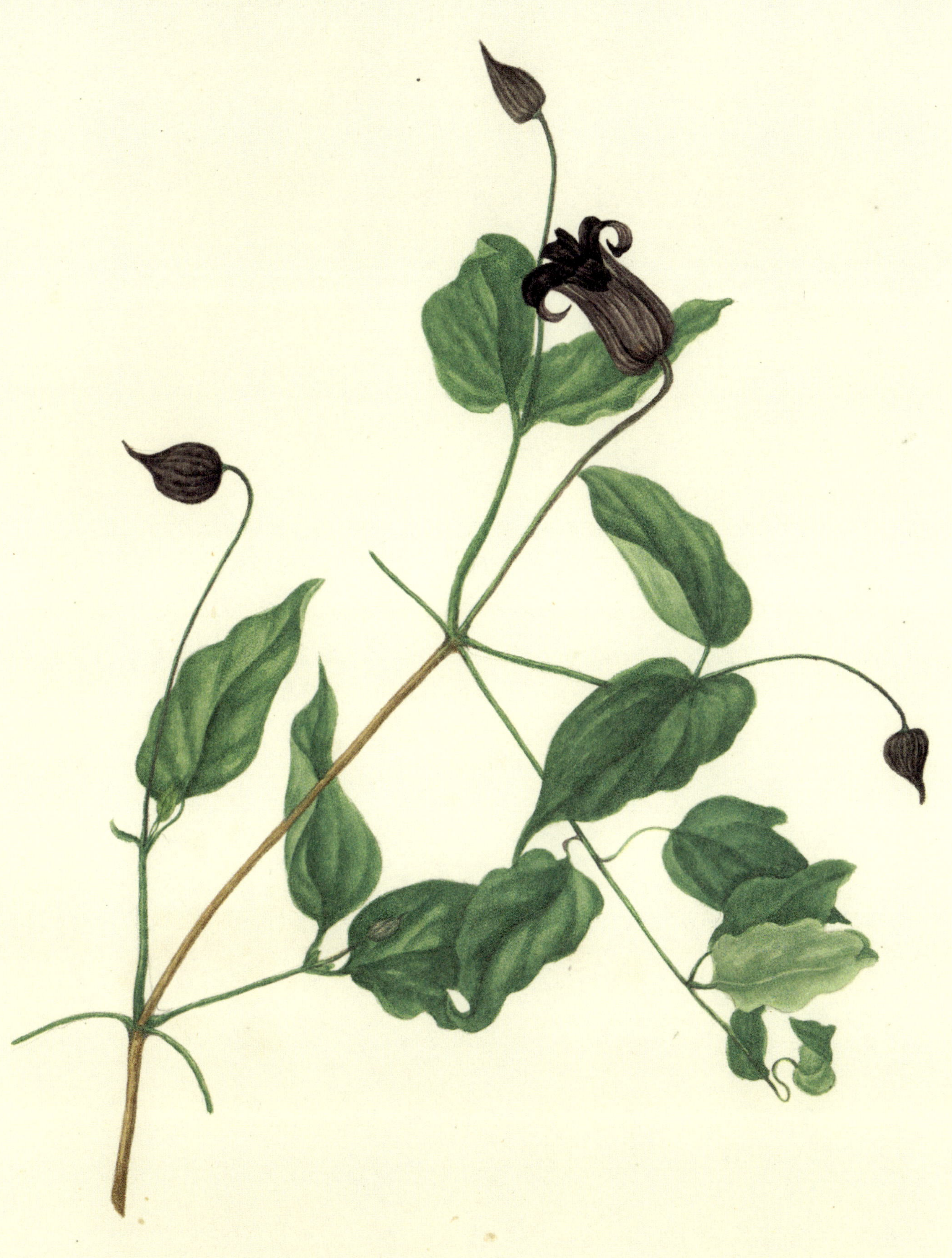

A plant from 4 to 6 feet in height, blooms from
sunset till sunrise, during the months of August
and September. grows upon the brink of running water.

No. 94

Yellow Evening Primrose or Flutter-mill — *Oenothera missouriensis* Sims.

A plant from 4 to 6 feet in height, blooms from sunset till sunrise, during the months of August and September, grows upon the brink of running water.

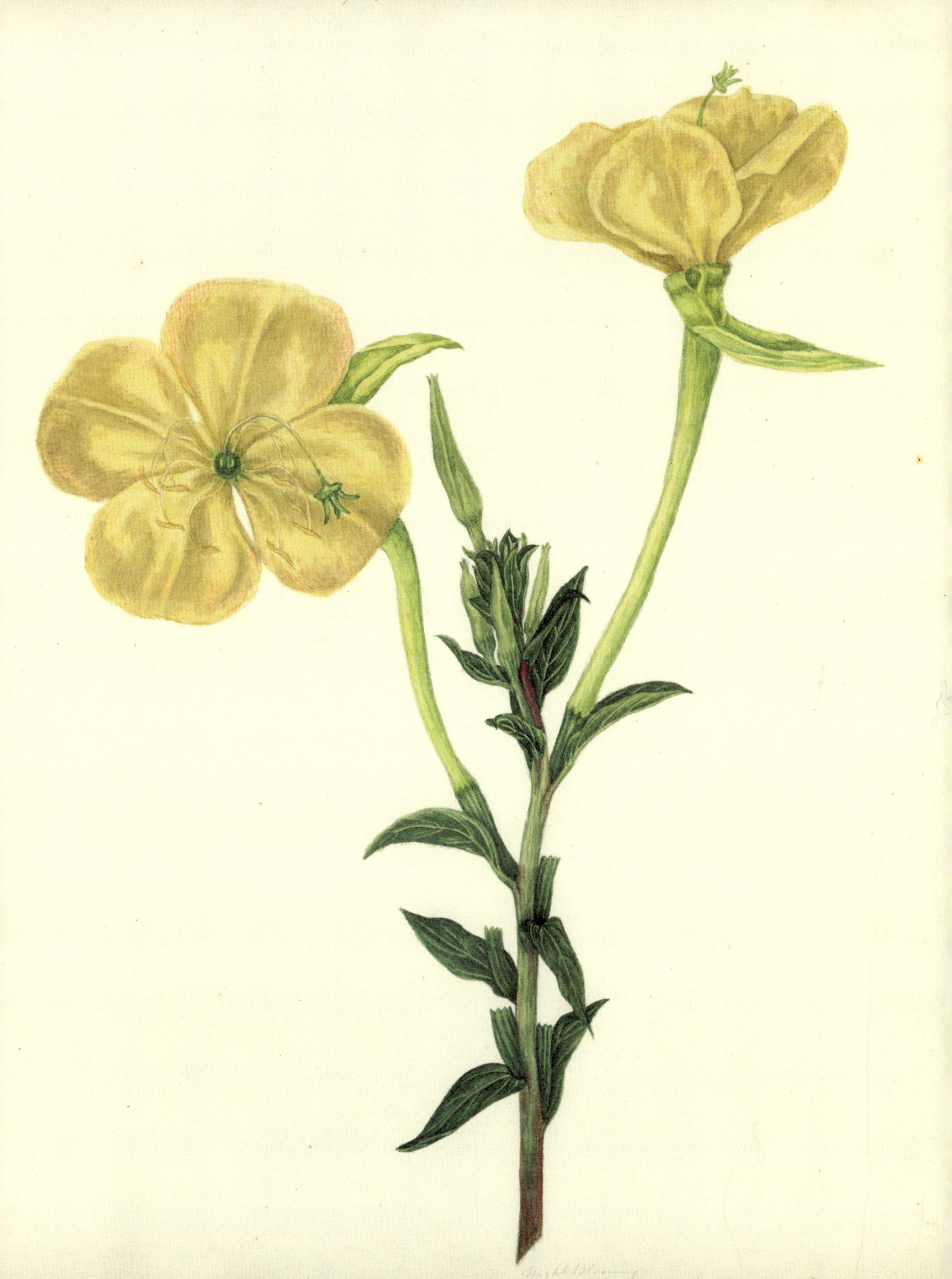
Night Blooming

A plant about 3 or 4 feet high, grows in rich woodlands. the apple has quite an agreeable flavour. The root is mucilaginous, and is frequently used for poultices, as a substitute for Slippery Elm. the flowers are seen from May till November, at the same time with the fruit.

No. 95

Turk's Cap or Mexican Apple — *Malvaviscus drummondii* Torr. and Gray

A plant about 3 or 4 feet high, grows in rich woodlands. The apple has quite an agreeable flavour. The root is mucilaginous, and is frequently used for poultices, as a substitute for Slippery Elm. The flowers are seen from May till November, at the same time with the fruit.

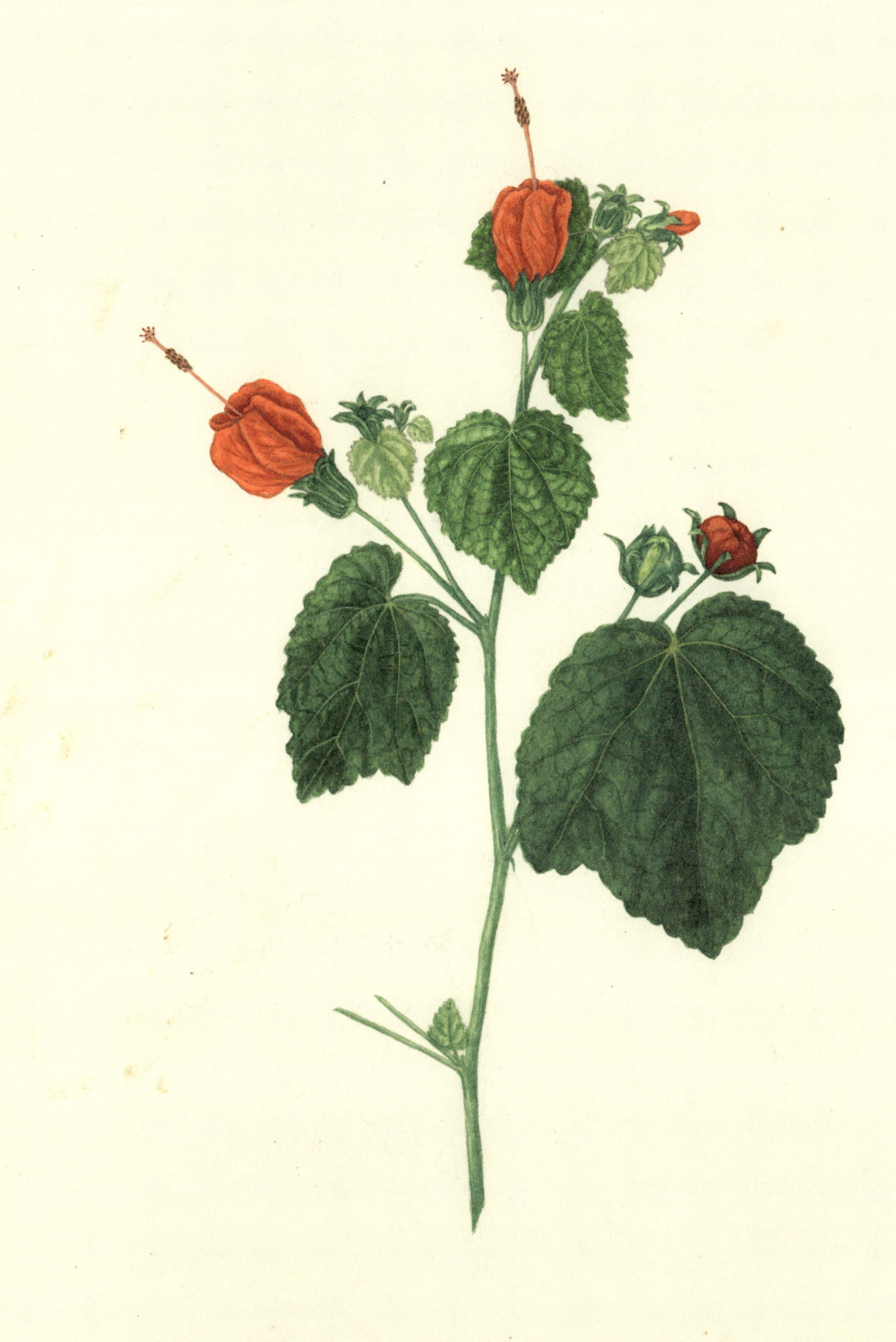

Cherokee Apple

Blooms from May till November

Salvia. Grows about 3 feet high in rich soil, and blooms from the 1st Sept till late in October the colour is a rare tint of blue.

No. 96

Blue Sage or Mealy Sage — *Salvia farinacea* Benth.

Salvia. Grows about 3 feet high in rich soil, and blooms from the 1st Sept till late in October the colour is a rare tint of blue.

10

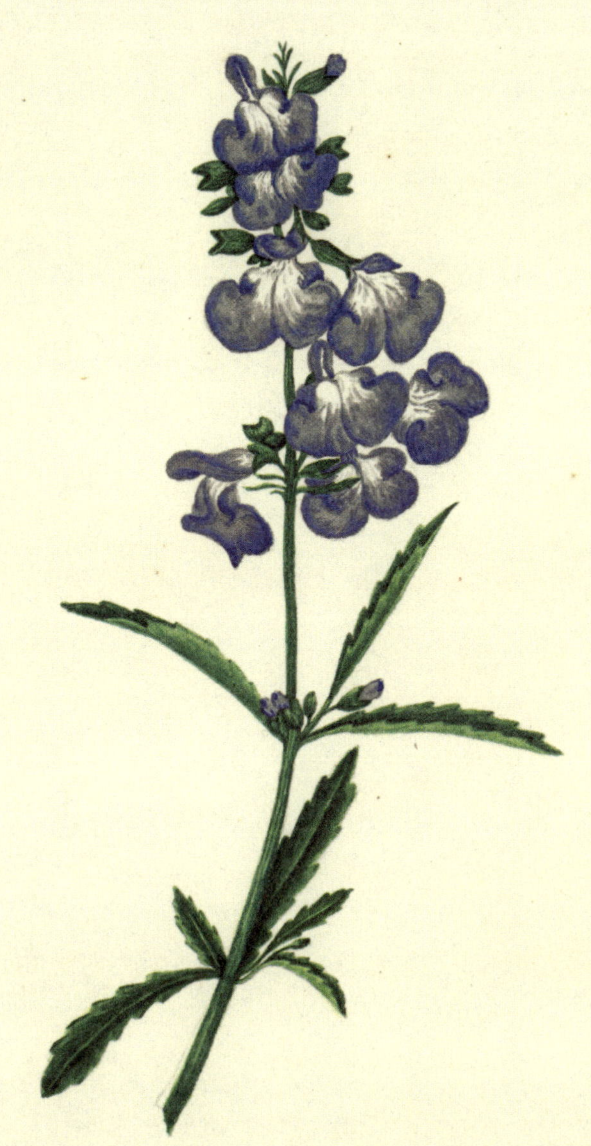

September 1st

2 Stamens Pistil & Germ of 42

A very beautiful and fragrant prairie flower, blooms during two or three weeks in October root-fibrous, Annual.

No. 97

Agalinus — *Agalinus gattingeri* Small (= *Gerardia gattingeri* Small)

A very beautiful and fragrant prairie flower, blooms during two or three weeks in October root-fibrous, Annual.

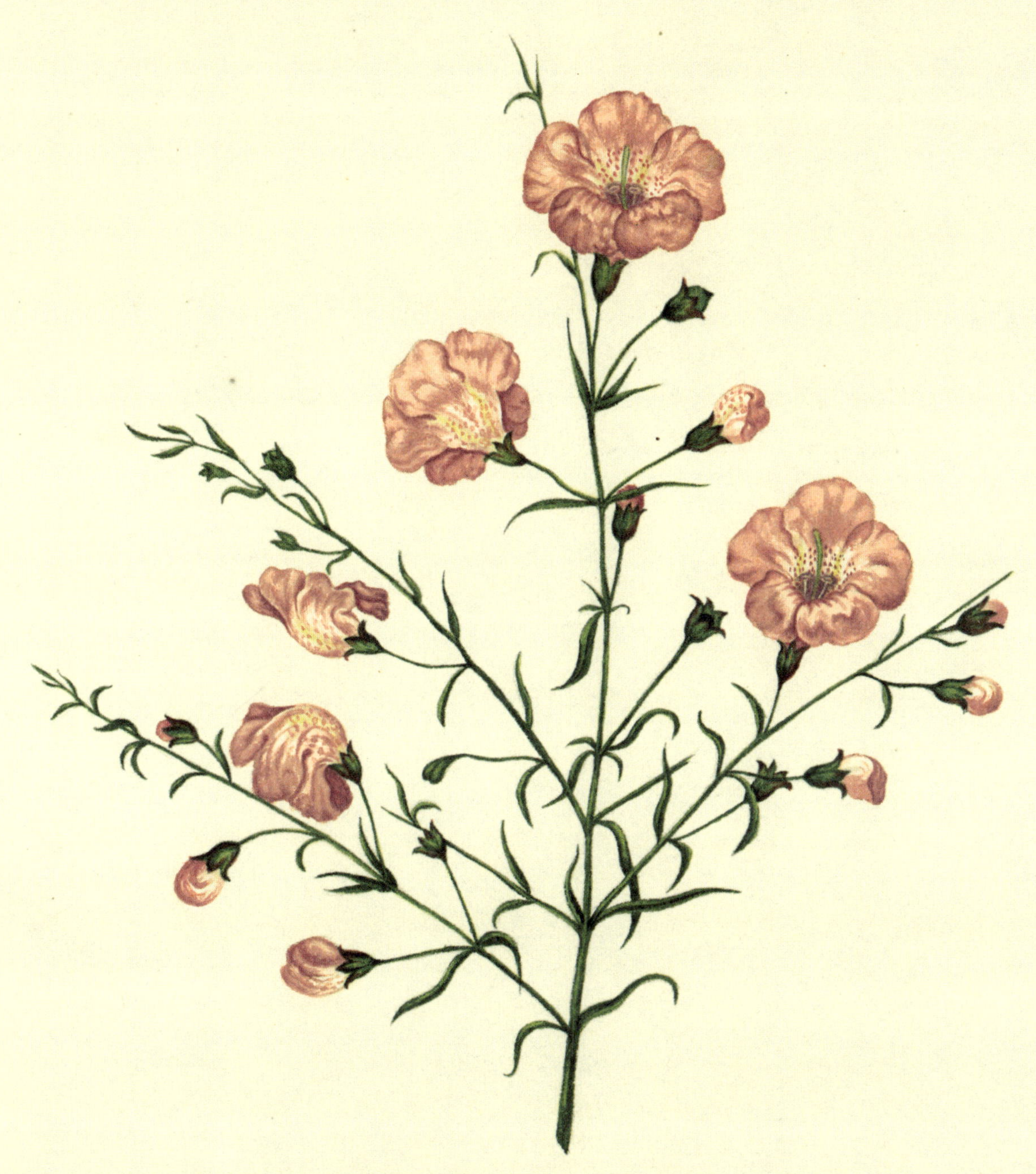

October 15th

Fragrant Prairie Flower

A plant growing about 4 inches high, blooms in November, is chiefly found on gravelly hill sides.

No. 99

Purple Wood Sorrel — *Oxalis violacea* L.

A plant growing about 4 inches high, blooms in November, is chiefly found on gravelly hill sides.

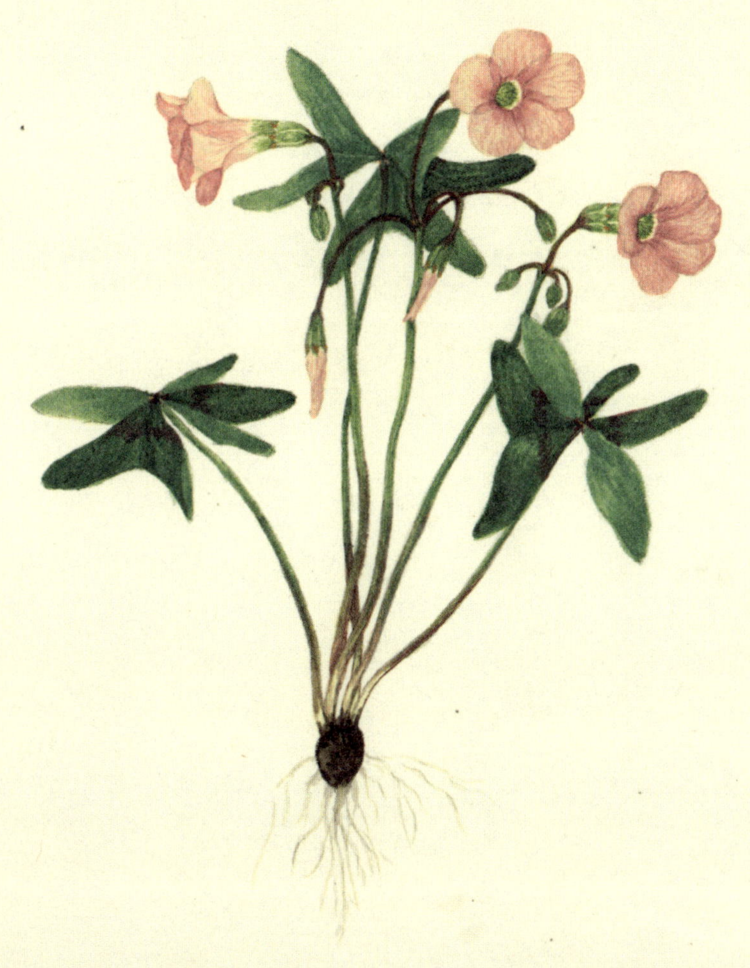

Species of Sorrel

Nettle, a flower resembling Jasmine, with the same odour, covered with nettles, grows equally well in poor as rich soils, blooms from April till November. Perennial and said to have a very large tuberous root.

No. 100

Bull Nettle — *Cnidoscolus texanus* Muell., Arg., Small (= *Jatropha texana* Muell., Arg.)

Nettle, a flower resembling Jasmine, with the same odour, covered with nettles, grows equally well in poor as rich soil, blooms from April till November. Perennial and said to have a very large tuberous root.

100

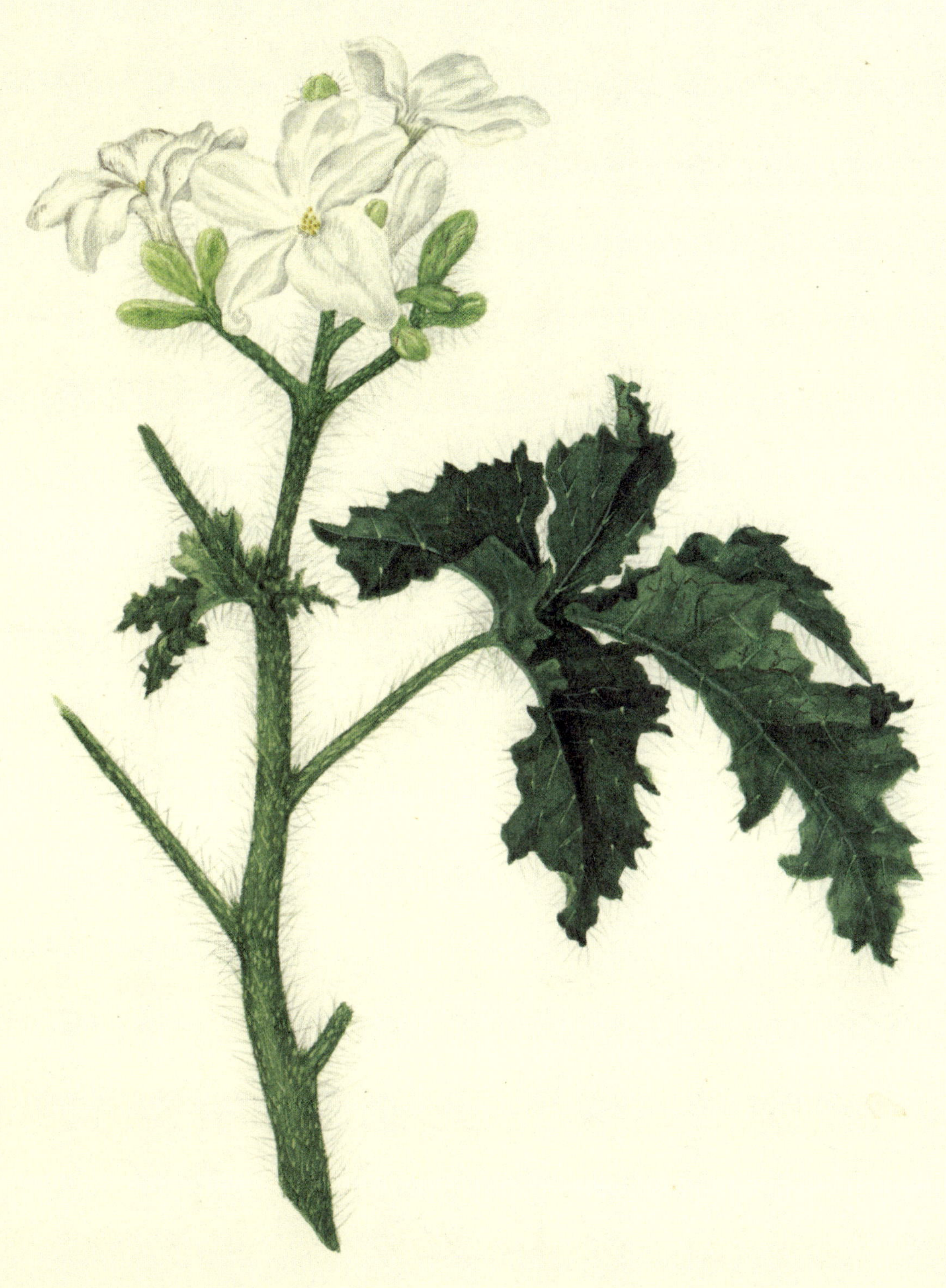

Jassamin Nettle

very fragrant

November 1st

The long drooping branches of this plant, are usually found, overhanging clear brooks, and river banks. it blooms in November, and is one of the last flowers of Autumn. December and January can seldom boast of wild flowers, unless the winter should be unusually warm, or on the southern coast, where every month has its own flora.

No. 101

Small-leaved Aster — *Aster oblongifolium* Nutt.

The long drooping branches of this plant, are usually found, overhanging clear brooks, and river banks. It blooms in November, and is one of the last flowers of Autumn. December and January can seldom boast of wild flowers, unless the winter should be unusually warm, or on the southern coast, where every month has it own flora.

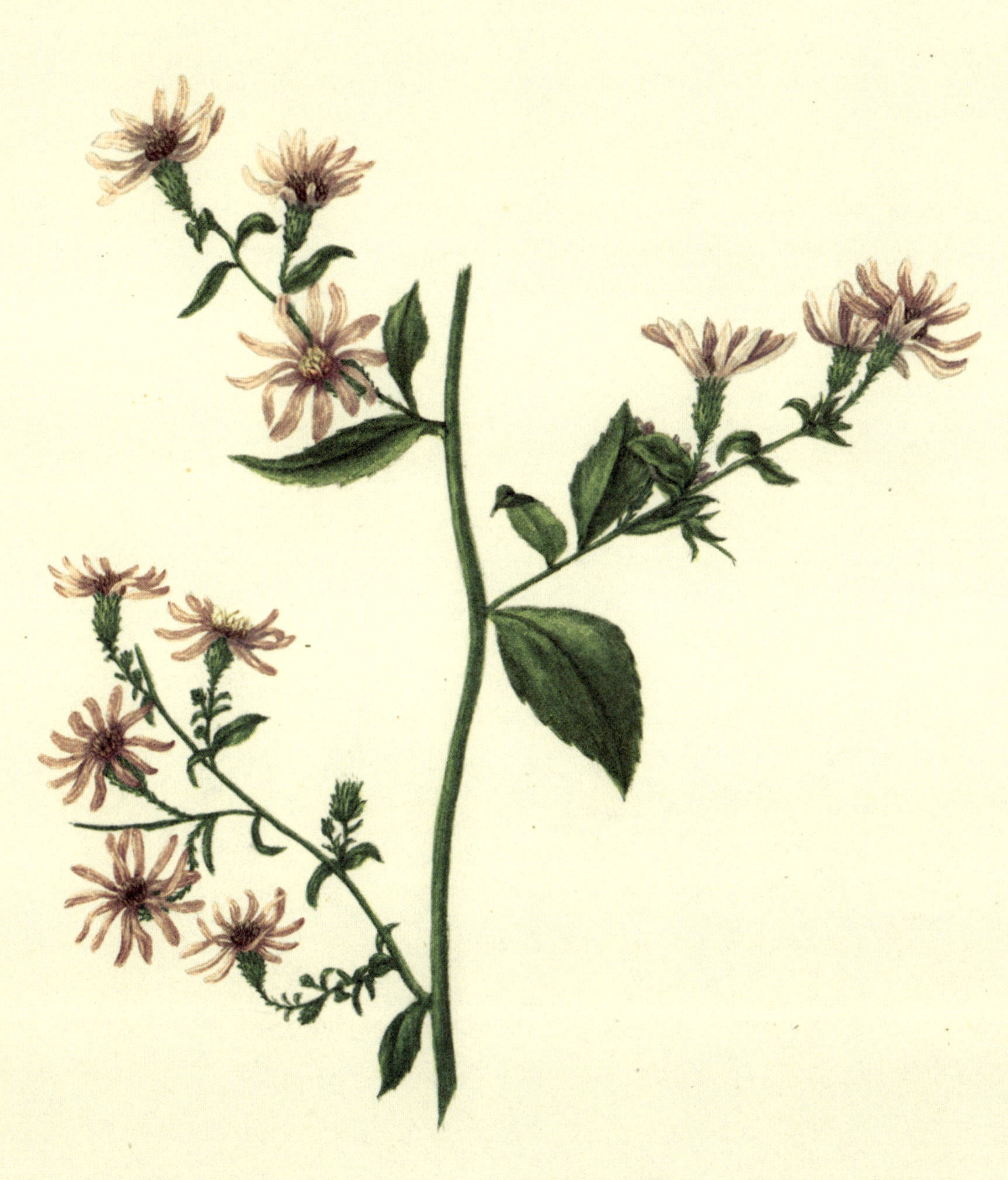

Mrs. Johnstone's letter to Mrs. Fisher dated October 18, 1894, mentions that "Four Plates have been stolen." Her handwritten descriptions of the four are reproduced on the opposite page.

A beautiful plant, which puts forth numerous blossoms, which are very frail, a gentle touch will send its flowers showering to the ground in salmon coloured wheels, all the petals are joined at their base, it is of short duration and is only seen in April, on the calcareous soils.

"Mustang Grape" native of Texas. a profuse bearer and of luxuriant growth, covering the tops of the tallest trees of the forest. it is tempting in appearance, and of an agreeable flavour, but leaves an unpleasant soreness in the mouth and throat after eating it. The wine which is made from it by the Germans of New Braunfels, resembles claret, if made with the addition of clarified sugar and a due proportion of water. the wine resembles "still Champagne". if the juice is pressed through the hand it will irritate the surface very unpleasantly.

A beautiful plant with a great profusion of bloom, grows on wet low lands, and upon hill sides, naturally irrigated, the root is very small, and fibrous, blooms in August and September.

A magnificent vine, of rich green, heavy laden with beautiful glossy, crimson berries. climbing over the undergrowth of the forests, twining round the branches, and pendant from their ends, it forms an exquisite forest-drapery, not to be equalled by the perfection of art. It is called "Texas Sarsaparilla", and its root is sometimes used as a substitute for the imported. It is in all its glory in October, and finds its most favourable locality in the sandy soil of the "Post Oak Woods"

ACKNOWLEDGMENTS

This book is the result of a number of people who recognized the beauty and historical significance of Eliza Griffin Johnston's talent and wanted to share it with everyone. Special appreciation goes to: The Daughters of The Republic of Texas Past Presidents General Nelma Toney Wilkinson, Madge Thornhill Roberts, and M. P. "Patti" Atkins; Past Custodians General Nancy McGuire Shurtleff, and Betty Sue Bird; Betty and the late John Stokes for the beautiful digitizational images of Eliza's wild flowers; Sylvia and Max Miller for introducing the Stokes to DRT; the DRT Headquarters & Museum Committee for their research and support; the DRT Headquarters & Museum Staff for their clerical contribution; and Luci Baines Johnson for her wonderful foreword.

BIBLIOGRAPHY

Barrett, Arrie "Western Forts of Texas. 1845-1861," West Texas Historical Association *Year Book,* VII (June, 1931), 115-39.

Bender, A. B., "Military Forts in the Southwest, 1848-1860", *The New Mexico Historical Review,* XVI, No. 2 (April, 1941), 125-47.

Bierschwale, Margaret, *Fort McKavett, Texas, Post on the San Sabá.* Salado, Texas, Anson Jones Press, 1966.

Crimmins, M. L. (ed.), "Colonel J. K. F. Mansfield's Report of the Inspection of the Department of Texas in 1856," *The Southwestern Historical Quarterly,* XLII (October, 1938), 122-48; (January, 1939), 215-57; (April, 1939), 351-87.

___________, "W. G. Freeman's Report on the Eighth Military Department," *The Southwestern Historical Quarterly,* LI (July, 1947), 54-58; (October, 1947), 167-74; (January, 1948), 252-58; (April, 1948), 350-57; (LII (July, 1948, 100-08; (October, 1948), 227-33; (January, 1949), 349-53; (April, 1949), 202-08; (January, 1950), 308-19; (April, 1950), 443-73.

Crimmins, Col. M. L., "Experiences of an Army Surgeon at Fort Chadbourne," West Texas Historical Association *Year Book,* XIV (October, 1938), 73-82.

Cullum, George W., *Biographical Register of the Officers and Graduates of the US Military Academy.* 2 vols. New York, 1868.

Danford, Robert M. (ed.), *Register of Graduates and Former Cadets, United States Military Academy.* New York, 1953.

Denis, Alberta Johnston, "Mrs Albert Sidney Johnston," *Texas Magazine,* I (May, 1897), 427-30.

____________, "Sketch of Albert Sidney Johnston," *Texas Magazine,* I (May, 1897), 426-29.

____________, *Spanish Alta California.* New York, Macmillan, 1927.

Eastman, Seth, *A Seth Eastman Sketchbook, 1848-1849.* Introduction by Lois Burkhalter. San Antonio. Marion Koogler McNay Art Institute, and Austin, University of Texas Press, 1961.

Frazer, Robert Walter, *Forts of the West: Military Forts and Presidios and Posts Commonly Called Forts, West of the Mississippi.*Norman, University of Oklahoma, 1955.

Hamersly, T. H. S., *Complete Regular Army Register of the United States.* Washington, D. C., 1880.

Hartje, Robert George, *Van Dorn, The Life and Times of a Confederate General.* Nashville, Vanderbilt University Press, 1967.

Heitman, Francis B., *Historical Register and Dictionary of the United States Army,* 1789-1903. 2 vols. Washington D. C., 1903.

Hopkins, Joseph G. E. (ed.), *Concise Dictionary of American Biography.* New York, Scribner's, 1964. See "Johnston, Albert Sidney," 505.

Johnson, Richard W., *A Soldier's Reminiscences in Peace and War.* Philadelphia, J. B. Lippincott Company, 1886.

Johnston, William Preston, *The Johnstons of Salisbury.* New Orleans, Press of L. Graham and Son, 1897.

___________, "Journal", in Barret Collection, Tulane University, New Orleans, Louisiana.

___________, *The Life of General Albert Sidney Johnston.* New York, D. Appleton and Company, Inc., 1878.

Malone, Dumas (ed.), *Dictionary of American Biography.* New York, Charles Scribner's and Sons, 1933. See "Johnston, Albert Sidney," Vol. X, 135-36.

McDermott, John Francis, *Seth Eastman, Pictorial Historian of the Indian.* Norman, University of Oklahoma Press, 1961.

Miller, E. V. D. (ed.), *A Soldier's Honor: Reminiscences of Major General Earl Van Dorn.* By his comrades. New York, Abbey Press, 1902.

National Archives Microfilm Publications, *Return from United States Military Forts, 1800-1916,* Microcopy 617. National Archives, Washington, D. C., 1965.

Austin, Texas, Post at, Roll 59, November, 1848-August, 1875.

Belknap, Fort, Roll 95, June, 1851-August, 1875.

Cooper, Camp, Roll 253, January, 1856-February, 1861.

Croghan, Fort, Roll 70, March, 1849-November, 1853.

Graham, Fort, roll 412, April, 1847-October, 1853

Phantom Hill, Fort, Roll 14, September, 1851-March, 1854.

Price, George F., *Across the Continent with the Fifth Cavalry.* New York, D. Van Nostrand Company, Inc., 1883.

Rister, Carl Coke, "The Border Post of Phantom Hill" West Texas Historical Association *Year Book*, XIV (October, 1938), 3-13.

_______________, *Robert E. Lee in Texas*, Norman, University of Oklahoma Press, 1946.

Roland, Charles P., *Albert Sidney Johnston, Soldier of the Three Republics.* Austin, University of Texas Press, 1964 (Contains material from the Johnston Papers, Barret Collection, Howard-Tilton Memorial Library, Tulane University, New Orleans, Louisiana.)

_______________, and Richard C. Robbins (eds.), "The Diary of Eliza (Mrs. Albert Sidney) Johnston: The Second Cavalry Comes to Texas," *The Southwestern Historical Quarterly,* LX (April, 1957), 463-500.

Schoolcraft, Henry Rowe, *Historical and Statistical Information Respecting the History, Conditions and Prospects of the Indian Tribes of the United States.* 6 Parts. Illustrations by Seth Eastman, Capt., U. S. A. Philadelphia, Lippincott, Grambo, and Company, 1851-1857.

Sibley, Marilyn McAdams (ed.), "With Albert Sidney Johnston in West Texas: Austin to Fort Chadbourne, March, 1855," West Texas Historical Association *Year Book*, XXXV (October, 1964), 121-45.

Smith, Justin, *The War With Mexico.* 2 vols. New York, Macmillan Company, 1919.

Webb, Walter Prescott, and H. Bailey Carroll (eds.), *The Handbook of Texas.* 2 vols. Austin, Texas State Historical Association, 1952. See "Johnston, Albert Sidney," Vol. I, 919.

Wortham, Louis J., *A History of Texas from Wilderness to Commonwealth.* 5 vols. Fort Worth, Wortham-Molyneaux Company, 1924.

OTHER SOURCES

Johnston, Albert Sidney, and Eliza Johnston, Archival material in Museum Case with letters, picrures and relics. Daughters of the Republic of Texas Museum, 510 East Anderson Lane, Austin, Texas.

Johnston, Albert Sidney, Archives and Files (Letters, News Clippings and Pictures) in Austin-Travis County Collection, Austin Public Library, Austin, Texas.

Johnston, Albert Sidney, Archives File of Clippings, Archives, University of Texas Library, Eugene C. Barker Texas History Center, Sid Richardson Hall, Austin.

Texas Indian Papers, Mss., Archives, Texas State Library, Austin, Texas.

INDEX TO FLOWERS

US $50.00
9 780764 338632 55000
ISBN: 978-0-7643-3863-2

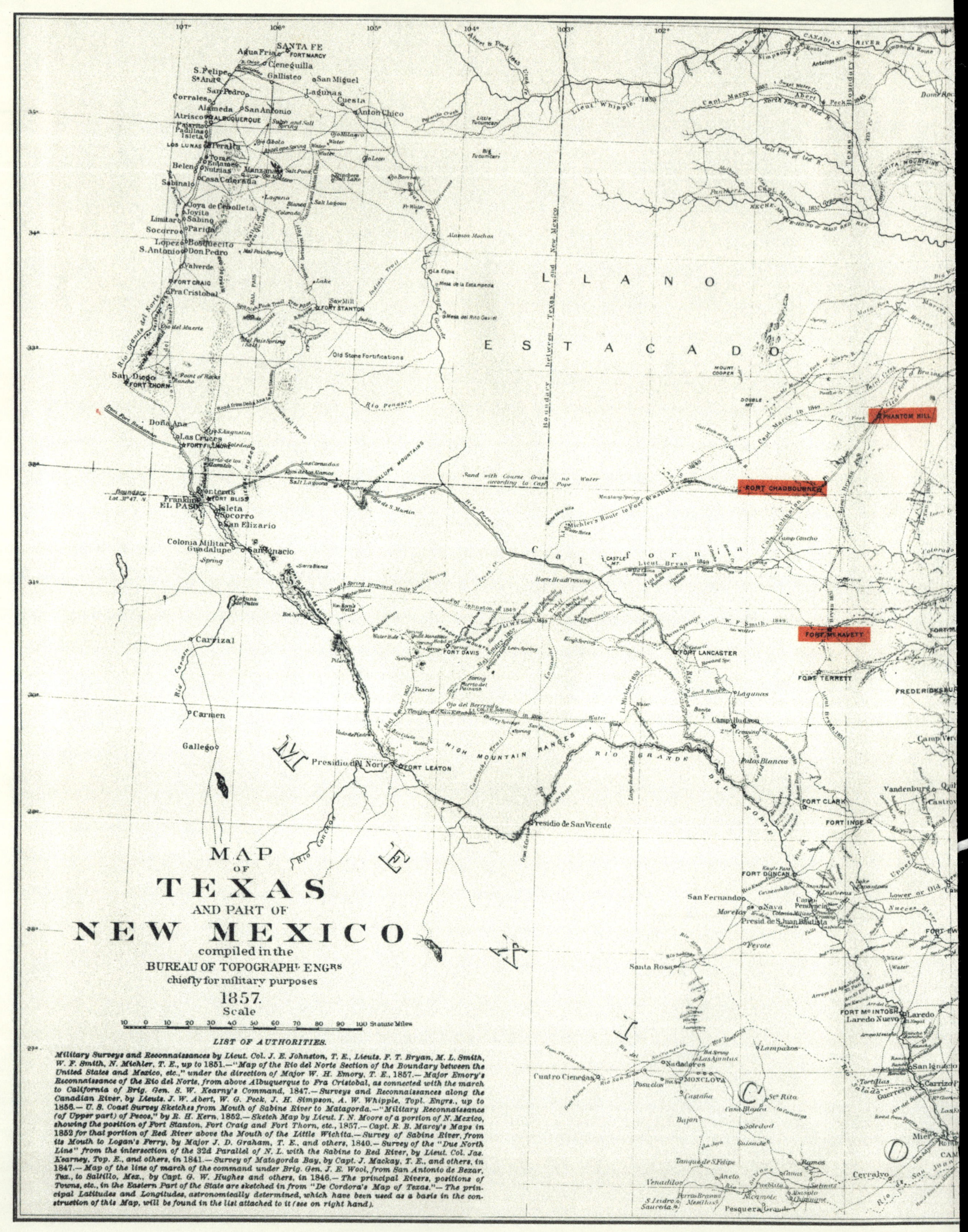
MAP
OF
TEXAS
AND PART OF
NEW MEXICO
compiled in the
BUREAU OF TOPOGRAPHL. ENGRS
chiefly for military purposes
1857.
Scale
10 0 10 20 30 40 50 60 70 80 90 100 Statute Miles
LIST OF AUTHORITIES.
Military Surveys and Reconnaissances by Lieut. Col. J. E. Johnston, T. E., Lieuts. F. T. Bryan, M. L. Smith, W. F. Smith, N. Michler, T. E., up to 1851.—"Map of the Rio del Norte Section of the Boundary between the United States and Mexico, etc.," under the direction of Major W. H. Emory, T. E., 1857.—Major Emory's Reconnaissance of the Rio del Norte, from above Albuquerque to Fra Cristobal, as connected with the march to California of Brig. Gen. S. W. Kearny's Command, 1847.—Surveys and Reconnaissances along the Canadian River, by Lieuts. J. W. Abert, W. G. Peck, J. H. Simpson, A. W. Whipple, Topl. Engrs., up to 1856.—U. S. Coast Survey Sketches from Mouth of Sabine River to Matagorda.—"Military Reconnaissance (of Upper part) of Pecos," by R. H. Kern, 1852.—Sketch Map by Lieut. I. N. Moore of a portion of N. Mexico, showing the position of Fort Stanton, Fort Craig and Fort Thorn, etc., 1857.—Capt. R. B. Marcy's Maps in 1852 for that portion of Red River above the Mouth of the Little Wichita.—Survey of Sabine River, from its Mouth to Logan's Ferry, by Major J. D. Graham, T. E., and others, 1840.—Survey of the "Due North Line" from the intersection of the 32d Parallel of N. L. with the Sabine to Red River, by Lieut. Col. Jas. Kearney, Top. E., and others, in 1841.—Survey of Matagorda Bay, by Capt. J. Mackay, T. E., and others, in 1847.—Map of the line of march of the command under Brig. Gen. J. E. Wool, from San Antonio de Bexar, Tex., to Saltillo, Mex., by Capt. G. W. Hughes and others, in 1846.—The principal Rivers, positions of Towns, etc., in the Eastern Part of the State are sketched in from "De Cordora's Map of Texas."—The principal Latitudes and Longitudes, astronomically determined, which have been used as a basis in the construction of this Map, will be found in the list attached to it (see on right hand).
LLANO ESTACADO
MEXICO
SANTA FE
FORT MARCY
ALBUQUERQUE
FORT CRAIG
FORT STANTON
FORT THORN
EL PASO
FORT BLISS
FORT DAVIS
FORT LEATON
Presidio del Norte
Presidio de San Vicente
HIGH MOUNTAIN RANGES
RIO GRANDE DEL NORTE
FORT LANCASTER
FORT CHADBOURNE
PHANTOM HILL
FORT McKAVETT
FORT TERRETT
FORT CLARK
FORT INGE
FORT DUNCAN
FORT McINTOSH
Laredo
MONCLOVA
San Fernando
Santa Rosa
Cuatro Cienegas
Boundary between Texas and New Mexico
Sand with Course Grass no Water according to Capt. Pope
Old Stone Fortifications
Rio Pecos